OCT 26 2004

The Boy Genius and the Mogul

Also by Daniel Stashower

Teller of Tales: The Life of
Arthur Conan Doyle

The Boy Genius

BROADWAY BOOKS / NEW YORK

and the Mogul

The Untold Story
of Television

Daniel
Stashower

For my father,

David L. Stashower,

who saw it at the 1939 World's Fair.

Cheer up sad world and wink,

It's kinda fun to be extinct.

—Lines scrawled in one of
Philo T. Farnsworth's
research journals

Contents

Preface xiii

One

The Death of Radio 1

Two

The Laboratory Pest 11

Three

The Messenger Boy 27

Four

Light from a Distant Star 43

Five

Tilting at Windmills 57

Six

The Battle of the Century 75

Seven
The Ideas in This Boy's Head......................91

Eight
Photographs Come to Life......................115

Nine
Dollars in the Thing.............................133

Ten
A Beautiful Instrument.........................153

Eleven
Priority of Invention............................185

Twelve
Now We Add Sight to Sound.....................213

Thirteen
The Lawyer Wept.............................239

Bibliography................................261

Acknowledgments.............................263

Index.......................................265

Preface

What the Future Telephot Will Look Like In Order to be Practical. Light R Throws Light on Speaker's Face and Is Reflected Into Lens L. Instead of a Mouthpiece, the Holes H of the Sensitive Transmitter Inside of Frame F Pick Up the Speech. The Picture of the Distant Person Appears on Screen S.

Television? The word is half Greek and half Latin.
No good will come of it.
—*The Manchester Guardian*

In 1910, when my grandmother was seven years old, Hugo Gernsback would come to the house and make alarming predictions about a device he called the "telephot." My grandmother was then living on Central Avenue in Cleveland, and Gernsback, a favorite cousin, often stopped off on his train trips from New York to Chicago, where he went to purchase radio equipment for his electrical parts company.

Gernsback had not yet attained fame as a pioneer of "science fiction," a term he is sometimes credited with having coined. His principal achievements—*Amazing Stories* magazine, of which he was the founding editor, and a truly awful science fiction novel entitled *Ralph 124C 41+*—still lay in the future. Already, however, he had cultivated a certain imaginative flair. A lean, dapper man who favored expensive suits and bright silk ties, Hugo would arrive with a giant box of Schrafft's chocolates under his arm and spin out wild tales of the future and the marvels it would bring. Robot doctors, retirement colonies on Mars, domed cities orbiting the earth—all of these were just around the corner. If a ringing telephone interrupted one of his stories, he invariably raised a finger of caution at my grandmother. "Hildegarde,"

An artist's impression from a 1918 magazine offers a glimpse of how a future television device, dubbed the telephot, *might operate.* THE ELECTRICAL EXPERIMENTER

he would say in his thick German accent, "fix your hair. It won't be long before the caller can see your face over the telephone wires."

The notion of a device that would enable one to see objects at a remote distance had been in play for many years at this point. The word "television"—from the Greek for "far" and the Latin for "seeing"—had begun to surface in learned journals and scientific texts, though a number of other phrases were also used to describe the strange concept: "hear-seeing," "audiovision," "visual listening," "radiovision," and "telephonography." Gernsback himself initially favored "telephot," though the word "television" crept into a 1909 issue of his *Modern Electrics* magazine, prompting a later claim that "before that time the designation had never been used." Family pride notwithstanding, I am constrained to admit that the term had already appeared in print at least ten years previously.

"There are certain inventions which, although not yet existent, we may take for granted will be invented some day," Gernsback wrote in his *Electrical Experimenter* magazine in 1918. "That they have not already appeared is by no means the fault of science, but simply because certain minor phases in the various endeavors have not as yet advanced sufficiently to make such inventions possible. Television, or 'remote seeing,' is one such invention. That such an invention is urgently required is needless to say. Everybody would wish to have such an instrument, and it is safe to say that such a device would revolutionize our present mode of living. Numerous inventors have busied themselves trying to invent an apparatus or machine whereby it would be possible to view visual scenes from a great distance. Strangely, the general public is not aware of their struggle, or the frontiers of science that they are seeking to conquer."

Stranger still, more than eighty years later, the story of that struggle remains largely unknown. The general public has only the vaguest notion of how—or by whom—television was created. Stop the average person on the street and he or she will be able to tell you in an instant who invented the lightbulb, or the telephone, or even the cotton gin. But the origin of television, an invention that did as much as any other to shape the twentieth century, is largely unknown. The names of Philo T. Farnsworth and Vladimir Zworykin occasionally pop onto the screen, but the overall picture remains fuzzy.

It is fair to say, as Gernsback predicted, that "remote seeing" did, in fact, revolutionize our present mode of living. In the wake of the World Trade Center and Pentagon disasters it is perhaps unnecessary to deliberate over the power of television, or review the many ways in which it has shaped the world. Much has been written about the impact, both good and bad, of television's omnipresence and immediacy, from the Nixon-Kennedy debates and Vietnam to O.J. and Jerry Springer. What is often lost, however, beneath the bland and often stupefying effect of television's usual content is the revolution contained within its tubes and diodes. The men who invented television are not responsible for *The Love Boat*. "We're in the same position as a plumber laying a pipe," David Sarnoff, the president of the Radio Corporation of America, once had occasion to remark. "We're not responsible for what goes through the pipe."

The process of laying that pipe would prove to be one of the most dramatic scientific quests—and bitter legal battles—of the electronic age. It has been argued that there was no single pioneer of television, and therefore no Kitty Hawk or Menlo Park, but rather a series of "Eureka" moments in various parts of the world. As with the development of space travel or the creation of the atom bomb, television is said to have evolved over a period of furious struggle and heated competition. That being the case, it is not surprising to find that there are many different versions of the story, each reflecting the self-interest of whoever is telling it. At the same time, the story tends to engender a great deal of flag-waving, and nearly every country in the world lays claim to the true and only "Father of Television"—Kenjiro Takayanagi of Japan, René Barthelemy of France, Dionys von Mihaly of Hungary, Boris Rosing of Russia, and John Logie Baird of Great Britain. All of these men, and many others, played a significant role. None of them, however, managed to gather all of the various pieces together into one definitive box.

The fundamentals of that box had been glimpsed a generation earlier by such nineteenth-century pioneers as Joseph May, who discovered the strange light-sensitive properties of the chemical selenium in

1872, and Paul Nipkow, who in 1884 patented a mechanical process of image-scanning that would form the basis of television experimentation for decades to come. Matters took a strange turn in 1880, when Alexander Graham Bell deposited a sealed dossier concerning a device called a "photophone" with the Smithsonian Institution. A rumor arose that the famed inventor of the telephone had now perfected a means of seeing by telegraph. In fact it was nothing of the sort—Bell was experimenting with the transmission of speech by means of a beam of light—but the mere suggestion of an Alexander Graham Bell "distant viewer" prompted a mad rush of inventors publishing their results. It is pleasant to note that in August of 1904 a patent application for a color television system was filed, by an inventor named Frankenstein.

Each would-be inventor had a different idea of what purpose the device might serve. Initially, very few had any notion that television might one day find its way into the home. Some experimenters envisioned it as a new method of exhibiting motion pictures or news events in public halls constructed especially for that purpose. Officials of the U.S. Navy, upon seeing a crude mechanical prototype in 1921, put television to work sending weather maps to ships at sea. Others, like Hugo Gernsback, imagined television as a means of one-to-one communication. A 1918 Gernsback article entitled "Television and the Telephot" was accompanied by a line drawing of a man clutching an old-style "candlestick" telephone, with an ear tube and clicker arm, that had been fitted out with a small screen resembling a hand-held mirror. In the screen, one could see the caller's sweetheart gazing back at him, with the ear tube of her own telephot pressed to her ear.

By the 1920s, scientists at the world's major electrical research laboratories began to realize that television was on the horizon, and a small handful grasped something of its potential to change the world, touching off what the radio pioneer Lee de Forest would call a "global horse race" to perfect a working system and, perhaps more important, be the first to bring it to market. In almost every respect, the evolution of television and its broadcasting networks anticipates the coming of home computers and the Internet. Then as now, there was a general awareness that a revolution was in the air, with fortunes to be made. In a similar manner, a dominant, polarizing figure stepped forward to seize control of the emerging industry, a man who was not only a technological visionary but also a man of business, willing to cut the legs out from under his competitors by whatever means necessary. At the helm of the Radio Corporation of America, David Sarnoff ruled the radio industry as an electronic fiefdom, with even the Federal Communications Commission held under tight control. He fully intended to exert the same authority over television.

Even as the struggle for power escalated, however, no one could be quite certain where the technology would lead. "What thrilling lectures on solar physics will such pictures permit!" exclaimed Lee de Forest in 1928. "What could be a more fitting theme for television than a quiet parade through some famous art gallery, pausing a moment before each masterpiece while some gifted commentator dwells briefly upon its characteristics, explains its meaning, and recounts the story of its creation? What could be more richly entertaining or more uplifting than such an experience? I see no other application."

The president of the British Broadcasting Corporation was no closer to the mark. "It will be admitted by all," he declared in 1925, "that to exploit so good a scientific invention for the purpose and pursuit of entertainment alone would be a prostitution of its powers and an insult to the character and intelligence of the people."

The theme of education and cultural improvement would continue for some time. Even George Bernard Shaw got into the act with a play called *Back to Methuselah,* in which a British prime minister holds a televised video conference with cabinet ministers in distant cities. A short-lived magazine called *All About Television,* which debuted in 1927, showed a young married couple settling down in their living room to watch a concert—the woman was shown in a formal gown and pearls, while her husband wore white tie and carried a top hat.

Others focused on the potential of broadcasting events of global significance. Speaking to *Screenland* magazine in 1928, William Paley, the "clever young president" of the Columbia Broadcasting Corporation, spoke of coming wonders: "Imagine seeing flashed upon the screen in simultaneous sight and sound and natural color an event of worldwide interest as it is taking place! Visualize World Series baseball games, football games, automobile and horse races, the instant they occur, on supersized stereoscopic screens! I predict that thousands of new theaters will spring up all over the country for the showing of televised news events alone." Indeed, it was feared by some—including General James B. Harbord, RCA's chairman of the board—that such broadcasting might rob live events of their interest. "There are apprehensions," Harbord declared in 1929, "in regard to this aspect. There are some people who fear that our future prize rings, baseball diamonds and football gridirons may be deserted except for a battery of television cameras."

The general public had more immediate concerns. In February 1929, a concerned reader wrote to the *Passaic Herald* to ask a pressing question: "Will you kindly inform me through your paper if by means of television or radiovision it is possible to look into apartments from adjoining apartments and watch the movements of people, as well as broadcast them, and if it is possible will you tell us how people can be protected against such operations and preserve the privacy which we are all entitled to in our home, be it a mansion or apartment?"

The following year, a reader voiced a similar concern in the pages of the *Cleveland News*: "I am so scared about 'television.' The telephone and radio were marvelous inventions but if it so be one can see a friend's face when miles distant, will they not soon invent some contraption to read a person's mind? Can we never have privacy? Could we not lock up our thoughts that they cannot be visualized and spoil our lives?"

For all of the confusion over what television would do, there was an even greater debate over how it would work. The earliest television sets made use of a mechanical system of transmission based on Paul Nipkow's 1884 patent for a whirling metal disk perforated with tiny holes. The Nipkow disk, when rotated in front of an illuminated image, allowed tiny segments of light and dark to filter through, each of which was converted into an electrical impulse by selenium or some other light-reactive chemical. At a nearby receiver, usually linked by wire, a second disk, rotating at precisely the same rate, converted the electrical impulses back into segments of light and dark, which could then be focused as an image on a viewing screen.

At best, these "Model T" televisions produced dim, flickering images on a screen not much larger than a postage stamp. Among the chief difficulties was the fact that the two whirling disks needed to be synchronized at speeds greater than 450 revolutions per minute, a feat that could seldom be accomplished with unreliable motors and belt drives. The challenge facing the early television pioneers, then, was to find a way to improve this synchronization between the transmitters and the receivers so that bigger and better images might be possible.

While many of the world's greatest scientists and research laboratories focused their energies on this goal in the 1920s, David Sarnoff began to look elsewhere for answers. A Russian immigrant named Vladimir Zworykin had convinced him that the future of television lay in a completely new direction. Zworykin, realizing that the mechanical systems could never be entirely perfected, resolved to achieve the same effect by means of an electronic scanning beam. At its core, this process would turn on the creation of a new type of glass tube, called an iconoscope, which would form the beating heart of the new technology. This tube, a direct descendant of Edison's incandescent bulb and De Forest's radio tube, held the promise of a revolution in mass communication.

If Zworykin succeeded, he would effectively hand control of the emerging television industry to David Sarnoff and the Radio Corporation of America. What Sarnoff did not know, indeed could not have known, as he pumped millions of dollars into Zworykin's electronic television initiative, was that someone else—armed with little more than a high school education and a stack of Gernsback magazines—had already thought of the idea.

His name was Philo T. Farnsworth, and he was fourteen years old.

The Boy Genius and the Mogul

One

The Death of Radio

By the spring of 1923, the Radio Corporation of America had put the finishing touches on a magnificent broadcasting tower on the roof of the Aeolian Hall, twenty-one stories above West 42nd Street in New York City. At the very top of the tower, above a cross-arm that stretched thirty-six feet across, stood a globe fashioned from strips of iron. It measured perhaps five feet in diameter, and the strips of iron were widely spaced in the manner of a hollow, loosely wound ball of yarn. The tower, along with a second broadcasting mast nearby, was intended as a statement of RCA's dominance of the radio industry, throwing a long shadow across Fifth Avenue.

On May 15 of that year, a tall, somewhat lanky man named Edwin Howard Armstrong could be seen climbing the tower's 115-foot access ladder. Armstrong wore a dark suit, a pair of glossy leather shoes, a silk tie, and a gray fedora pulled low against a stiff crosswind. Earlier, he had swung upside down by his legs from the tower's cross-arm. Now, scrambling to the top of the open sphere, he braced one foot under a strip of iron and kicked the other into the air, waving gleefully at a photographer on the roof below.

Armstrong had every reason to feel on top of the world. His in-

Edwin Howard Armstrong, the radio pioneer, displays a "portable" suitcase receiver on a beach excursion in 1923. BETTMANN/CORBIS

novative circuit designs had transformed the radio industry, and made him a wealthy man at the age of thirty-two. His high-wire posturing—an impulse he indulged whenever an opportunity presented itself—was simply a giddy expression of his status at the pinnacle of the broadcasting world. "Armstrong," asked an engineer who witnessed one such display, "why do you do these damned fool things?"

"Because," Armstrong replied, "the spirit moves me."

David Sarnoff, then the general manager of RCA, was not amused. "If you have made up your mind that this mundane world of ours is not a suitable place for you to be spending your time in, I don't want to quarrel with your decision," Sarnoff wrote in a letter to Armstrong, "but keep away from the Aeolian Hall towers or any other property of the Radio Corporation."

Sarnoff had good reason to be concerned, as his fortunes were largely entwined with those of Armstrong. Ten years earlier, on January 30, 1913, the twenty-two-year-old Armstrong had brought Sarnoff to a rickety transmitting station at Belmar, on the New Jersey coast. The station belonged to the American Marconi Company, and Sarnoff, at the age of twenty-one, was Marconi's chief inspector.

Sarnoff had come to this isolated station, which was little more than a crude shack, to evaluate a powerful radio receiver unit, invented by Armstrong, that employed a new type of regenerative feedback circuit that would become known as the oscillating audion. Then as now, the primary function of a radio was to convert radio waves into small electrical pulses which, when amplified, could be converted into recognizable sound. At the time, however, distant radio signals could seldom be heard above the ever-present crackle of background static from naturally occurring electromagnetic waves. Armstrong had discovered a means of cycling part of a received signal back and forth through the receiver and amplifier, magnifying the strength of the signal many times over. Armstrong's discovery, if it held up, would allow for radio communication over greater distances than ever before.

It proved to be a bitterly cold night, but Sarnoff soon forgot his discomfort. He watched with mounting excitement as Armstrong crouched over the receiving unit and, after a moment's tinkering, pulled in a remarkable message: "Lightning bad. Shall ground aerial wires." Sarnoff could scarcely believe what he was hearing; the message had originated in Honolulu.

The two young men would spend the entire night—thirteen hours in all—huddled over Armstrong's receiver, pulling in radio signals from around the world. Years later, Sarnoff's memory of the experience moved him to uncharacteristic raptures: "Well do I remember that memorable night at the Belmar station when, by means of your 'magic box,' I was able to copy the signals from Honolulu," Sarnoff wrote in a letter to his friend. "Whatever chills the air produced were more than extinguished by the warmth of the thrill which came to me at hearing for the first time signals from across the Atlantic and across the Pacific."

At first glance, the two men seemed unlikely allies. Armstrong, a native New Yorker from a well-to-do family, would remain a fiercely independent inventor in the mold of Edison and Marconi. Sarnoff, a Russian Jewish immigrant who had literally worked his way up from the mailroom, was poised to become the archetype of the American tycoon, a man who would devote his life to the goals and interests of his corporation. Even so, the alliance they forged at Belmar would not only shape the lives of both men, but also help to determine the future of mass communication in the United States. Armstrong's feedback circuit, together with a subsequent innovation called the superheterodyne, an elegant technique that could improve reception and tune a radio at the same time, would soon make him a millionaire. As the largest holder of RCA stock, Armstrong would become a fixture in Sarnoff's life—both in the office, where Armstrong courted and married Sarnoff's secretary, and at home, where Armstrong visited so frequently that Sarnoff's family dubbed him "the coffee man."

For a time, Armstrong reveled in his good fortune. He took a grand tour of Europe—"Arriving in England on Saturday" he cabled a friend, "with the contents of the Radio Corporation's safe"—and bought himself a lavish Hispano-Suiza automobile. Even as he surveyed his dominion from atop the RCA broadcasting mast, however, there remained one unconquered summit. For all of the accomplishments and refinements of Armstrong and fellow radio pioneers such as Lee de Forest and Reginald Aubrey Fessenden, radio communication was still hampered by the constant din of background static. The problem was so pervasive that it was the custom for newspapers to run weather forecasts alongside their radio listings, to give the home listener an idea of the likely effect of adverse conditions.

It was a subject that Sarnoff and Armstrong often discussed during their coffee chats. "Give me a little black box," Sarnoff said on one occasion, referring to Marconi's original "black box" radio apparatus, "but get rid of the static." Armstrong, believing this to be the sole remaining obstacle in radio broadcasting, calmly accepted the challenge.

With the confidence of youth, Armstrong initially expected a quick solution. In fact, more than ten years would pass before his labors brought results. In December of 1933, Armstrong once again summoned David Sarnoff to see his latest miracle. Sarnoff, now the president of RCA, appeared at Armstrong's laboratory, in the basement of Philosophy Hall at Columbia University, expecting to see some new gadget or tube that would filter out bothersome background noise from radio carrier waves. Instead, Armstrong had found a way to alter the waves themselves, creating a fundamentally new form of radio communication. Instead of modulating the amplitude, or intensity, of a radio carrier wave, Armstrong had developed a means of modifying its frequency, or interval. If one imagined radio signals as ocean waves, Armstrong had found a way to control the rate at which they washed up on the beach—changing the frequency, rather than the size. In time, this form of transmission would be known as frequency modulation, or FM.

The implications of Armstrong's breakthrough were stunning. "This is not an ordinary invention," Sarnoff declared. "This is a revolution." Determined to claim this latest innovation for RCA, Sarnoff immediately placed the company's new experimental laboratories atop the Empire State Building at Armstrong's disposal—in effect putting Armstrong at the peak of the world's tallest broadcasting mast. To all outward appearances, it seemed that Armstrong had scored another technical triumph.

All was not as it seemed. Much had changed in the world of broadcast communications while Armstrong had been locked away in the basement of Philosophy Hall. The emerging technology of television, which had been only a faint crackle of static when Armstrong started his work, now threatened to drown him out. Up to this point, Sarnoff had been cautious in his approach to television, fearing that a premature commitment would undermine RCA's hugely profitable radio operations. Initially, the laboratory atop the Empire State Building had been dedicated to television experiments. By canceling the television operations and turning the facility over to Armstrong, Sarnoff was sending a clear and carefully modulated signal to the business community—radio was here to stay. This strategy promised not only to preserve RCA's dominance of the industry, but also to give Sarnoff's research scientists more time to perfect a commercially viable television system.

It soon became apparent, however, that Sarnoff couldn't afford to drag his feet any longer. Armstrong's FM system, if adopted, would carry a staggering price. In order to take up FM as the new standard of radio, the entire industry would have to be overhauled, and existing radio sets would have to be scrapped. At a time when huge amounts of money were needed for television research, RCA could not afford to sacrifice its radio revenues. At the same time, Sarnoff realized that his television initiative was no longer the only game in town. Others were working to perfect television technology, and if some other company got there first, RCA might find itself required to buy licensing rights and equipment from a rival.

Accordingly, Sarnoff took a new line. The work on FM radio would be shelved while RCA renewed its commitment to television. Sarnoff assured Armstrong that this would only be a temporary interruption, and even offered to employ FM technology in the television initiative. For the moment, however, RCA had to tend to the bottom line. Armstrong was told to remove his equipment from the Empire State Building. It was not the first time Armstrong had been ordered off an RCA broadcast mast, and he had reason to hope that all would end well.

Matters came to a head at the annual RCA stockholders' meeting in May 1935. While Armstrong waited expectantly for some mention of the FM revolution, Sarnoff instead made a dramatic announcement that the company would commit $1 million to its television research program. Treading a fine line so as to avoid upsetting the radio partisans, Sarnoff indicated that "while television promises to supplement the present service of broadcasting by adding sight to sound, it will not supplant or diminish the importance and usefulness of sound broadcasting." As objections were raised, Armstrong rose to his feet. Sarnoff, he reminded them, had guided the company through the dark days of the depression. "I think you would have been wiped out if it hadn't been for him," Armstrong declared. "I tell you, I wouldn't have his job for five hundred thousand dollars a year. I don't agree with everything, for I have a row on with him now. I am going to fight it through to the last ditch. I just wanted to tell you what you owe to Sarnoff."

In the end, Sarnoff got his way, and the following day he sent a letter of thanks to Armstrong. "Doubtless I have made many mistakes in my life," he wrote, "but I am glad to say they have not been in the quality of the friends I selected for reposing my faith."

For all of that, it soon became clear that Sarnoff would give no further support to the development of FM. Undeterred, Armstrong resolved to proceed on his own. Only six months later, on November 5, 1935, he arranged a lecture before the New York chapter of the Institute of Radio Engineers. After addressing his audience for some little while, Armstrong quietly played his trump card: "Now, suppose we have a little demonstration." The curtains parted to show what appeared to be an ordinary radio receiver. As Armstrong switched the unit on, the audience heard the usual sound of broadcast static. Then, as Armstrong turned a knob, the unit fell strangely silent. For a moment it seemed as if the radio had gone dead, but then the sound of an announcer's voice issued from the speaker: "This is amateur station WQAG at Yonkers, New York, operating on frequency modulation at two and a half meters." A collective gasp could be heard from the audience of engineers; the announcer's voice had come through so clearly that he could easily have been present in the room. Armstrong gestured for silence as the demonstration continued. The sound of a glass of water being poured came over the radio's speaker, followed by the crumpling of a piece of paper. Armstrong had made his point—these sounds could not possibly have been distinguished against a background of AM static.

Encouraged by the enthusiastic reception, Armstrong went ahead with plans to build his own FM transmitting station in Alpine, New Jersey. When completed, the station's 425-foot broadcast tower would be visible across the Hudson River in New York City—even from David Sarnoff's palatial suite of offices on the fifty-third floor of the RCA building.

The project would require much of Armstrong's energy and resources, and he liquidated most of his personal fortune—including a huge block of RCA stock—to make the funds available. Unfortunately, an even greater portion of his energies would soon be absorbed in litigation with RCA over the use of his patents. In time the case wound up in court, where the question of FM became a decisive issue. For some time, RCA had been claiming to have developed its own system of frequency modulation without any help from Armstrong. Now, speaking before a judge, Sarnoff insisted that his engineers had "done more to develop FM than anybody in this country, including Armstrong." Seated with his lawyers, Armstrong regarded his former friend with an expression of undisguised contempt.

The suit would drag on for years. "They will stall on this thing until I am dead or broke," Armstrong would often say. His wife and many of his friends urged him to accept a settlement, but for Armstrong it had become a matter of honor—one that required a clear legal victory. By 1953, Armstrong's patents and licenses had expired, and his legal bills and research expenses had drained his fortune. His health began to suffer and his behavior grew erratic. On one occasion he came to believe that someone had poisoned his food and insisted on having his stomach pumped. On another, his wife fled the house as Armstrong lashed out with a fireplace poker.

On January 31, 1954, two months after the incident with the fireplace poker, Armstrong sat down and jotted a note to his wife. "I am heartbroken because I cannot see you once again," he wrote. "I deeply regret what has happened between us. I cannot understand how I could hurt the dearest thing in the whole world to me. I would give my life to turn back to the time when we were so happy and free." He added a few lines about the state of his finances, then closed: "God keep you and may the Lord have mercy on my soul."

This done, Armstrong removed the air-conditioning unit from his bedroom window, put on a scarf and gloves, and stepped out of his thirteenth-story window.

David Sarnoff wept openly at Armstrong's funeral. "I did not kill Armstrong," Sarnoff had told one of his engineers on learning of the tragedy, but clearly the news had shaken him. Forty years had passed since the two men had huddled together in the transmitting station at Belmar, ushering in the era of modern radio. In Armstrong's view, Sarnoff had betrayed not only his friendship but also his ideals. To Sarnoff's way of thinking, however, it was only business. The profits from RCA's radio operations had been fueling television research for years. FM would have derailed that effort and jeopardized Sarnoff's plans to dominate this new and potentially limitless market. At that point, Howard Armstrong became simply another obstacle in Sarnoff's path.

Before Sarnoff could seize control of television, however, he would have to deal with another bright young inventor who was standing squarely in his way.

Two

The Laboratory Pest

SAY FELLOWS
GET INTO
RADIO-TELEVISION
AND
TALKING PICTURES

Let me tell you how I can quickly train you, NOT by book study, but by actual shop training on real Radio, Television and Talking Picture equipment in 12 WEEKS in the great shops of COYNE in Chicago.

Here at Coyne you don't need advanced education or experience and many of my students earn while learning. After graduation I give them lifetime employment service. Here at Coyne too you get individual instruction and you can start anytime.

Radio offers jobs as Designer, inspector and tester, salesman, and in installation work, operator of a broadcasting station, wireless operator on a ship, with Talking Pictures theatres — with Television Laboratories and studios. Television alone will soon be calling for thousands of trained men.

Come to Coyne here in Chicago and prepare for one of these jobs the quick and practical way BY ACTUAL SHOP WORK.

It's a shame for any fellow to go thru life as an untrained man working at small pay, and never even sure of a steady job, and when he does work working at any old price they want to pay him.

You can avoid this. You can be a trained man and have a real future. Mail the coupon today, and I'll send you my big FREE book and tell you how you can be a success just as hundreds of my graduates are. Address

H. C. LEWIS, President
Radio Division, COYNE ELECTRICAL SCHOOL
500 S. Paulina St., Dept. 20-7n, Chicago, Ill.
Send me your Big Free Radio and Television Book, and tell me how I too can make a success in Radio.

Name..

Address..

City...State.....................

Each day for more than a week, Philo T. Farnsworth waited outside Justin Tolman's classroom at Idaho's Rigby High School and begged to be admitted to the senior chemistry course. Farnsworth would arrive early, having been up since four o'clock to get in an hour of study before his morning farm chores. After riding four miles from home on horseback, he would lie in wait for Tolman on the front steps of the school, or near the faculty lounge.

Farnsworth, tall and wiry, had turned fifteen in August 1921. His drumming hands and tapping feet gave an impression of nervous energy, though his mode of speech was often slow and hesitant. Friends recalled him as having "wonderful blue eyes," along with "sandy-colored hair that had a tendency to curl" and a "broad, infectious smile."

Farnsworth's broad smile had little effect on Justin Tolman. The chemistry teacher admired the boy's enthusiasm, but repeatedly turned him down. Farnsworth's family had only recently moved to Rigby, a small farming community in eastern Idaho, and the newly enrolled freshman had missed half of the school year. It was enough, Tolman reasoned, that the boy should try to catch up with the rest of the freshman class. Taking on a senior's workload was clearly out of the question.

An early radio magazine advertisement urges readers to get in on the ground floor of television. RADIO-CRAFT MAGAZINE

"I looked at him and laughed," Tolman would later recall. After explaining, somewhat impatiently, that the course was available only to seniors, Tolman tried to reason with the eager new arrival. "Now you, a freshman, come in here thinking you can carry the regular work of a senior, and in addition make up the work that these boys and girls have been struggling with for almost five months. Such a thing cannot be done. Come back two years from next September and we will have plenty of room and we will be glad to have you."

Farnsworth would not be put off. He returned the next day and pleaded his case again, this time producing a note from his freshman science teacher attesting to his advanced study. At length Tolman gave in, agreeing to let Farnsworth sit in on the class without credit, and only if he promised to keep quiet.

Farnsworth couldn't stop himself from participating in the class. When the teacher posed a question about the previous week's assignment, only Farnsworth seemed to know the answer. When a chemical equation had the class stumped, Farnsworth supplied the missing information. By the end of the first class, Tolman realized that Farnsworth's natural talent for science far exceeded his own. "A week had hardly passed before I found myself going to school a little earlier in the morning and coming home a little later at night so that this boy might receive special instruction and have more laboratory time to make up the work of the first semester. This he did in a few weeks' time."

Soon, the teacher and his enthusiastic student had moved beyond the established curriculum. Farnsworth seemed especially fascinated by radio waves and light-sensitive chemicals, and many of his questions centered on those two areas. He sat motionless at a desk in the front of the classroom as Tolman filled the blackboard with chemical symbols.

The sessions often lasted well into the night. "The custodian of the building called him the laboratory pest," Tolman recalled. "He complained that I let him stay so late at night that they never had a chance to clean up, and if they did, he came so early the next morning the place never looked clean."

Throughout his life Tolman would play down his role in Farnsworth's scientific flowering, cheerfully admitting that half the time he couldn't follow what the boy was saying. It is clear, however, that Farnsworth cherished the opportunity to learn from the older man. "Philo's questions were apt to come at any time and any place," Tolman said. "He generally had a question or two after each class, but he would also stop me in the hall, on the campus, or on the street. We would make drawings on the blackboard, scraps of paper or anything we had handy as we tried to explain to each other what we meant. Other times I was able to place in his hand books that gave him the information. I recall one of these books had to deal with the cathode ray. This book he all but wore out."

One day, as he was passing along the corridor outside of a study hall, Tolman heard the sound of Farnsworth's voice. School rules forbade talking during study hall, but Farnsworth could nevertheless be heard addressing his fellow students in animated tones. Tolman paused with his hand on the doorknob, expecting to hear an elaboration of that week's chemistry assignment. Instead, Farnsworth was outlining the basic principles of Einstein's theory of relativity. It is fair to say that Einstein's theorems, which were only just gaining mainstream acceptance at the time, would not have been on the basic reading list for Rigby High. For whatever reason, Farnsworth felt that his fellow students could not go another day without a quick overview. As he spoke, an abrupt transformation came over him. Normally shy and taciturn, he became, in the words of a fellow student, "as fiery and silver-tongued as any preacher." Tolman, standing in the corridor outside, saw that Farnsworth's teenaged audience was hanging on every word.

/ / /

Farnsworth's scientific erudition was certainly improbable. In 1921, as Farnsworth cobbled together a working knowledge of cathode rays and electromagnetic waves, his family did not even own a radio. In fact, the Farnsworths had only recently moved to a house equipped with electricity. At the time, one in four households in the United States was a farm, and only 2 percent of farm households had electric power. Even the most primitive crystal radio set was a tremendous novelty. For all of the advancements made by Lee de Forest and Edwin Howard Armstrong, very few Americans had heard voice transmissions, as most message traffic was still carried out by Morse code. The majority of the country's five thousand radio operators were amateurs, or "hams," and the first licensed station in the United States, Pittsburgh's KDKA, had started up only one year earlier.

Nor was the Farnsworth family itself a likely font of scientific inspiration. Farnsworth's grandfather, for whom he was named, had been one of Brigham Young's lieutenants, helping to build the original Mormon Temple in Nauvoo, Illinois, and later trekking west to join in the settlement of the Great Salt Basin. The family drew strength from their Mormon ideals through many years of hardship and privation, eventually settling at a place called Indian Creek, near Beaver, Utah, where Philo Taylor Farnsworth II was born on August 19, 1906, in a log cabin built by his grandfather.

Farnsworth's father, Lewis, was a farmer who had married his mother, Serena, two years earlier, following the death of his first wife, who had left him with four children. In time, Lewis and Serena would have five more children. Lewis and his older sons worked the land while the women spun wool and cotton. The family moved from place to place as circumstance and work conditions dictated, sometimes with young Philo at the reins of a horse-drawn wagon filled with crated hens and piglets.

Against this background, Philo Farnsworth seemed unlikely to bloom into a scientific prodigy. Almost from the first, however, there were signs which could not be ignored. When the boy was three, his father took him to a railroad terminal to see a locomotive. Farnsworth, who up to that point had only traveled by horse, was initially terrified by the clanking of the engine, and promptly covered his ears and hid his face in his father's coat. The train's conductor, seeing the boy's terror, invited him up into the cab and showed him the furnace and flues, patiently explaining how the engine's power was generated. Arriving home that evening, young Philo asked for a pencil and paper. Settling himself at the kitchen table, the three-year-old made a detailed drawing of what he had seen that afternoon, with a particular emphasis on the locomotive's internal workings.

At the age of six, Farnsworth announced his intention to follow in the path of Thomas Edison and Alexander Graham Bell, whose achievements had been described for him by his older siblings. "I guess I had decided it would be nice to become an inventor when I first saw a hand-cranked telephone and gramophone," he later said. "These things seemed like magic to me." At night, he pored over the pages of the Sears, Roebuck & Co. catalog, marveling over such fascinating and novel devices as the Conley Stereoscopic Camera with genuine red Russian leather focusing bellows and the Oxford Cylinder Talking Machine.

In one sense, the young Farnsworth's dream of becoming an inventor made perfect sense. As Edison himself observed in 1908, the world had entered a "renaissance of invention," with new innovations being recorded at a fantastic rate. Each day's newspapers seemed to bring word of some fresh contrivance or refinement, ranging from the radio, motion pictures, and the automobile to the tea bag, cellophane, and the safety razor. Less obvious to the general public, however, was a change in the nature of the inventive process. As the English philosopher Alfred North Whitehead observed, "The greatest invention of the nineteenth century was the invention of the method of invention," meaning a shift away from the solitary inventor in his isolated lab to the well-funded, well-organized efforts of large research centers. Even Edison himself, seemingly the very model of the eccentric individualist, had long since established his research facility at Menlo Park, where he coordinated the efforts of a large and carefully trained staff. Seen in this context, Philo Farnsworth's boyhood ambitions take on an added shading—he longed to pattern himself on Edison and Bell, but the era of the solitary inventor was quickly fading.

In the spring of 1919, the Farnsworth family moved to a 240-acre farm near Rigby, Idaho, owned by one of Farnsworth's uncles. Farnsworth, now twelve years old, was thrilled to discover a Delco battery generator that provided a basic, if unreliable, source of electric power for the farm's hay stackers and grain elevator. "I couldn't wait to find out how power was made," Farnsworth later recalled, and when the local repairman, a man by the name of William Tall, appeared to service the generator, Farnsworth hovered nearby asking questions. On occasion, it was thought, Farnsworth would intentionally disable the system to bring Mr. Tall out for further interrogation. In time, however, the family would be able to dispense with the repairman altogether—the boy was soon able to take the generator apart and put it back together again.

Before long, his new electrical knowledge found its way into Farnsworth's daily round of chores. At one stage, he found an old discarded motor near the farm and managed to restore it to working condition—a process that involved an intricate hand-winding of the electrical coils. He then attached the motor to the wooden handle of his mother's washing machine, thereby relieving himself of the tedious job of hand-churning the dirty clothes. Eager to create more labor-saving devices, he began scavenging for spare parts wherever they might be found. "We never had an alarm clock that worked," his sister Agnes once remarked.

Lewis Farnsworth did his best to encourage his son's tinkering. He made time for regular trips to the library, where the boy steadily worked his way through every available science book. At night the two of them would lie on their backs in a meadow and gaze up at the stars while Lewis recited the names of the constellations. The younger Farnsworth read everything he could find on astronomy, marveling over the seemingly incomprehensible distance represented by light from familiar stars.

In the attic of the Rigby farmhouse, Farnsworth uncovered a stack of scientific and technical magazines stretching back several years, apparently stashed away by a former tenant. "I was in seventh heaven," he would recall. Farnsworth never recorded the titles of the magazines in this treasure trove, but at the time there were only a limited number in existence—*Scientific American, Popular Science, Technical World,* and *The Electrical Experimenter,* among a handful of others. Many of these magazines featured a hodgepodge of technical information and embryonic science fiction. A typical issue of *The Electrical Experimenter,* edited by Hugo Gernsback, offered articles ranging from the practical—"The Vacuum Detector and How It Works"—to the wildly fanciful, such as Gernsback's plan for a pair of "Future Goggles," which promised to release the "untapped potential of human cerebration."

Farnsworth also found lengthy descriptions of the work of the radio pioneers whose achievements would inspire him, such as Nikola

Tesla's innovative work with magnetic fields; Lee de Forest's creation of the famous audion tube, which amplified radio signals and generated oscillations; and Reginald Aubrey Fessenden's groundbreaking broadcast of the first program of speech and music in 1906, the year of Farnsworth's birth. "Captain Edwin Howard Armstrong Is 'Over There,' " ran a headline in a 1918 issue of *The Electrical Experimenter.* "Like so many other of his fellow citizens, the heroic Mr. Armstrong has answered the call of his country in the present struggle," noted the accompanying article. "His skill in the radio art will prove of supreme value to the U.S. Signal Corps." These colorful tributes transformed electrical engineers into dashing men of action, blending the best elements of Tom Swift and Horatio Alger's Ragged Dick.

Even the paid advertisements seemed calculated to fire the imagination, especially in the wartime issues. One, for a glorified box kite, described in breathless terms the danger posed by that "dark behemoth of the sky" the Zeppelin rigid airship: "The Terror of the Old World—The Possible Destruction of the New. Learn New Aeronautical Ideas: Defend Fort Totten." Another advertisement offered an "electrically illuminated boutonniere" in the shape of an American flag, powered by a bulky flashlight case carried in a coat pocket. Had Farnsworth been able to avail himself of Gernsback's Future Goggles, he would have found a dark portent among the pages of these magazines. By late 1919, nearly every scientific and technical magazine carried a large advertisement for the wares on offer from the Radio Corporation of America. "Our laboratories are working around the clock to produce a startling new array of life-enhancing devices," ran a notice in an early issue of *Radio News.* "Our products are certain to have a profound effect on the quality of your everyday life." Farnsworth could scarcely have imagined how resonant those words would become.

At least some of the articles found in these magazines would have set Farnsworth's mind turning toward the concept of "telephonography," or television. As early as 1917, a handful of science writers were describing the rudiments of television technology as it existed at the time. The November issue of *Literary Digest* featured an article entitled "German Device for Seeing Wireless Signals," setting out the basic principles of the whirling mechanical scanning device known as the Nipkow disk. Later that year, an *Electrical Experimenter* article entitled "How I Telegraph Pictures" elaborated on the theme. Illustrated by a grainy "telegraph picture" of President Woodrow Wilson, the article described a mechanical process of breaking down a photograph into tiny segments for transmission, "translating the light and the shade of the picture into pulsations or variations of an electrical current." At the other end of the transmission, the photograph would be put back together by "a means of successively recording these pulsations or variations in the form of what appears to be gradations of light and shade." In the author's judgment, however, this process could be managed only with still pictures, not moving images. "The process of 'television' is at present impossible for both mechanical and electrical reasons," he explained, because the scanning mechanism would have to go over each frame of film, top to bottom, at least four hundred times per second. No mechanical device, he reasoned, would ever be capable of such speed. "This is the mechanical difficulty of 'tele-vision,' " the author concluded. The telegraphing of still photographs, therefore, seemed to him to be a "more fruitful field."

In September 1921, Farnsworth likely saw an article in *Scientific American* entitled "Transmitting Photographs and Drawings by Radio." The story described the efforts of the French experimenter Edouard Belin to transmit photographs between St. Louis and New York City. Previously, Belin had succeeded in doing so by means of existing telegraph lines. Now he proposed to achieve the same effect by means of radio waves—in other words, wireless facsimile transmission. While the use of radio waves marked a giant leap forward, Belin's apparatus remained, at heart, a mechanical one, and therefore limited by the finite speed of whirling metal disks.

Ironically, the way forward could be glimpsed in remarks made years earlier by the British engineer A. A. Campbell Swinton, an authority on electrical and steam power. In 1908, responding to an article in the British science journal *Nature* about the possibility of "distant electric vision," Swinton proposed that the difficulties might be resolved "by the employment of two beams of kathode rays, one at the transmitting and one at the receiving station, synchronously deflected by the varying fields of two electromagnets." After expanding on the idea, Campbell Swinton concluded that the means of achieving this did not yet exist, "but should something suitable be discovered, distant electric vision will, I think, come within the realm of possibility."

The remarks of Campbell Swinton, reprinted in a later issue of *The Electrical Experimenter,* introduced a profound new element into the static cloud of television theory. In discussing "kathode"—or cathode—rays, Campbell Swinton was referring to the current of electrons, or electron beam, emitted by a negatively charged electrode in a vacuum tube, such as the De Forest audion tube. In other words, Campbell Swinton was proposing to replace mechanical television workings with a stream of electrons in some sort of special vacuum tube, controlled by magnets. It remained only to invent such a tube, a prospect that would have seemed hugely unlikely in 1908. More than ten years later, when young Philo Farnsworth had his first exposure to the concept, Campbell Swinton remained dubious. The difficulty with television, he told the Radio Society of Great Britain in 1920, was that "it is probably scarcely worth anybody's while to pursue it. I think you would have to spend some years in hard work, and then would the result be worth anything financially?"

For Farnsworth, poring over his magazines long into the night, television seemed well worth pursing, with the potential for unlimited financial gain. "I was only thirteen when I began studying the problem," he later said. "It wasn't long before I realized that whoever solved it would make a fortune." What began as an interesting scientific puzzle soon became an intense preoccupation, and Farnsworth's greatest concern was to learn more of the basic science necessary to move forward. For this, he needed money to buy science books.

Farnsworth had always been willing to do extra work to raise spending money, including trapping muskrats and selling their fur, but he seldom earned enough to buy the expensive technical books he wanted. A possible source of income presented itself in the September 1921 issue of *Science and Invention* magazine, formerly *The Electrical Experimenter.* Under the heading "Motor Hints," editor Hugo Gernsback called for budding inventors to submit ideas for "enhancing the

safety and comfort of the modern automobile," with a specific emphasis on the prevention of auto theft. "We have not been at all satisfied
with the class of suggestions we have been receiving lately in this department," the editor declared. "Most of the devices that are suggested
are very crude, and while some of them may be original, they are so
impractical that not one in a hundred motorists would think of using
or installing such a device." Gernsback then went on to relate the
shocking statistics of auto theft in New York City, where as many as
fifteen cars fell prey to auto thieves each day. "This is a terrible loss and
must be stopped at all cost," he insisted.

Farnsworth had encountered no more than a handful of automobiles in his life. Only a few months earlier, Warren G. Harding had
been the first president-elect to ride to his inauguration in an automobile, a Packard Twin-Six. A Chevrolet "Four-Ninety" open touring
car could be had for $645, and the latest accessories for the venerable
Model T Ford included a fuel gauge, a speedometer, and a "Warn-U"
signal—better known as a taillight. For Farnsworth, the prospect of
even owning a car, much less creating a practical invention for one,
must have seemed fairly remote. Even so, he desperately wanted to
win the contest and claim the $25 prize. The problem began to occupy
his thoughts during the tedious patches of his farm chores. In later
years Farnsworth would declare that the "solitude of the open country was most conducive to thought and reflection." It would perhaps
be just as accurate to say that he was an imaginative boy saddled with
hours' worth of repetitive tasks, and it is not surprising that his
thoughts often wandered far from the job at hand. One of his duties at
the time was the plowing of the farm's potato fields, for which he used
a disk-cutter plow behind a team of three horses. Using three horses
saved time, but it also carried risks—some time earlier, a neighboring
farmer had been killed when a horse startled and knocked him against
the sharp points of the plow.

Farnsworth's father frequently cautioned him to be careful and pay
attention to his plowing, but one day as Farnsworth progressed with
his work his mind drifted off into contemplation of the problem of
auto theft. Distracted, he did not notice that one of the reins of his
horse team had slipped from his fingers and was trailing along on the

ground. Coming upon the scene from a distance, Lewis Farnsworth saw that the horses and plow were now out of balance, so that any sudden movement might cause his son to stumble forward into the disk cutters. Walking as swiftly as he dared, the elder Farnsworth intercepted his son and took up the fallen rein. The boy did not seem to notice that he had been in any danger. "I've got it!" he shouted. "I really think it will work!"

Lewis Farnsworth, angry at his son's carelessness, refused to discuss the matter until later that night. Only then, after the boy had apologized for his inattention, did he explain the reason for his sudden outburst in the potato field. "I've been reading about electrons and how to magnetize metals," Farnsworth explained to his father. "I think if I were to magnetize the ignition of a car, you wouldn't be able unlock it unless you also magnetized the key."

Within days Farnsworth had mailed off plans for a "magnetized anti-theft ignition system" to *Science and Invention,* and in February of the following year it was announced that "Mr. P. T. Farnsworth" had taken the top prize. "Not one person in a thousand would ever tumble to the fact that this switch operates in the way it does," ran the editorial explanation, adding that the motorist need only to remember to carry a magnet on his person in order to activate the switch.

It is unlikely that the readers of *Science and Invention* realized that Mr. P. T. Farnsworth would be using a portion of the winnings to buy his first pair of long pants. Farnsworth had recently joined a small dance band as a violinist, and was embarrassed to be seen performing in his knickers. With the balance of his winnings, along with the proceeds from his violin playing, Farnsworth added to his library of science journals and books.

By this time, Idaho's foremost boy inventor had enrolled at Rigby High and begun his after-hours studies with Justin Tolman. It would be some time, however, before Tolman realized where Farnsworth's studies were taking him. "Looking back," Tolman said, "I realize that nearly every question he asked me had some bearing on the problems of television. I see now that it was all coming together in that head of his."

From his science journals, Farnsworth had learned the basics of mechanical scanners such as the Nipkow disk and the limited work being done with these devices by would-be television innovators around the world. The efforts of Edouard Belin and others suggested that it might be possible to broadcast television signals over radio waves rather than telegraph wires, though many other sources—such as the article on telegraphing pictures—raised doubts that mechanical scanners would ever be suited to this task. Inspired by the theories of writers such as Campbell Swinton, Farnsworth's thoughts had turned to electronic scanning, leading him to read and reread the volume on cathode rays he had borrowed from Tolman. It was these thoughts and concepts, some contradictory, others purely theoretical, that churned through Farnsworth's head as he went about his farm chores each day.

One afternoon, as Farnsworth was mowing a field of hay, his mind once again drifted off into the realm of abstract science, though this time he managed to keep a tight grip on the reins of his horse team. The solution to a workable system of television seemed no closer, but at least the problem helped to pass the time as he guided the horses back and forth across the field. Now, as he turned to look back over the freshly mown hay, a peculiar thought came to him. The hay had fallen into neat rows, each line alternating in direction from the one above. It suddenly struck him that it might be possible to invent a device that would read images electronically rather than mechanically, by scanning them in horizontal rows—one line at a time, just like the rows of hay. With the right kind of tube, one would be able to break down a complex image into a series of simple lines, just as the human eye scans the pages of a book, and then put them back together again in a second tube at the other end, a process Farnsworth would liken to "capturing light in a bottle."

Needless to say, this inspiration marked a substantial leap forward from the "magnetized anti-theft ignition system," and the stakes were considerably greater than $25 and a pair of long pants. Farnsworth kept his ideas to himself for a considerable time while he gathered more information. At length, he decided he needed a second opinion.

One afternoon in late February of 1922, Justin Tolman arrived for one of his usual after-school tutoring sessions and found that Farnsworth had covered the blackboard with schematic drawings and mathematical equations. Setting down his books, Tolman asked what all of this represented. Television, Farnsworth answered—a new kind of television. Tolman was vaguely familiar with the term, and had read something about the work being done with Nipkow disks. He asked Farnsworth if he was working along those lines. "It can't be done by mechanical means," Farnsworth answered. "I propose to do it by wholly electrical means, by manipulating electrons."

Earlier, during Farnsworth's impromptu lecture on the theory of relativity, Tolman had been struck by the seemingly effortless manner of the young man's speech and his obvious passion for the ideas. Now, as Farnsworth sought to explain a radical theory of his own, Tolman was struck by an even greater sense of conviction. Farnsworth stood at the blackboard and began outlining his system step by step. He knew that a photoelectric material, such as selenium, released a stream of electrons whenever light hit its surface. Cathode rays would do the opposite, changing invisible electrons into glowing light. These two effects, Farnsworth reasoned, would make television possible. He envisioned a special vacuum tube with a light-sensitive surface inside. Under the proper lighting conditions, the tube would react to the light and dark areas of any object placed before it, and convert this information into a series of electrical impulses. These electrical impulses could then be transmitted to a receiver—by wire, initially, but ultimately by radio waves. At the receiver, a second tube would convert the electrical impulses back into light. The light would glow faintly in some areas and brightly in others, according to the intensity of the signal received. If a sufficient number of these light and dark areas could be transmitted, they might be assembled to form a recognizable image. In this manner, a picture of the object scanned by the first tube would be reproduced by the second tube—providing, in effect, pictures by radio.

Farnsworth realized that the biggest obstacle would be to find a means of accomplishing this complex procedure quickly enough to be practical. If the picture could be broken down and transmitted in tiny elements, and if those elements could be reassembled in an orderly and nearly instantaneous sequence, the human eye would be fooled into thinking it was seeing the entire image all at once. Later, Farnsworth used a newspaper photograph to elaborate the point. "If you had a reading glass you would see that this picture is made up of many small dots," he explained. "There are probably 250,000 dots in such a reproduction. To transmit a picture of like quality over television, each of these dots must be picked up separately and sent in sequence. To fool the eye, all this must be done in a fraction of a second. To get smooth motion as in motion pictures, we must probably send the pictures at the rate of thirty a second. In other words, to do the thing successfully we must register and transmit 250,000 variations every thirtieth of a second. That means something like 7,500,000 changes in intensity every second."

No whirling mechanical disk would ever be fast enough to achieve this, Farnsworth reasoned, but it might be accomplished by means of electronic scanning, controlled by magnetic coils, that could perform the operation in an orderly, line-by-line fashion, just as hay might fall into alternating rows behind a horse-drawn mower. It would require an extraordinarily complex and entirely new type of vacuum tube, Farnsworth told Tolman, but he believed the basic elements were scientifically sound.

In time, Farnsworth would come to call this tube the "image dissector," after the manner in which it dissected whatever it saw into lines of light. Now, as he went over his design point by point with his chemistry teacher, Farnsworth emphasized the advantage that his system had over the others he had read about in his magazines. "The whole secret is controlling electrons," he said. "Control their speed, control their direction, change light—or pictures—into electricity and electricity into pictures at the other end, and you'll have television." Later still, he would sum it up in a single phrase: his system had no moving parts.

For some time, Farnsworth and Tolman huddled together at the chalkboard. At one stage, as Farnsworth clarified a particular point, he reached for the closest sheet of paper—a page from Tolman's notebook—and jotted down a crude sketch of his proposed camera device. Tolman studied the sketch for some moments. He could see nothing wrong with his student's reasoning. "He asked if I could not give him a suggestion that would help him realize his ambition," Tolman recalled. "Looking him in the eyes, I replied, 'Study like the devil and keep mum.' "

Soon enough, the school custodian would arrive and wash away the latest scribblings of Rigby's "laboratory pest," but Farnsworth had won his first convert. "It meant a lot to me," he would say in later years. "It meant I could move forward."

For all of that, neither Farnsworth nor Tolman could possibly have grasped the full import of what had been accomplished. At the moment he conceived the idea of electronic scanning, Farnsworth made an intuitive leap that would place him ten years ahead of nearly every other television innovator in the world. He had rejected, by the age of fifteen, an entire system of technology to which other scientists would devote their lives.

For the moment, Tolman could only shake his head. "It was clear that Farnsworth had moved beyond my ability to help him," he said. "I doubt if there were a handful of big thinkers in the entire world at that time who could have fully understood his ideas."

In fact, Tolman may have been exaggerating. At that time it would be fair to say that there was only one other person in the world working on Farnsworth's level. Unfortunately, that man would soon be working for David Sarnoff.

Three

The Messenger Boy

While his classmates at Rigby High followed the exploits of such sports stars as Jack Dempsey and Babe Ruth, Philo Farnsworth tracked the heroes of radio engineering. At the local library Farnsworth boned up on the accomplishments of such pioneers as Michael Faraday and Joseph Henry, who broke new ground with electrical currents, and the German physicist Heinrich Hertz, who first demonstrated the existence of radio waves. With his radical television ideas firmly in mind, Farnsworth also read up on the men who had invented and refined the vacuum tube—John Ambrose Fleming, Karl Ferdinand Braun, and Lee de Forest, among others.

Of all the tales of innovation that inspired Farnsworth, the story of Guglielmo Marconi would prove to be the most engrossing. "He was a keen, eager boy," ran one account, "with little formal training. Yet somehow this bright-eyed Italian lad confounded the cherished precepts of science by sending radio waves through the trackless ether."

Farnsworth, who also intended to confound the cherished precepts of science, found much to admire in the tale of Marconi's rise to fame and fortune. Born in 1874 to an Anglo-Irish mother and a wealthy Italian father, the young Marconi was raised on his family's es-

David Sarnoff, age twenty-one, mans his radio post at the John Wanamaker department store in 1912, the year of the Titanic *disaster.* BETTMANN/CORBIS

tate outside Bologna. Like Farnsworth, the boy passed much of his free time with electrical experiments and science journals, and later managed to wangle his way into an advanced science course at the University of Bologna.

Like many experimenters of the time, the young Marconi developed a fascination with "Hertzian," or radio, waves. There had been much speculation about the potential of these waves, and it was believed that they might somehow be used as a means of communication over great distances. While still in his teens, Marconi began adapting Hertz's experiments—featuring a spark-gap transmitter and a loop aerial receiver—in the hope of sending radio waves across the "trackless ether."

Over time Marconi developed a device known as the "black box" transmitter, which, when hooked up to a Morse telegraph key, could send out dots and dashes as radio signals. For a receiver, he adapted recent innovations by the French scientist Edouard Branly and the British physicist Oliver Lodge. A thin glass tube, with a metal rod at each end, was attached to his loop aerial. Whenever radio waves struck the aerial, metal filings inside the tube would cling to the rods, completing an electrical circuit. The gadget, known as a "coherer" for the manner in which the filings cohered to the rod, could be hooked up to a ringing bell or to a "Morse inker," a machine used by telegraphers to record coded signals onto a strip of paper.

Marconi refined his system over a period of two years. Though he himself had not originated any of the scientific theory behind wireless communication, he had the vision to see how existing concepts could be used as never before. "My chief trouble," he would later write, "was that the idea was so elementary, so simple in logic, that it seemed difficult for me to believe that no one else had thought of putting it into practice."

Through a careful process of trial and error, Marconi gradually lengthened the range of his transmissions. At first he could ring a bell at the other side of a room, then across an open field. As the range increased, he found he could send wireless signals over the horizon, well beyond the line of sight. A farmer's rifle shot, echoing over the hills, signaled that his message had been successfully received.

In time, Marconi felt ready to demonstrate his achievements for the public. When Italian authorities expressed no particular interest, Marconi's mother decided to trade on her family connections—she was a Jameson, of the Irish distilling family—in order to try their luck in Britain. Marconi and his mother arrived in London in February 1896, along with two trunks filled with radio equipment.

Within weeks, Marconi's mother had arranged for her son to give a demonstration for Sir William Preece, the chief engineer of telegraphs for the Post Office, the controlling authority over telegraph and telephone communication in Great Britain. The tests began in a small room at the London Post Office, then progressed to Salisbury Plain, where Marconi sent a radio signal over a distance of nine miles. The British officials were properly impressed. By the end of 1897, the twenty-three-year-old Marconi was a director of a corporation bearing his name—the Marconi Wireless Telegraph Company, Ltd. He would later remark, "The calm of my life ended then."

The story of Marconi's achievements traveled well over the horizon, and newspapers across Europe began reporting on his doings on an almost daily basis. With remarkable flair, Marconi parlayed his sudden celebrity into a series of publicity stunts, each promoting the power and range of his radio apparatus. He gave a well-publicized demonstration for members of Parliament, and established a wireless link across the English Channel to a receiving station in France. As Prince Edward recovered from an appendectomy aboard the royal yacht, Marconi equipment transmitted news of his progress to Queen Victoria on the Isle of Wight. Perhaps the crowning achievement came in December 1901, when Marconi traveled to Newfoundland and successfully received a radio signal from a Marconi transmitting station in England. "This was the young Italian's crowning glory," noted an account in *Radio-Craft* magazine, "for the ingenuity of a single man had now conquered the mighty Atlantic Ocean."

Marconi seemed to take a particular pleasure in conquering the ocean. Soon he began to travel regularly to New York—where the local press dubbed him the "Sorcerer of the Airwaves"—and he took a close interest in the running of his British company's newest subsidiary, the American Marconi Wireless Telegraph Company, known familiarly as American Marconi. One evening in December of 1906, Marconi appeared at the company's branch office on William Street, in lower Manhattan. As he left to inspect a laboratory a short distance away, a fifteen-year-old office boy stepped out of the office behind him. Seizing the opening, the boy introduced himself as Marconi's newest employee.

His name was David Sarnoff. Within moments, Sarnoff had managed to apprise Marconi of his aspiration to become a telegraph operator, and perhaps he even displayed the telegraph key that he had purchased with money from one of his first pay packets, so as to be able to practice Morse code long into the night. Marconi instantly warmed to the young office boy. "We were on the same wavelength," Sarnoff liked to say of the encounter.

Marconi took Sarnoff to see the company's laboratory on Front Street and gave him access to the technical library maintained there. By the time they parted, Sarnoff had volunteered to be Marconi's personal errand boy during his visits to New York. Among his duties would be arranging deliveries of flowers and gifts to Marconi's many female acquaintances around the city. By all accounts, Sarnoff handled this job with discretion and dispatch. Within months, Marconi personally approved Sarnoff's promotion to the position of junior wireless operator, at a salary of $7.50 per week. Sarnoff was on his way.

Through the years, David Sarnoff has generally been characterized as either a brilliant corporate visionary or a ruthless robber baron. Neither portrayal does him full justice. Over the course of his long career he would combine an intuitive grasp of coming technology with an uncanny business acumen—part dreamer, part bean-counter. "In others," Governor Nelson Rockefeller was to say, "the word 'visionary' meant a capacity to see a mirage. In David Sarnoff, the word 'visionary' meant a capacity to see into tomorrow and to make it work."

"All life is a risk," Sarnoff himself would say. "I learned it earlier than most."

Sarnoff was born in 1891 in Uzlian, a shtetl in Russia, in the province of Minsk. His father, Abraham, was a housepainter and paperhanger; his mother, Leah, came from a long line of rabbis. When David was four years old his father set off for America, promising to send for his wife and three sons when he had earned the money for their passage. It would take nearly five years. During that time, the boy lived in complete isolation from his mother and brothers in a village one hundred miles away, studying with one of his great-uncles to become a Talmudic scholar. For more than four years he gave himself over to the rigorous discipline of religious study from dawn to dusk, memorizing two thousand words of the Talmud every day and seldom venturing outside except to walk to temple. Although he would credit this early training with giving him the mental toughness to succeed in business, Sarnoff would also carry a certain sense of joyless isolation into adulthood. "I guess I was hermetically sealed off from childhood," he once remarked.

In 1900, at the age of nine, Sarnoff learned that his father had gathered the $144 needed to purchase four steerage tickets for passage to America. He rejoined his family in Uzlian and prepared for the long and difficult journey to New York. As the family boarded a ship that would carry them to America, the boy saw his mother's hamper of kosher food, which had somehow gotten mixed up with the other baggage, disappearing into the vessel's hold. Realizing that he and his family would have nothing to eat if the hamper went below, he instinctively dove after it—landing, as luck would have it, on a pile of soft luggage. A sailor threw him a rope and hauled young Sarnoff and the precious hamper to safety. "Boy," the sailor declared, "you're going to do all right in America."

The long sea crossing left Sarnoff with a lasting memory of "sweaty bodies close-packed and the stench of vomit." Much the same conditions awaited him in New York. Abraham Sarnoff settled the family in a three-room railroad flat on Monroe Street on the Lower East Side, where they shared a dank and grimy bathroom with as many as fifteen other people. "It was like being tossed into a whirlpool," Sarnoff recalled, "a slum whirlpool, and left to sink or swim."

The prospects for the future could not have seemed especially bright. Abraham Sarnoff was suffering from tuberculosis, and worked only sporadically. Within days of his arrival, young David was competing with other Jewish boys to sell and deliver Yiddish-language newspapers. He rose at four each morning to get a jump on the competition, and shortened his route by running along the rooftops of the neighborhood's tightly packed tenement buildings. When the deliveries were made, he devoted the rest of the day to learning English, which he did with uncommon speed. For years he would carry a pocket dictionary everywhere he went, so that he might master any unfamiliar words he encountered.

By the time Sarnoff reached the age of fourteen, two more younger siblings had arrived to strain the family's finances. With his father's health in a steady decline, the burden of supporting the family now transferred to David, the eldest son, with the result that his formal education ceased in the eighth grade. Somehow—perhaps through the intervention of an anonymous benefactor—he found the money to purchase a newsstand at 46th Street and Tenth Avenue, in Hell's Kitchen, where his younger brothers and ailing father helped to sell papers.

In 1906, at the age of fifteen, Sarnoff planned to better his circumstances by branching out into a career in journalism. He now had a truly exceptional command of English—so exceptional that he had become a successful debater at the East Side Educational Alliance—and saw no reason to settle for a job at one of the Yiddish papers he sold in Hell's Kitchen. "More than anything in the world," he later recalled, "I wanted to rise above that ghetto background." With that goal in mind, Sarnoff brushed off his only suit and headed south to Herald Square, determined to get a job at the *New York Herald.*

Presenting himself at the offices of the *Herald,* Sarnoff inquired about job openings. He soon learned that he was in the wrong place; instead of the *Herald,* he had mistakenly wandered into the lobby of the newspaper's sister organization, the Commercial Cable Company. As fate would have it, there was a job opening for a messenger boy. Sarnoff immediately accepted, and was soon traveling across the city on a bicycle in a messenger boy's uniform carrying cablegrams.

Sarnoff would soon be fired for refusing to work on the Jewish High Holidays. This was more a matter of finance than religious conviction; he could earn more money singing in the temple choir than he could delivering cablegrams. Even so, though the Commercial Cable job lasted only a few months, Sarnoff had now resolved to become a telegraph operator. Acting on a tip from a former coworker, he presented himself at the William Street office of American Marconi. He carried his own personal telegraph key and wore his hair swept back to make himself appear older. "Could you use a man as a junior operator?" Sarnoff asked. "No," came the reply, "but we could use an office boy."

Sarnoff accepted immediately—resolving, quite literally, to work his way up from the mailroom. In Russia, Sarnoff had studied the Talmud from morning to night, and had gone to bed without supper if he failed to recite his daily portion. At American Marconi, he applied himself with the same sense of rigor. He pored over technical journals. He grilled the wireless operators about their technique. He studied the business correspondence that flowed into the company's filing system, mastering not only the content but also the corporate style in which they were written. After work, he took night courses. At home, he sat up in bed with his telegraph key, practicing his key taps late into the night.

By the time Guglielmo Marconi himself arrived at the William Street office to hand Sarnoff his big break, the fifteen-year-old office boy knew as much about the workings of the company as any other employee. Over the coming months, Sarnoff's cunning and diligence would see him through a series of postings, ranging from an isolated communications outpost on Nantucket to an assignment aboard a transatlantic steamship. By the time Sarnoff's father passed away the following year, sixteen-year-old David had managed to sell his newsstand at a profit and move the family out of the railroad tenement.

All the while, Sarnoff continued his regimen of self-improvement, often through correspondence courses, studying not only business and finance, but also technology, with an emphasis on advanced mathematics and electrical engineering. Sarnoff also made a careful study of Marconi himself, resolving to pattern his own career on that of the man he was to call "the benefactor of all the world." Marconi repaid the attention by fostering his young errand boy's interest in science, making time for detailed theoretical discussions of radio interference and electromagnetic waves. "David," Marconi once told him, "we know how things work, but we don't know *why* they work."

By 1912, a series of promotions had brought Sarnoff to a position as manager of a Marconi station at the top of the John Wanamaker department store at 9th Street and Broadway. Sarnoff's duties were not especially strenuous, as most of the message traffic was carried out with the store's main branch in Philadelphia, for the purpose of providing customers with a demonstration of the marvels of wireless communication. While not as impressive as some of his earlier postings, the Wanamaker's assignment would prove to be a turning point in the young operator's life. As Sarnoff would later tell it, he was the only operator manning his post on Sunday, April 14, when a fateful message came across the wires: "*Titanic* sinking fast."

"I have often been asked what were my emotions at that moment," Sarnoff wrote. "I doubt if I felt anything at all during the seventy-two hours after the news came. I gave the information to the press associations and newspapers at once, and it was as if bedlam had been let loose. Telephones were whirring, extras were being cried, crowds were gathering around newspaper bulletin boards. The air was as disturbed as the earth. Everybody was trying to get and send messages. Some who owned sets had relatives or friends aboard the *Titanic,* and they made frantic efforts to learn something definite. Finally, President Taft ordered all stations in the vicinity except ours closed down so that we might have no interference in the reception of official news. Word spread swiftly that a list of survivors was being received at Wanamaker's, and the station was quickly stormed by the grief-stricken and curious. . . . It seemed that the whole anxious world was attached to my earphones during the seventy-two hours I crouched tensely in that station. I felt my responsibility keenly, and weary though I was, could not have slept."

Later, the publicity department of the Radio Corporation of America would improve on Sarnoff's account: "The eyes of the whole world, it seemed, along with its fears and hopes, were fixed on young Sarnoff and his earphones. For three days and three nights, without sleep and virtually without food, Sarnoff remained glued to his earphones, while a horrified world hung on his every word. . . . Not until he had given the press the names of the last survivors, seventy-two hours after he had picked up the first distress signal, did the exhausted operator relinquish his earphones."

The image of the dedicated young wireless operator glued to his post was one that Sarnoff would cherish for the rest of his life. "The *Titanic* disaster brought radio to the front," he would often say, "and also me." It was certainly true that the catastrophe would make radio communication indispensable at sea. Sarnoff's role, however, is more difficult to verify. Although the story has become an integral part of the Sarnoff legend—recounted in *Time, Forbes, Fortune,* and *The Saturday Evening Post*—it is largely false. In fact, it is by no means certain that the Wanamaker post was operating on Sunday evening as the grim news first came over the wires, since the store itself would have been closed—raising the possibility that Sarnoff did not become involved until the following morning. Moreover, his name does not appear in the extensive coverage of the tragedy in the *New York Times,* the *Herald,* or the *Wall Street Journal.*

Still, there is no question that Sarnoff did play a role in bringing bulletins to an anxious public, and undoubtedly he kept a long vigil at his post, like many other wireless operators in the city, trying to pull the names of survivors out of the cloud of conflicting reports. One newspaper, the *New York American,* struck a deal with Wanamaker's for exclusive rights to its information about the *Titanic.* Sarnoff's name appears as one of three "expert wireless operators" who "captured scores of messages concerning the wreck." Be that as it may, by the Wednesday after the tragedy the Marconi Company had shut down most of its message centers to reduce radio interference, leaving only four in operation. The Wanamaker's station was not among them.

Sarnoff is certainly not the only person in the history of American business to embellish his résumé, but few have done so to greater effect. Over the coming years, the story of his part in the *Titanic* drama would underscore his role as a defining figure in the evolution of electronic communication. It was a position he would occupy for six decades.

If Sarnoff was sometimes a little hazy about his past, he had a remarkably clear vision of the future. By the end of 1915, he had risen to the position of chief inspector of American Marconi. Conscious of his new status, Sarnoff composed a remarkable memo. "I have in mind a plan of development which would make radio a household utility in the same sense as the piano or phonograph," he wrote. "The idea is to bring music into the house by wireless. The problem of transmitting music has already been solved in principle, and therefore all the receivers attuned to the transmitting wavelength should be capable of receiving such music. The receiver can be designed in the form of a simple 'Radio Music Box' and arranged for several different wavelengths, which should be changeable with the throwing of a single switch or pressing of a single button. The 'Radio Music Box' can be supplied with amplifying tubes and a loudspeaking telephone, all of which can be neatly mounted in one box. The box can be placed on a table in the parlor or living room, the switch set accordingly, and the transmitted music received."

This was extraordinary stuff for 1915, a time when even the clear transmission of Morse code was by no means assured. In combining his technical knowledge with his extraordinary business acumen, Sarnoff not only anticipated the development of radio as an instrument of home entertainment but also went on to sketch out the fundamentals of network broadcasting, rather than point-to-point communication, with large numbers of families receiving from "a single transmitter." Sarnoff then described the manner in which listeners might receive "lectures at home which can be made perfectly audible; also, events of national importance can be simultaneously announced and received. Baseball scores can be transmitted in the air by the use of one set installed at the Polo Grounds."

The now legendary "Radio Music Box" memo would, in years to come, establish Sarnoff as a technological visionary. Even at his most fanciful, however, he kept his eye firmly fixed on the bottom line, suggesting a retail price of $75 per radio unit. "There are about 15 million families in the United States alone," he wrote, "and if only 1 million, or 7 percent of the total families, thought well of the idea, it would mean a gross business of about $75 million." Sarnoff also foresaw "secondary sources of revenue" in terms of advertising for the Marconi Company and increased circulation of its house magazine.

As it happened, it was an idea for which the world was not yet prepared. With the United States preparing to enter the war in Europe, American Marconi found itself all but overwhelmed with orders from the U.S. Navy. Sarnoff's memo, which called for a top-to-bottom reorganization of the company and its priorities, was far too radical for serious consideration. Ironically, Sarnoff's commitment to working within a corporate framework would postpone his greatest innovation, while independent inventors such as De Forest and Fessenden were free to push ahead. By the time Sarnoff's superiors came around to his way of thinking, the company would have to hustle to overtake their smaller, less entrenched competitors.

In the meantime, Sarnoff was far from idle. As a new general manager, Edward Nally, took the helm of American Marconi, Sarnoff acquired new responsibilities. Although Nally had a strong background in cable communication, he was relatively ignorant of wireless operations. For months Sarnoff had been an instructor at the Marconi Institute, teaching new recruits how to operate and sell the company's equipment. Now, after hours, Sarnoff tutored his new boss in the same techniques. Soon, Sarnoff had established himself as Nally's right-hand man, becoming not only the company's chief inspector but also the assistant chief engineer and contract manager.

Sarnoff reveled in his growing prominence and prosperity. He began to take greater care with his personal appearance, acquiring a number of off-the-rack suits that offered a reasonable facsimile if not the actual expense of Guglielmo Marconi's hand-tailored wardrobe. A gold watchchain could be seen draped across his expanding stomach, and a fat cigar was often clipped between two fingers. A homburg and a walking stick were arranged on a rack in the corner of his office. In keeping with his new station, Sarnoff moved his family a second time, settling his mother and siblings in a modern apartment in the Bronx, complete with electric lights, hot water, steam heat, and indoor plumbing. Eager to wipe away all traces of Hell's Kitchen, he instructed his mother to get rid of every stick of her old furniture.

Some elements of his old life could not be so easily discarded. As an aspiring telegrapher on William Street, Sarnoff had been dismissed by the older operators as a useless "Jew Boy." The intolerance intensified as he moved up through the ranks, which is hardly surprising at a time when no less a figure than Henry Ford was funding newspaper diatribes such as "The International Jew: The World's Problem." In later life Sarnoff would speak publicly on the responsibility of being "a Jew whose lot it has fallen to be in the public eye in America." For the moment, conscious of his status as the only Jewish executive at American Marconi, Sarnoff worked to minimize the emphasis on his background, taking particular care to Americanize his accent.

His mother had other ideas. When a family of French immigrants joined her local synagogue, Leah Sarnoff resolved to play matchmaker. Her son would claim that it was love at first sight when he was introduced to Lizette Hermant, a blond Parisian who was then in her early twenties. Her English was limited, as was Sarnoff's French, but apparently the young communications specialist managed to get his message across. He cheerfully submitted to a lengthy courtship under the supervision of the Hermant family, followed by a wedding at the Bronx synagogue on July 4, 1917. Sarnoff would henceforth refer to his anniversary as the day "I lost my independence."

Even as he settled into married life, purchasing a home in Mount Vernon, north of the city, Sarnoff's career acquired a new focus. President Wilson's declaration of war in April 1917 sent Sarnoff hurrying to enlist in the armed forces. Now twenty-six, he angled for a commission in naval communications and was bitterly disappointed when the application was refused—his services as a civilian, overseeing the installation of wireless apparatus on navy vessels, were judged to be essential to the war effort. Not satisfied with a civilian role, Sarnoff made a second, even more energetic effort to enlist, vowing to succeed even if it meant becoming a buck private in the army. Only the direct intervention of the navy's top engineer, Admiral R. S. Griffen, kept him out of boot camp. "Exemption is considered absolutely necessary," Griffen wrote in a cable to the draft board, "in order that the fleet will not suffer delays due to unsatisfactory deliveries in existing contracts."

Denied his commission, Sarnoff nevertheless became a key figure in the war effort. He was now in control of a staff of more than seven hundred employees, supervising the shipboard communications of some six hundred vessels. When President Wilson ordered a government takeover of all wireless facilities in the United States and its possessions, Sarnoff began to divide his time between New York and Washington, where he advised various government and military agencies on communications strategies.

Radio was to play a decisive role in the conflict. As German U-boats succeeded in cutting Britain's undersea cables, wireless communication became America's only reliable link to Allied commanders, as well as to its own military forces abroad. At a Marconi installation in New Brunswick, New Jersey, the navy erected a massive 200-kilowatt transmitter, the most powerful in existence, capable of providing clear voice transmission across the Atlantic. In January 1918, when President Wilson laid out his Fourteen Points plan as the basis for a peace settlement, the New Brunswick transmitter broadcast the text to Europe. For Sarnoff, who was present for the transmission, it was a forceful confirmation of his assertion set out in the Radio Music Box memo that "events of national importance can be simultaneously announced and received."

The message was not lost on American Marconi's competitors. The leaders of the American electrical industry—Westinghouse, General Electric, and the American Telephone and Telegraph Company—began pouring greater resources into their technical laboratories, setting the stage for a bruising postwar power struggle. Up to this point, the wireless industry had been mired in a chaos of conflicting patents and incompatible technologies, leaving much of the impetus in the hands of amateur operators. The government takeover had imposed a sense of order and purpose, with the navy establishing a virtual monopoly over not only the equipment but also the associated patents.

With the signing of the armistice in November 1918, the government proved reluctant to surrender control. The following month, Navy Secretary Josephus Daniels appeared before Congress proposing a bill to "secure for all time to the Navy Department the control of radio in the United States," allowing the military to "continue the splendid work it has carried on during the war." The precedent was clear, Daniels argued, since every other nation capable of wireless communication had already established a government monopoly.

Reaction was decidedly mixed. "Having just won a fight against autocracy," declared one congressman, "we would start another auto-cratic movement with this bill." Prominent radio executives, including Edward Nally of American Marconi and Owen Young of General Electric, joined the fray, and the bill soon died in committee.

Having lost its bid to retain control, the government let it be known that a private monopoly might be looked upon with favor. Matters soon came to a head over a powerful new piece of equipment. A General Electric engineer named Ernst Alexanderson had devised a revolutionary type of radio alternator—an electric generator to pro-duce alternating current—which had been a key component in the Marconi tower at New Brunswick. Sarnoff himself had declared it to be the finest in the world, with the result that in 1919, American Marconi's parent company, Britain's Marconi Wireless Telegraph Company, placed a $5 million order for twenty-four Alexanderson al-ternators.

When General Electric's Owen Young notified the government of the proposed sale, alarms sounded. President Wilson himself was said to oppose the deal, and Franklin D. Roosevelt, then assistant secretary of the navy, asked Young to confer with navy officials before taking any further action. In essence, the government objected to handing over control of a piece of key American technology to the British. The war had greatly enhanced America's mass communications capabilities, and it was thought that this single transaction would forfeit America's gains and tip the scales back toward Britain's prewar domination of the industry. Navy Secretary Josephus Daniels now led a charge to "fight against British monopoly," summoning the key figures of the Ameri-can communications industry to Washington.

With American Marconi largely controlled by its British counter-part, it was clear that it would be difficult to keep the Alexanderson al-ternator out of foreign hands. Over the next few weeks, a dramatic proposal emerged. General Electric would reject the order from British Marconi and place the alternator under American control. To help compensate General Electric for the lost sale, the navy would put its own valuable wartime research patents into a communal pool, to-gether with those controlled by General Electric and those held inde-pendently by American Marconi. Each of the participants in this agreement would have free use of all the patents, sweeping aside many layers of competitive restrictions. The patent pool would be controlled by a new subsidiary of General Electric, to be created through a buyout of American Marconi stock—effectively severing the American company from its British parent. The new company would be called the Radio Corporation of America.

Within three months, a team of negotiators, including American Marconi's Edward Nally, hammered out an agreement that transferred British Marconi's controlling stock of the American subsidiary to General Electric for $3.5 million. On October 17, 1919, the Radio Corporation of America was incorporated, with bylaws that emphasized its nationalistic agenda—its executives were required to be American citizens and no more than 20 percent of its stock could be held by foreigners. Owen Young became chairman of the board, Edward Nally was appointed president, and twenty-eight-year-old David Sarnoff would serve as commercial manager. From the first, Young and Nally had agreed that the new company must "control as many patents as there is a possibility of our owning or using," and the patent pool soon expanded to include Westinghouse, the American Telephone and Telegraph Company, and even the United Fruit Company, which had done some pioneering work in linking its banana boats and plantations by wireless.

For Sarnoff, the message was clear—whoever controlled the patents controlled the industry. In the years to come, as he rose through the ranks of RCA, he would never deviate from this basic business philosophy. In time he would accumulate a vast store of technology patents, and those he could not acquire he would find a way to circumvent. "The Radio Corporation does not pay royalties," he would often say. "We collect them." It was a dictum that would shape his career—and the industry—for the next fifty years.

There would be only one exception.

Four

Light from a Distant Star

Roughly four miles up the Provo Canyon in northern Utah, there is a famous double cataract waterfall called Bridal Veil. Even before Highway 189 made the falls more accessible to tourist traffic, Bridal Veil was a place well known to nature hikers, picnickers, and, especially, courting couples. It was here, one Saturday in 1923, that young Philo T. Farnsworth brought seventeen-year-old Elma Gardner, a young woman whom he considered to be the "swellest" in all of Utah.

Elma Gardner was, literally, the girl next door. The Farnsworth family had left Rigby for Provo earlier that year, with Lewis Farnsworth once again seeking better working conditions. Provo, known as Utah's "Garden City" for its many fruit orchards and other greenery, was in the midst of an economic boom, owing in part to the opening of the Ironton steel mill that year. Along with the increased employment prospects, Serena Farnsworth hoped that Provo, being the home of Brigham Young University, might offer more in the way of educational opportunities for her children. Eventually the family settled in one half of a duplex home in the north end of town. Elma Gardner's father had worked with Lewis Farnsworth for a time on a construction job, and when the other half of the duplex became vacant, the Gardners moved in.

Philo T. Farnsworth, seen here in 1930 at the age of twenty-four, was hailed as a "boy genius" in the press. BETTMANN/CORBIS

Elma, known as "Pem" to her friends, was a vivacious and quick-witted young woman. She had a particular fondness for music and spent much of her free time at the family piano. Her striking good looks bore a passing resemblance to those of Clara Bow, who had made her screen debut the previous year.

Although they were neighbors, Pem did not know Philo Farnsworth as well as she would have liked. She had grown close to his sister Agnes, however, and often heard stories of the brilliant older brother who had big plans for the future. Years later, Pem would recall the vivid impression Farnsworth made when she first saw him in the family kitchen: "He radiated a sense of strength and vitality," she recalled, and he had "the deepest blue eyes I had ever seen. I had to agree with Agnes—he was certainly a brother to boast about."

Their date at Bridal Veil began poorly. Farnsworth had brought a pair of horses to carry them into the canyon, and Pem, hoping to impress him with her riding ability, chose the more spirited of the pair and promptly found herself splayed flat on the ground. Flustered, she traded mounts with Farnsworth, grateful that he had not laughed at her unladylike display.

Arriving at the waterfall, Pem could not help but feel that her date seemed somewhat distant. She knew that he played the violin in a dance band, and she asked him how he had happened to take it up. Farnsworth warmed to the subject. As a boy, he told her, he had carefully saved his pennies over a period of several months, hoping to buy a bicycle from the Sears catalog. At the last minute, his grandmother urged him to order a violin instead, and with some reluctance he agreed. Initially the violin had seemed a poor substitute, but over time Farnsworth began to enjoy the instrument. With practice, he believed, he might even aspire to follow in the footsteps of Fritz Kreisler, a popular composer and concert violinist of the day. However, Farnsworth said, apparently gathering his resolve, he had not brought his date up to Bridal Veil to discuss music.

"That's good," said Pem with a nervous laugh. "I was beginning to wonder what you brought me up here for."

It is perhaps fair to say that most young men would have responded with action rather than words, but Farnsworth had, in fact, brought his date to this isolated and romantic spot for a discussion of electromagnetic wave transmission. He spoke for some time, pacing up and down beside the stream, trailing his fingers through the air to show the movement of electrons and occasionally making diagrams in the dirt with a stick. Pem, who had never heard the word "electron" before, much less the unfamiliar "television," did her best to follow what he was saying. She could plainly see, by the intensity of his manner, that the subject had great importance to him. She also sensed apprehension and vulnerability, as though he were revealing some embarrassing family secret. She would later learn that another girl for whom he had cared had dismissed his ideas as nonsense talk, telling him that the man she married would have to be "going somewhere."

Pem listened with a growing sense of wonder. Though she had only a dim understanding of Farnsworth's ideas, she found herself enthralled by his earnest conviction. "Had he told me he could fly to the moon," she recalled, "I would have believed he could find a way."

In fact, Farnsworth did harbor hopes of leading an expedition into space, but he did not say as much to Pem that day. At the time, it was all he could do to keep shoes on his feet. The move to Provo marked a period of tremendous upheaval, with Farnsworth struggling to continue his education while holding down a series of odd jobs.

For a time he worked as a railroad electrician for the Oregon Short Line. As a boy he had been thrilled by the sight of a gleaming locomotive; now he found himself clinging precariously to the runner rail of a moving engine as it passed over the switching points, reaching out with one hand to adjust the focus of the headlights. He performed this task even in rainy weather, when the threat to life and limb was all too vivid, as evidenced by the many injuries and empty sleeves to be seen among his fellow railroad workers. Farnsworth hated the work, but the salary allowed him to take correspondence courses from the University of Utah, along with a radio engineering class from the newly established National Radio Institute. "Men! Here's the 'dope' you've been looking for!" proclaimed an advertisement for the course. "Earn BIG MONEY in work that is almost ROMANCE!"

Farnsworth's dreams of earning big money left very little time for romance, and for a time Pem was left to wonder whether her dashing young admirer had forgotten her. Instead of playing the field, however, Farnsworth was busily devising a new type of radio dial, capable of more sensitive tuning. His father, being of a cautious nature, warned him that such ideas were "too valuable and fragile, and could be pirated easily." The elder Farnsworth provided money so that his son could take out a patent by mail, through one of the many patent lawyers who advertised in the pages of *Science and Invention* magazine. Unfortunately, the lawyer Farnsworth selected—whose advertisement appeared beside notices for "Anti-dyspepsia tonic" and "Ukulele Lessons While You Sleep"—proved to be a shady character. Farnsworth never recovered his father's money, and he resolved to educate himself on matters of patent law, in the hope of avoiding future difficulties.

By the fall of 1923, in keeping with Justin Tolman's advice to "study like the devil and keep mum," Farnsworth had quit the railroad and was doing his level best to continue his education. In Provo he enrolled at the Brigham Young High School and, at the same time, also managed to sign on at Brigham Young University as a special student, working as a janitor to help cover expenses. Farnsworth was only seventeen at the time, and if he had a precocious grasp of advanced science and engineering, his knowledge of basic liberal arts was that of an average high school student. He was aware of the imbalance and was eager to improve himself where he felt deficient. At the same time, he recognized that his television ideas, however promising, were still largely theoretical. He hoped that his university courses would provide the basic knowledge he needed to bring his theories into practice. Although Farnsworth knew of no direct competition, he was troubled by a nagging certainty that someone somewhere must be thinking along similar lines.

To help organize his thinking, Farnsworth developed a habit of jotting down random ideas in a succession of flip-top pocket notebooks. Some of these notebooks survive, offering a snapshot of the young Farnsworth's zeal. Notes on Falstaff and Longfellow are interspersed with drafts of a letter to the Intermountian Electric Company, inquiring about having radio dials rebored to accommodate a particular brass bushing. A basic freshman reading list—"Finish *Twelfth Night* for Monday"—is followed by a strangely animated analysis of Coulomb's law governing the attraction between electrical charges, adorned with frantic directional arrows and exclamation points.

Farnsworth would later say that he confided in some of his Brigham Young professors about his ideas for television. There is no indication that he was taken entirely seriously, though by the end of his time there he had been given free access to the university's laboratory facilities. Farnsworth also spent time at the local utility plant, hoping to pick up spare work while learning the fundamentals of power generation, and he happened to be on hand one day when the main generator broke down. As a boy he had astonished his family by repairing the Delco battery generator at the Rigby farm. Now he found himself working on a larger scale. "Experts were unable to solve the trouble," ran a later account in the Utah *Deseret News*. "Philo stepped forward, asked permission to fix the machinery, and set to work. Soon everything was running smoothly, and the offer of a job followed immediately."

For all his hard work, Farnsworth's time at Brigham Young would in many ways be the most carefree period of his life. He participated in school drama productions, played first violin with the chamber orchestra, attended church regularly, and even found time to learn the piano. As the first semester wound down for the Christmas holidays, Farnsworth looked forward to getting a crack at advanced physics in the coming term.

As the holidays approached, however, all was not well at home. Returning from a ground-clearing project in Idaho, Lewis Farnsworth was caught in a sudden storm and forced to drive his horse team through a savage blizzard. He arrived home with a crust of ice over his clothing and was soon feverish with pneumonia. As his father's condition worsened, Philo took up a vigil at his bedside, recalling the nights they had spent watching the heavens in Rigby, tracking light from distant constellations. Now, as the hours lengthened, Philo spoke again of light traveling from one place to another, carrying coded images in the form of electricity, a passage no less incredible to him than the birth of star.

Lewis Farnsworth died on January 8, 1924, at the age of fifty-eight, leaving his son with much of the responsibility of caring for the family. As his grief-stricken mother withdrew into her bedroom for several weeks, Farnsworth kept up a brave front for his younger siblings. At night, however, he grappled with the loss, often rising from bed and walking three miles to stand at his father's grave. "My father's death was a great shock to me," he later said. "I was extremely unsettled for some time."

Indeed, Farnsworth's life was changed forever, and among the first casualties was his dream of obtaining a college education. Farnsworth mopped floors and sawed lumber in an attempt to continue at Brigham Young, but in the end it was all he could do to finish high school. Unable to find work, he enrolled in the U.S. Naval Academy at Annapolis, Maryland, scoring second in the nation on the entrance examination. The navy seemed to offer a chance of continuing his studies while earning money to send home. As with so many of Farnsworth's ideas, the theory was good, but extremely difficult to reduce to practice. Farnsworth could not adapt to military life, and soon obtained an honorable discharge on the grounds that he was needed at home to support his widowed mother. In part, the decision to leave after a few months was a matter of protecting his future interests. On reaching Annapolis, he realized that he would be obliged to turn over any future inventions—and associated patents—to the United States government. His earlier episode with the radio tuner dial had taught him a great deal about patent law; Farnsworth left the academy determined to maintain control of his ideas at all costs.

Along with this fresh set of convictions, Farnsworth also brought a new name back to Utah. When his fellow cadets saddled him with the nickname "Fido," he decided to drop the *o* from his first name. He would be known as Phil Farnsworth from that point forward. In the wake of his father's death, Farnsworth also had a more relaxed attitude toward the Mormon faith and no longer attended church regularly. Though he would return to the fold in his later years, he now preferred to observe the faith in his own manner.

Throughout 1924 and 1925, as he scrounged for work wherever he could find it, Farnsworth saw his hopes of television work dimming. He knew that without the proper education or training he couldn't possibly hope to sign on with any of the large engineering firms, far less compete with them as an independent researcher. As his family's financial situation worsened, he left Provo for Salt Lake City in search of better opportunities. Pem Gardner's brother Cliff went along with him; the two young men shared a rented room and pooled their incomes, sending much of what they earned back to their families.

In Salt Lake, Farnsworth and Gardner tried to start up a business selling and repairing radio sets. "Radio repair is fun and E–Z!" claimed a notice in *Radio News,* but their experience proved otherwise. Although radio had begun to take hold in Utah, it was by no means the "everyday household utility" envisioned by David Sarnoff. Parts were difficult to obtain, and whatever money Farnsworth and Gardner managed to earn they were forced to plow back into their inventory. Once again Farnsworth fell back on menial labor; he and Gardner signed on with the city's street-sweeping crew, rising before dawn each day to take to the roads with push brooms.

On weekends, Farnsworth traveled back to Provo to see Pem Gardner, although it seemed to her that his move to Salt Lake had placed their courtship on a low boil. Often they would sit around the piano in the Gardners' living room and play music—Pem at the keyboard, her brother Cliff on trombone, and Farnsworth sawing away at his Sears violin. By all accounts, Fritz Kreisler had little to fear from Phil Farnsworth, but Pem liked the wistful expression that came over him as he played.

One weekend Farnsworth brought home a radio set from Salt Lake and threw a party for his friends. The apparatus was still judged to be a considerable novelty; many of Farnsworth's guests had never heard one before, and at least one of his friends felt that the experience warranted a seventy-five-mile drive from Idaho. As the group crowded in for a better view, Farnsworth spun the tuning dial and brought in a music broadcast from a distant station. After a moment, one announcer's voice broke in to dedicate three selections to Phil Farnsworth and party in Provo, Utah. When the music finished, Farnsworth spun the dial again and stood back as an announcer in Los

Angeles dedicated a further three selections to the Provo party, followed by another set of songs broadcast from Cincinnati. Farnsworth, it emerged, had written to each of the stations in advance with his requests. His guests—and Pem in particular—were suitably impressed.

At Friday-night mixers on the Brigham Young campus, Pem would track the state of their relationship by the number of dances Farnsworth claimed. One night they swept out of the hall and danced all the way home along the sidewalk, but Farnsworth then dropped her at her door with a polite tip of his hat. Farnsworth often spoke of his big plans for the future, but Pem recalled feeling an agonizing sense of uncertainty over whether she would have any place in them.

In spite of his big plans, as 1925 drew to a close, Farnsworth appeared firmly mired in a rut. Each month he nervously paged through the latest issues of *Radio News* and *Science and Invention,* half expecting to see an announcement of a breakthrough in electronic television. By this time the major research laboratories on the East Coast had begun to take an interest in mechanical systems of television transmission. It seemed to Farnsworth that they were all flailing around in the dark, but the solution was close at hand, and inevitably one of them would stumble across it sooner or later. Farnsworth, meanwhile, was still sweeping streets in Salt Lake City. At the age of eighteen, he was tortured by a sense of being washed up before he had ever truly begun. At one stage he considered writing up his ideas on television and trying to peddle them to a science magazine. "He thought he might be able to get one hundred dollars if he worked it right," Cliff Gardner recalled. Even that modest ambition seemed beyond his reach, however, and Farnsworth never proceeded with the idea.

On Christmas Eve of 1925, Cliff and Pem Gardner took Farnsworth and his sister Agnes to see their grandparents in Salem, twenty miles south of Provo. Pem's sister Verona was dating a young man who had his own automobile, and the six teenagers made the journey through a frigid winter snowstorm. At long last, Pem recalled, her eighteen-year-old suitor made his move. Driving home from Salem, he drew her close in the backseat of the car and declared his intentions: "Pem," he said, "I think we were made for each other."

As fate would have it, the car ran out of gas at that precise moment. More than sixty years later Pem remembered, with an undiminished sense of awe, that it seemed as if the entire world had stopped along with the car. "I hadn't dared dream this would ever happen," she said simply. By the time the car got back on the road, the two had promised themselves to one another. "Later, when he left me at my door, I could have jumped to the roof and shouted my love for him," Pem insisted. "He had held me in his arms and kissed me!"

For a time, the couple kept their feelings quiet, though in the weeks to come Farnsworth left a series of gifts and keepsakes—flowers, candy, and the sheet music to the recent Irving Berlin release, *Always*. Somehow, to Pem's everlasting wonder, he managed to find the money to present her with a diamond engagement ring the following February, on her eighteenth birthday. She protested vigorously that he would have to take it back—he couldn't possibly afford it, and she didn't want the expense to further derail his education. Farnsworth wouldn't hear of it. "I didn't want to give you a ring we'd both be ashamed of when we're rich," he said. "And we will be."

For all his confidence, there was little to indicate that Farnsworth would ever be solvent, far less rich. In Salt Lake, the radio business continued to struggle, and Farnsworth took on additional odd jobs to keep afloat. By the spring of 1926, he had signed on with a pair of professional fund-raisers named George Everson and Leslie Gorrell, who were in town to organize the local drive for the Community Chest charities.

George Everson had started his career as a social worker, turning to fund-raising on the advice of a colleague in San Francisco. A florid-faced man with a brush mustache, Everson was forty years old when Farnsworth met him. Leslie Gorrell, his younger partner, had only recently graduated from Stanford University. The two men had worked together for two years, and their usual pattern found them arriving in town to take a survey of the local businesses. They would then rent office space and hire some local staff to help organize the campaign. The job might take three or four weeks, at the end of which the two men would move on to their next assignment. There was little to indicate, as they reached Utah, that the Community Chest job would be differ-

ent from any other, and if Everson's car had managed to reach Salt
Lake under its own power, they would never have taken any particular notice of young Phil Farnsworth.

Everson's car, a Chandler roadster, had thrown a bearing as he and
Gorrell crossed over the state line into Utah. They put the car in for
repairs and completed the journey by bus, not wanting to delay the
start of the campaign. In Salt Lake, they found space for their headquarters and advertised for temporary staff. Farnsworth signed onto
the survey team, mapping out the commercial districts for more efficient canvassing, while Cliff Gardner was hired as an office boy.

When Everson's mechanic called several days later to say that the
roadster was ready to be picked up, Farnsworth volunteered to go and
collect it. Two days passed without word from him. "Finally," Everson
recalled, "at the end of the third day, when I was almost distracted with
worry about him and the car, a long-distance telephone call from
Provo came in. It was Phil."

"'Where are you?' I asked with some impatience."

"'I'm in Provo,' he replied. 'The bearing burned out again. I
couldn't get it fixed, so I pulled out the piston and have limped into
here on five cylinders. I'll be in late tonight.'"

Several mechanics had tried and failed to repair the faulty bearing.
Farnsworth—who had not only invented an antitheft device but had
the long pants to prove it—diagnosed the problem immediately.
"Farnsworth impressed me as knowing more about the car than the
man who made it," Everson recalled, "so I asked him to go along with
me and give instructions to the mechanic for its repair."

It had now dawned on Everson that Farnsworth was no ordinary
teenager. "Young Farnsworth at this time looked much older than his
nineteen years," Everson would later say. "He was of moderate height
and slight build and he gave the impression of being undernourished.
He skin lacked the glow of health that is typical of boys his age. There
was a nervous tension about him that was probably the result of financial worry and frustration in making headway in his scientific pursuits.
Around the Community Chest office he had the appearance of a clerk
too closely confined to his work."

One night, after working late into the evening to complete a large mailing, Everson found himself sitting around a conference table with Farnsworth, Gorrell, and Cliff Gardner. The four workers "started a sort of bull session," Everson recalled. "I asked Phil if he planned to go on to school."

Everson saw at once that he had touched a nerve. "I can't afford it," Farnsworth said quickly. After a moment, he added, "I've been trying to find a way to finance an invention of mine, but it's pretty tough."

"What is your idea?" asked Gorrell.

Farnsworth hesitated. "It's a television system," he said.

Everson and Gorrell exchanged a glance. "What's that?" Everson asked.

"It's a way of sending pictures through the air in the same way we do sound," Farnsworth explained. "I thought of it when I was in high school."

Understandably, Everson and Gorrell did not instantly pounce on the idea. The notion seemed fanciful at best, if not actually absurd, and for the moment they took no further interest in the boy who wanted to send pictures through the air. Farnsworth, for his part, immediately regretted having said even this much. Although Everson regarded the subject as nothing more than "the interesting daydream of an ambitious youngster," Farnsworth pleaded with both men to keep quiet about what he had told them. Farnsworth's protective instincts—perhaps more than the idea itself—intrigued the two fund-raisers. Gorrell, who had a background in mechanical engineering, decided that they should explore Farnsworth's idea and "find out what it's all about." A few nights later they took Farnsworth to dinner and asked to hear more.

"As the discussion started," Everson wrote, "Farnsworth's personality seemed to change. His eyes, always pleasant, began burning with eagerness and conviction; his speech, which usually was halting, became fluent to the point of eloquence as he described with the fire of earnestness this scheme that had occupied his mind for the last four years. He became a supersalesman, inspiring his listeners with an ever-increasing interest in what he was saying."

Everson and Gorrell were hardly strangers to the art of salesmanship, but even so they could not help but be swept up by Farnsworth's passion. The idea itself, however, was foreign territory. "When the discussion began I hardly knew what the word 'television' meant," Everson admitted. "I had read somewhere that a man by the name of Baird was doing some experimental work in the transmission of pictures, and that this new art was called 'television.' Otherwise it seemed so far removed from reality that I hadn't given it any thought."

Listening to Farnsworth that evening, he could not help but wonder if this outlandish concept might actually be possible. Almost at once, however, Everson was troubled by a practical concern: "I thought that if Farnsworth, with little more than a high school education and a background of pioneer communities, had conceived this idea of electronic television, surely the great laboratories such as General Electric and Bell must have hit upon the same scheme, and were probably developing it in secret."

When Everson asked about the potential competition, Farnsworth fell silent. Following Justin Tolman's advice, Farnsworth had not previously divulged his ideas to anyone but his teachers, his closest friends, and members of his family. His teachers had asked purely scientific questions about the prospects for success, and his friends and family, who had limited interest in electronic image scanning, had simply listened with indulgent patience. Now, for the first time, someone had asked him a business question. Farnsworth realized that Everson and Gorrell were taking him seriously.

At the same time, Everson had given voice to his darkest fear. Farnsworth had never for a moment doubted that he could make his ideas work. What kept him awake at night was the gnawing fear that someone else—someone in a well-financed corporate lab—was plugging away at the idea while he swept the streets of Salt Lake City. Looking across the table at Everson and Gorrell, he knew that he had been handed an opportunity, and he appreciated how fragile and fleeting such moments could be. Anything less than a full, informed answer would make him seem naive and ill prepared. Still, if Farnsworth dwelled too long on the obstacles that lay in his path, he was likely to scare Everson and Gorrell away. Whatever the risks, however, he felt duty bound to give a candid assessment of the potential competition.

He spent a moment gathering his thoughts. Then he took a deep breath, and began talking.

Five

Tilting at Windmills

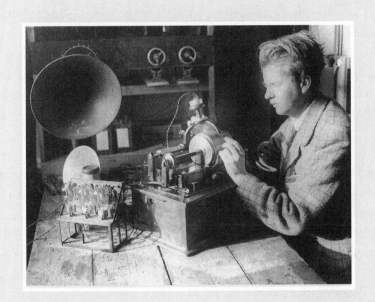

*It's the old story over again. The inventor gets the
experience and the capitalist gets the invention.*

—Charles Francis Jenkins

In November 1922, just a few months after Farnsworth disclosed his television idea to Justin Tolman, he came across a disturbing article in the pages of *Scientific American*. It described the "wondrous strides" being made by a fifty-five-year-old inventor named Charles Francis Jenkins, who earlier that year had applied for a patent to cover his system of transmitting pictures by wireless. Under the title "Motion Pictures by Radio," the *Scientific American* article explained in breathless terms the "startling character of the idea" and went on to assure its readers that the invention "opens up the possibility of broadcasting the image of a man."

For Farnsworth, the possibility of broadcasting the image of a man would not have been especially startling. What really caught his attention was the article's emphasis on the manner in which the Jenkins apparatus made use of "light and electricity, both moving at velocities of 186,000 miles per second." To Farnsworth, this undoubtedly sounded as though Jenkins had tumbled onto his idea of "capturing light in a bottle." In fact, the Jenkins system, though ingenious, was nothing more than a modification of Paul Nipkow's mechanical apparatus, substituting a pair of glass prismatic rings for the whirling metal disk. The

John Logie Baird, the tireless pioneer of mechanical television, is seen here tinkering with his apparatus in 1927. BETTMANN/CORBIS

rings, spinning in opposite directions, offered a means of bending and shaping a beam of light for more effective scanning, rather than shooting the light through the holes of the Nipkow disk. It was a substantial advance, but the Jenkins technique still relied on mechanical movement, while Farnsworth remained convinced that the ultimate success could only be achieved with "no moving parts."

For the moment, however, the Jenkins apparatus was the only game in town. The device, which Jenkins would eventually call a "teloramaphone," had been on his mind for more than a quarter of a century. As a young man, Jenkins had designed a new type of movie projector called a "Phantoscope"—employing an early version of his prismatic rings—which offered a dramatic improvement over its chief competitor, the Edison Kinetoscope. Unlike the Edison model, the Jenkins machine produced images that were free of bothersome flicker, a problem that had been an early obstacle to commercial development of motion pictures.

It appeared that Jenkins was on his way to fame and fortune. Then, mysteriously, the only working Phantoscope was stolen from his home, possibly by one of his partners, and soon appeared under an ironclad patent as the "Edison Vitascope." Jenkins won a court battle over the device—receiving a $2,500 payment, followed by a gold medal of recognition from the Franklin Institute—but all credit for the invention went to Edison. "I'll know better next time," Jenkins declared.

With the Edison payout in his pocket, Jenkins set himself up as an "all-purpose inventor," eventually amassing more than four hundred patents on devices ranging from a wagon-wheel jack to disposable milk bottles. At the turn of the century he unveiled a steam-driven automobile on the streets of Washington, D.C. It traveled so slowly, Jenkins recalled, that small boys were literally able to run rings around it—"with derisive thumbs at their noses."

In 1910, having traded this conveyance for a comparatively sprightly Model T, Jenkins decided to revive his flagging inspiration with a coast-to-coast road trip. Being of a precise turn of mind, Jenkins resolved to make the journey in the most literal sense possible. In Atlantic City, he drove his car onto the beach and backed the rear wheels into the waters of the Atlantic. He then drove due west until the front wheels were resting in the Pacific. Along the way, Jenkins allowed himself to reflect on the lessons of the Phantoscope, and how he might yet turn the inspiration to a more lasting advantage. As early as 1894, he had conceived of a notion he called "Radiovision," a process for "transmitting images to a distance by electricity." It now occurred to him, not for the first time, that he might be able to combine the Phantoscope with Radiovision, adapting the glass rings of the movie projector to a television scanning system.

It would be some time before the pieces came together. In 1921, after more than a decade of further experimentation, he established the Jenkins Laboratories in Washington, D.C., for the purpose of developing "radio movies" to be broadcast for entertainment in the home. By May of the following year he had succeeded in sending still photographs by radio. A few months later, Jenkins held a demonstration for a select audience of military officials, broadcasting a picture of President Harding from the navy's radio station in Anacostia, Virginia, to a newspaper office in Philadelphia. The navy brass were impressed; they snapped up the device with the intention of sending weather maps to ships at sea.

"Television has now been perfected," declared S. R. Winters in the pages of *Science and Invention*. "This arresting statement, when seriously employed by any individual other than the accredited originator and inventor of the motion-picture machine would smack of sensationalism. However, when C. Francis Jenkins of Washington, D.C., possessor of the Elliott Cresson gold medal, awarded by the Franklin Institute of America for his original contribution to motion picture mechanics, announces that he has discovered a means for transmitting photographs and motion pictures through space, the public lends an attentive ear."

Indeed, transmitting the image of Harding had put Jenkins on the map, but, as even he admitted, the entertainment value diminished upon repeated viewings. Determined to press ahead until his system could accommodate moving images, Jenkins returned to his lab. By June 1925, Jenkins declared himself ready to broadcast "readily recognizable moving objects"—a phrase that would loom large in patent battles to come. A group of Washington notables, among them the heads of the Bureau of Standards and the Commerce Department, gathered at the Jenkins Laboratories for what were believed to be the first moving images ever broadcast. Barely visible through a field of static, a dim, hazy snippet of motion could be seen bubbling up on Jenkins's ten-by-twelve-inch screen—the slowly turning blades of a windmill.

In Utah, Farnsworth learned of the breakthrough in the pages of *Radio News,* yet another Hugo Gernsback publication. "I have just left the laboratory of Mr. C. Francis Jenkins of Washington, D.C.," Gernsback told his readers, "and am still under the influence of what I consider to be the most marvelous invention of the age." Gernsback gave an animated description of the manner in which he had seen his own hand "projected by radio," and then went on to discuss the potential applications of the device: "The day will come when you will be able to sit at home and witness a baseball game as it is being played five thousand miles away, or you will be able to sit at home and not only listen to, but also actually see an opera as it is being sung and acted. In future wars, it will be possible for an Admiral to witness a naval battle and to follow it with his own eyes, although his battleship squadron may be thousands of miles away."

If the pursuit of "remote seeing" had at first seemed quixotic, the "Windmill Broadcast," as it came to be known, appeared to mark television's coming of age. Jenkins was hailed as "the father of television" in the *New York Times,* and *Scientific American* described the event as "the dawn of a new epoch."

"Congratulations were in order," Jenkins admitted, "but they seemed to be given in a rather awed manner as the unfathomable possibilities of this new extension of human vision came to be more and more realized."

It would have required a great deal of imagination to fathom those possibilities from what the observers saw on Jenkins's viewing screen. His prismatic scanner produced images that were so crude as to be little more than silhouettes, with no light and dark shadings at all, rather like the portrait cuttings made by carnival entertainers of the day. Jenkins was keenly aware of the limitations of his apparatus and felt certain that he would soon be able to refine the images. For the moment, however, he took considerable pride in having given "the first public demonstration of radiovision."

Here, Jenkins was sadly mistaken. An energetic Scottish engineer named John Logie Baird had achieved much the same thing two months earlier, in the electrical goods section of a London department store.

At first glance, John Logie Baird seemed even less likely than Philo T. Farnsworth to make his mark as a television pioneer. Two years previously, toward the end of 1923, Baird had arrived in Hastings, on the southeastern coast of England, to nurse himself back to health following a nervous collapse. "Coughing, choking and spluttering, and so thin as to be almost transparent, I arrived at Hastings station," he later recalled, "assets totaling two hundred pounds, prospects nothing. What was to be done? I must invent something."

His early efforts in this line could not have been called promising. First he developed a "rustless" razor made of glass, but the initial tests were discouraging. "After cutting myself rather badly," he wrote, "I decided to try pneumatic soles." The idea of inflatable shoes struck him as a natural extension of the pneumatic tire, which had only recently been introduced, and promised to remove some of the "bothersome knocks and jolts" from the daily business of walking. Accordingly, Baird purchased a pair of extra-large boots and placed semi-inflated balloons in the soles. "I walked a hundred yards in a succession of drunken and uncontrollable lurches," he recalled, "followed by a few delighted urchins, then the demonstration was brought to a conclusion by one of my tyres bursting."

Undaunted, Baird decided to turn his attention to something he considered less difficult. At dinner with his friend Guy Robertson—whose resemblance to a portrait of Mephistopheles had won him the nickname "Mephy"—Baird outlined his latest brainstorm: "Well, sir," he declared over raisin pudding, "you will be pleased to hear that I have invented a means of seeing by wireless."

"Oh," replied Mephy, "I hope that doesn't mean you are going to become one of those wireless nitwits. You can't afford to play about, you know."

Mephy's concern was not unwarranted, as there was little in Baird's background to suggest that he might succeed. The son of a parish minister, Baird was born on the west coast of Scotland in 1888. After taking a degree from a technical school—with an extra year tacked on because of "lack of ability and stupidity"—Baird worked his way through a series of menial jobs, eventually becoming an engineer's assistant in Glasgow. Baird later insisted that he might well have lived out the rest of his life in this comfortable if unexciting post had he not fallen madly in love with a young Glaswegian woman who lived near his rooming house. Baird now felt an overpowering need to better his circumstances and prove himself a worthy suitor. His methods of doing so led him to peculiar extremes. First he took a notion to market a hemorrhoid "specific" devised by a friend. This endeavor came to grief when Baird tried the "mysterious white ointment" on himself: "I was unable to sit down for some days." Not long afterward, Baird's career as a city engineer ended in spectacular fashion: while attempting to create industrial diamonds in a pot of cement, Baird tapped into an electrical main and blew out much of the city's power supply. He tendered his resignation and, with few other options available, decided to become a full-time inventor.

Baird's health had always been precarious, rendering him unfit for service during World War I. Disappointed by the rejection, he decided to make his contribution by means of the "Baird Undersock"—a thin cotton sheath, treated with borax, to be worn under the ordinary sock with the idea of wicking away moisture to keep the foot dry. To promote the item, Baird hired a platoon of women to march through Glasgow wearing sandwich boards that read: "The Baird Undersock for the Soldier's Foot."

Although the undersock enjoyed a modest success, Baird was not able to persuade his lady friend of his future prospects. Downcast, he succumbed to another of the bronchial ailments to which he was prone, despite the protection of the Baird Undersock. With his health at a low ebb, he decided to seek his fortune in warmer climes, promising to return and claim his beloved once he had invented something of lasting value.

With this goal in mind, the young inventor set off for Trinidad, where he lost a great deal of money in a scheme to export the local fruits for jam and preserves. He washed up in London, where he recouped some of his losses with "Baird's Speedy Cleanser," a cheap yellow soap that he marketed to hotels and boardinghouses. Buoyed by this upturn, he traveled to Glasgow to claim his love, only to discover that she had married in his absence. Baird's response was typically unorthodox. Upon discovering that the young lady still had feelings for him, he confronted her husband and hammered out a genteel agreement by which each enjoyed her company for several months of the year, with alternating holidays.

Baird was similarly accommodating in his business practices. When a cheaper soap called "Hutchinson's Rapid Washer" threatened to overtake his Speedy Cleanser, Baird invited Hutchinson for drinks at the Café Royal, where the two men decided to throw in together. Before the merger could take effect, however, Baird's health gave out completely. He allowed himself to be bought out so that he could remove himself to the relatively restful environment of Hastings. There, in 1923, he set to work on television. "The only ominous cloud on the horizon," he later wrote, "was that, in spite of the apparent simplicity of the task, no one had produced television."

Baird had little money, no laboratory facilities, and only a narrow experience of electrical engineering. Nevertheless, within eighteen months he had fashioned a working mechanical television. An account published in 1933 gives some sense of his improvisational genius: "An old tea-chest, purchased for a few coppers and carried through the Hastings streets, formed a base to carry the motor which rotated the exploring disk, while an empty biscuit box housed the projection lamp. Scanning discs were cut out of cardboard, and the mountings consisted of darning needles and old scrap timber. The necessary lenses on the optical side of the apparatus were procured from bicycle shops at a cost of fourpence each, while electric motors ready for the scrap-heap were pressed into service on duties for which they were never intended and were entirely unsuited. One or two old hat boxes were also utilized, and the whole conglomeration of bits and pieces was precariously held together with glue, sealing-wax and odd lengths of string."

Incredibly, it worked. Initially the images were no better than

Jenkins's silhouettes, so Baird busied himself with finding money to re-fine the system. Baird drew inspiration from a potential backer who told him that he would have "all the money you want" if he was able to transmit the image of a living face from one room to the next. Using the head of a ventriloquist's dummy named "Stookie Bill," Baird tried every conceivable method of wringing a recognizable image out of his Nipkow disk transmitter, eventually enlarging the scanning disk to an enormous eight-foot diameter. "On more than one occasion lenses broke loose," he recalled, "striking the walls or roof like bomb shells. The apparatus would then get out of balance and jump from one side of the lab to the other until it was stopped or the disk tore itself to pieces. I had some exciting moments."

These exciting moments seldom found favor with Baird's land-lords, and he moved frequently in the early days of his experimenta-tion. At one stage, after a 2,000-volt explosion blew him across a room, Baird was obliged to remove himself from Hastings. Returning to London, he found a small room in a fifth-floor attic on Frith Street, in Soho.

By now the work on his television prototype had left him in such financial straits that he frequently went without food. Desperate for working capital, Baird made the rounds trying to drum up publicity in order to attract backers. At the offices of the *Daily Express* newspaper, he was treated as a potential lunatic—"Watch him carefully," declared the editor, "he may have a razor hidden!" He fared no better at Britain's Marconi Wireless Telegraph Company, where the general manager, who owed his livelihood to the efforts of a young inventor not unlike Baird, declared that he had no interest whatsoever in tele-vision—"not in the very slightest degree."

Help arrived from an unusual quarter. Gordon Selfridge, of the world-famous Selfridges Department Store, presented himself at Frith Street in March 1925 asking to see Baird's apparatus. Baird happened to have the device working tolerably well at the time and was able to show Selfridge a crude transmission—the faint outline of a paper mask. Impressed, Selfridge asked Baird to demonstrate the system for three weeks in the electrical section of his store. Selfridges printed up a cir-cular to announce the "First Public Demonstration of Television" and went on to explain, "Television is to light what telephony is to sound—it means the INSTANTANEOUS transmission of a picture, so that the observer at the 'receiving' end can see, to all intents and purposes, what is a cinematographic view of what is happening at the 'sending' end."

Anticipating the potential for disappointment, given the crude state of Baird's apparatus, Selfridges offered a careful qualification: "The apparatus here demonstrated is, of course, absolutely 'in the rough'—the question of finance is always an important one for the inventor. But it does, undoubtedly, transmit an instantaneous picture. The picture is flickering and defective, and at present only simple pictures can be sent successfully; but Edison's first phonograph announced that 'Mary had a little lamb' in a way that only hearers who were 'in the secret' could understand—and yet, from that first result has developed the gramophone of today. Unquestionably the present experimental apparatus can be similarly perfected and refined."

This lowering of expectation proved to be necessary. During the three weeks of demonstrations, Baird managed to transmit only the crudest images, little better than bare outlines of shapes, and nothing that approached his desired goal of a "living human face." Even so, this hastily organized publicity stunt served to secure Baird's place in history as the man who gave the world's first public demonstration of television. For the present, however, Baird was far more concerned with the fee he received for his services. Selfridges had thrown him a lifeline of £25 per week, allowing him to continue with his work for a little while longer. When the demonstration period concluded, Baird withdrew to his Soho walk-up and resumed his experiments.

It was there, in October 1925, that Baird managed to resolve the "streaky blob" on his receiving screen into a recognizable image of "Stookie Bill," his ventriloquist dummy. "I had got it!" he recalled. "I could scarcely believe my eyes, and felt myself shaking with excitement." Running down to street level, Baird grabbed hold of an office boy named William Taynton and dragged him upstairs to sit in front of the transmitter. When the boy balked at the bright lights and fearsome-looking apparatus, Baird fished into his pocket for a half crown.

Taynton reluctantly consented—becoming, as Baird would claim, "the first face seen by television."

On January 26, 1926, an extraordinary group assembled in the street outside Baird's makeshift laboratory. It included a number of influential journalists, such as the science editor of the *Times,* along with some forty members of Britain's Royal Institution, an organization devoted to the advancement of science. In keeping with the solemnity of the occasion, the visitors arrived in evening dress. "This gorgeous gathering found that they were expected to climb three flights of narrow stone stairs," Baird recalled, "and then to stand in a narrow draughty passage, while batches of six at a time were brought into the two tiny attic rooms which formed my laboratory."

This was to be the official debut of the Baird system, and in spite of the cramped quarters the demonstration proved a great success—apart from the dismay of one of the elderly visitors when his long white beard became entangled in the whirling Nipkow disk. For Baird, it was a watershed moment. Only a few weeks earlier he had been tossed out the offices of the *Daily Express.* Now he found himself hailed as a "modern Galileo," while visitors swarmed from across the country to witness the miracle of Frith Street—everyone, said Baird, "from the office boy to the Prime Minister." The *New York Times* declared that "the international race for the perfection of television has been won by Great Britain." *Radio News* confirmed the verdict: "After countless experiments and years spent in research, Mr. J. L. Baird of London has at last succeeded in making his system of television a practical proposition." Even A. A. Campbell Swinton, who had theorized on the potential of the cathode ray nearly twenty years earlier, now came around to Baird's way of thinking. "I have been converted! I have been converted!" he cried after seeing the Baird system in action.

Phil Farnsworth, who was still doing odd jobs in Salt Lake City when he read of Baird's accomplishment in *Radio News,* had not been converted. For all of the favorable press, Farnsworth remained unshakable in his conviction that Baird's Nipkow disk scanner would never be practical. Nevertheless, Farnsworth could not help but admire the ingenuity and determination that had wrung an actual image from a hat box and a darning needle. In time, Farnsworth would have the opportunity of saying so in person.

It had been a fairly simple matter for Farnsworth to keep tabs on the progress of both Baird and Francis Jenkins. Both were independents, which obliged them to stage frequent public demonstrations, with as much press coverage as they could muster to attract investors. Reading the press reports from Utah, Farnsworth felt reassured that both Baird and Jenkins were spinning their disks in vain. There was always the danger that one of them would abandon the mechanical approach in favor of an all-electronic system, but at present it didn't seem likely.

A far greater concern was Dr. Ernst Fredrik Werner Alexanderson, celebrated as "the man who made radio circle the globe," who in 1925 announced his intention to conquer the problem of television once and for all. Similar statements from Baird and Jenkins had not caused Farnsworth much anxiety. Dr. Alexanderson, the chief engineer of the Radio Corporation of America, was an entirely different matter. Farnsworth had no doubt whatsoever that RCA had the talent—and, more importantly, the resources—to bring an all-electronic system of television to the public. His only hope, as he followed Alexanderson's confident pronouncements in the pages of *Radio News*, was that the elder statesman of wireless communication was looking in the wrong place.

Ernst Alexanderson, who made his reputation at General Electric, was a man of such idiosyncratic habits that, according to one colleague, even Albert Einstein would have found him "a bit eccentric." Born in Sweden, Alexanderson studied engineering at the Royal Institute of Technology in Stockholm. Upon graduation in 1902, Alexanderson joined twenty-five of his classmates in departing for Schenectady, New York, the home of General Electric's main laboratory, which was then considered to be the white-hot center of the world's electrical research.

Within three years of his arrival, Alexanderson had devised the famed radio alternator which had been a key feature in "throwing a human voice across the ocean" and which had figured so prominently in the formation of RCA. "The alternator," Alexanderson would later say, "was one of the inventions I had to make in order to hold my job." In the end, Alexanderson not only held his job but acquired several others as well. Although RCA controlled the patents to his work, Alexanderson's compensations were munificent. In addition to his position at General Electric, he became the first chief engineer of RCA, which brought his combined salary to a staggering $20,000 in 1919— a sum that even Phil Farnsworth, with all his dreams of future riches, could scarcely have contemplated.

With his disheveled blond hair and handlebar mustache, Alexanderson made a vivid impression. Famously absentminded, he would occasionally lapse into Swedish while greeting a colleague and had to be reminded that English was favored in Schenectady. Once, upon meeting a familiar-looking woman in the street, Alexanderson bowed politely before the young woman revealed that she was, in fact, his daughter.

During one such period of mental abstraction, Alexanderson conceived of a process by which television could be achieved "using only apparatus that already exists at present." As early as 1917, he had explored the possibility of transmitting pictures into the cockpits of military aircraft, as the roar of the engines often drowned out radio communication. By 1923 he was hard at work on a method of sending still pictures across the Atlantic, which led in turn to "the possibilities of transmitting moving pictures by radio."

Alexanderson was dismissive of the work of Baird and Jenkins. In December 1924, when David Sarnoff was considering buying up the Jenkins patents, he consulted his chief engineer. Alexanderson, who had already reconnoitered the Jenkins lab, advised against it. "Mr. Jenkins makes certain claims for television which he has not substantiated," Alexanderson reported. "The demonstration which I saw in Washington two years ago was very crude and so far as I have been able to learn he has not made much progress in that time." He went on to assure Sarnoff that "we will control this situation provided that we are the first to give a practical demonstration."

Alexanderson had reason to be confident. He was making huge strides in his effort to send photographs across the Atlantic by radio, which he judged to be the crucial first step toward a television system.

Although the process took twenty minutes, it marked a dramatic improvement over similar designs by other experimenters. Alexanderson recognized, however, that the process still had a long way to go before it could be developed into television. "From moving picture practice we know that the realization of this idea would require the transmission of a series of pictures at the rate of sixteen per second," he told *Science and Invention* magazine in 1925. "It is a long way from twenty minutes to one-sixteenth of a second. It means that we must work almost twenty thousand times faster than we do now. How long it will take to attain this end I do not venture to say. Our work has, however, already proven that the expectation of television is not unreasonable and that it may be accomplished with means that are in our possession at the present day."

The knowledge that the formidable Ernst Alexanderson, the titan of radio, had turned his attention to television can only have horrified young Phil Farnsworth. Though Farnsworth had yet to conduct his first experiment in 1925, he was now squaring up against a research juggernaut that combined the resources and manpower of Westinghouse, General Electric, and the American Telephone and Telegraph Company. Under the banner of RCA, Alexanderson and his team had access to every significant patent and laboratory facility in the United States, along with a virtually unlimited research budget. Farnsworth, by contrast, had a shoebox filled with tubes and wires, and a copy of *The Boy's Book of Electricity.*

What Farnsworth could not have known, upon reading Alexanderson's confident statements to the press, was that the older man's efforts would, for the time being, place a choke hold on RCA's television initiative. Soon enough, David Sarnoff would have cause to reevaluate the ideas of his chief engineer. For the moment, however, RCA took its cues from Alexanderson, whose thinking had not carried him much beyond the terrain of Baird and Jenkins.

Unlike Baird and Jenkins, however, Alexanderson recognized the vast hurdle that stood in his way. "At the root of this situation is the fact that we have to depend upon moving mechanical parts," Alexanderson would tell the American Institute of Electrical Engineers in December 1926. "If we knew of any way of sweeping a ray of light

back and forth without the use of mechanical motion, the solution of
the problem would be simplified. Perhaps some such way will be discovered, but we are not willing to wait for a discovery that may never
come."

/ / /

Alexanderson had no way of knowing that a teenage farm boy from
Utah had already conceived of just such a ray of light. For the moment, he was content to forge ahead with mechanical apparatus, leaving Farnsworth to conclude that every other television researcher in
the world was pumping a dry well. Sitting with George Everson and
Leslie Gorrell at their restaurant conference in Salt Lake, Farnsworth
drummed his hands on the table as he emphasized the point: television
could be accomplished only by stripping away the mechanical parts,
and only he had a viable plan to do so. "If mechanical parts are used,
the results will be crude and blurred," Farnsworth insisted. "I propose
to do it by manipulating electrons within vacuum tubes."

The two older men were greatly impressed by Farnsworth's vast
knowledge of what the potential competition had achieved, but several doubts remained. "It was all so highly abstruse," Everson recalled,
"yet told with such conviction, that although I was in no position to
evaluate the merits of the invention, I was tremendously impressed
with the amazing knowledge of the youth and his certainty that he
could accomplish what he had proposed."

Even so, Everson could not be certain whether he was dealing
with an imaginative boy or a genuine visionary. As the session broke
up late that evening, Farnsworth had no idea where matters stood.
Once again, he asked that the discussion be kept confidential. "The
idea hasn't been patented," he said. "I haven't had the money."

Here, Farnsworth was speaking a language that Everson and Gorrell could understand. "Actually," Everson said, "have you anything to
patent yet? Don't you have to make a thing work before you can get a
patent on it?"

Farnsworth, still smarting from his misadventure with the mail-
order patent lawyer, had now read up on the matter. A patent on a television system or any of its various components, he explained, would

guarantee him the exclusive right of ownership for a period of seventeen years, allowing him time to get his television system into production and earn money from it. At the same time, he could also license his patent rights to other manufacturers in return for royalties. The process of securing patent rights, as Farnsworth understood it, involved the creation of a working model—or "reduction to practice"—in order to demonstrate that the apparatus worked as claimed.

Everson considered the matter. "What do you think it would cost to build up a first model of your scheme?"

Farnsworth replied that he couldn't be certain.

"Well, think it over," said Everson. "Maybe if the cost isn't too great we can find the money to do it."

With that, he and Gorrell said good night and climbed into the Chandler roadster. Farnsworth did not appear to notice their departure. For some moments he stood alone on the sidewalk outside the restaurant. For once, his drumming hands and tapping feet were perfectly still.

Over the next few days, even as the fund-raising campaign picked up steam, Farnsworth bombarded Everson and Gorrell with information about television. "Phil, with superb salesmanship, snatched every opportunity to give us further details of his plans," Everson recalled. "Any scrap of paper would suffice for him to draw out scratchy designs of some part of his system."

Everson now felt a growing determination to help Farnsworth nail down a patent. During a lull after an especially vigorous campaign meeting, Everson found himself in an expansive mood. Turning to Farnsworth, he asked again how much money it would take to produce a working system. This was the moment of truth, and Farnsworth knew it. "It's pretty hard to say," he answered slowly, "but I should think five thousand dollars would be enough."

Everson weighed the figure carefully. "Well," he answered, "your guess is as good as any. I surely have no idea what is involved. I have about six thousand dollars in a special account in San Francisco. I've accumulated it with the idea that I'd take a long-shot chance on something, hoping to make a killing. This is about as wild a gamble as I can imagine. I'll put that up to work this thing out. If I win, it will be fine, but if we lose I won't squawk."

Everson would prove as good as his word. Six thousand dollars was a great deal of money in 1926, and Everson had decided to bet it all on a nineteen-year-old boy. In the years to come he would never once squawk, even though Farnsworth's estimated budget would prove to be wildly optimistic. "Farnsworth made me believe," Everson said. "He was so confident, so modestly self-assured, that you just couldn't help but rally behind him."

Over the next few days, the three men drew up a partnership agreement. Although he had put up no money, Farnsworth was given a 50 percent share in the enterprise, with the understanding that he would devote himself full time to the project. Everson and Gorrell were to split the remaining shares, with Gorrell promising to help cover Everson's losses if the project failed. Both men agreed that Farnsworth would owe nothing if the money was lost.

None of the three partners had even the slightest notion of what lay ahead. Everson believed that it would simply be a question of following Farnsworth's blueprint—a matter of a few weeks, perhaps. Farnsworth, though supremely confident, suspected that there might be a few technical hitches along the way. Gorrell was simply along for the ride. "The three of us were as ill-prepared for the venture under consideration as anyone could possibly be," Everson later admitted.

For the moment, all three felt a powerful sense of purpose, and once the deal was signed, events moved at a tremendous pace. Everson and Gorrell's next job would be taking them to Los Angeles. Farnsworth, realizing that he had exhausted the technical resources available to him in Utah, readily agreed to come along and set up a laboratory in California, where he would have ready access to better materials and scientific libraries. As the arrangements were finalized, however, Farnsworth threw his new partners a curve. He could not possibly come to Los Angeles, he insisted, without his fiancée. Everson attempted to reason with him, suggesting that it might be best to put the marriage on hold until the television enterprise had shown some progress. Farnsworth wouldn't hear of it. He found a telephone and placed a call to Provo: "Pem, darling," he said, "can you be ready to be married in three days?"

If Pem's response was incredulous—"You've got to be kidding!"— it was mild compared to that of the young couple's parents. Farnsworth traveled to Provo, where his considerable powers of persuasion were sorely tested as he tried to convince his mother and Pem's father to allow the marriage to go forth. In the end they relented, and on May 27, 1926, the couple were married by a local church authority at the Gardners' home. Farnsworth's mother was obliged to cosign the marriage license, as the groom was under the age of consent.

The newlyweds planned to leave for California the following day. Farnsworth had borrowed Everson's roadster so that he and Pem could drive back to Salt Lake City and spend their wedding night in a hotel by the train station. Realizing that he did not have enough money for the coming journey, Farnsworth was forced to make an ungallant retreat from the bridal suite in order to seek out Everson for a loan. The two men fell into a lengthy planning session for the Los Angeles lab, leaving young Mrs. Farnsworth alone on her wedding night.

Straggling back to the hotel several hours later, Farnsworth was quick to apologize for abandoning his bride. However, he warned, such absences were to be expected from time to time. With sudden intensity, he grasped her by the shoulders and fixed her with a grave expression. "Pemmie," he declared, "I have to tell you there is another woman in my life—and her name is Television."

If the pronouncement strikes the ear as a bit mannered and self-conscious, it must be remembered that Farnsworth was not yet out of his teens. He was not a man given to rhetoric, but it is cheering to note that at least on his wedding night, he wished to capture something of the moment, and convey a sense of destiny in the journey they had undertaken.

The moment would be brief.

Six

The Battle of the Century

On July 2, 1921, heavyweight champion Jack Dempsey, the famed "Manassas Mauler," climbed into the ring at Boyle's Thirty Acres in Jersey City, New Jersey, before a crowd of some ninety thousand boxing fans. His opponent, attired in an elegant gray silk robe, was Georges Carpentier, the French light-heavyweight known as "the Orchid Man." At stake was the heavyweight championship, a $1 million gate, and David Sarnoff's career.

Legendary promoter Tex Rickard had whipped up an unprecedented level of interest. Billed as the "Battle of the Century," the fight took on the trappings of a contest of good versus evil. Carpentier, who had flown combat in World War I, was presented as the "champion of righteousness," while Dempsey, who had been labeled a draft dodger during the war, took on the role of the scowling villain.

At ringside, an anxious David Sarnoff paced through a makeshift announcer's booth, checking the placement of an RCA microphone and telephone link. Though he cautiously described his efforts as experimental, Sarnoff was attempting something his superiors had dismissed as "just plain crazy"—a live sports broadcast to an estimated 300,000 Americans. If successful, the broadcast would jump-start

David Sarnoff, left, and his mentor, Guglielmo Marconi, tour a Long Island transmitting station in 1933. BETTMANN/CORBIS

RCA's stalled radio initiative and propel Sarnoff to the fore of mass communications. If not, Sarnoff might well find himself out of a job.

In the first year of RCA's existence, Sarnoff had watched with mounting frustration as others took control of the emerging radio industry. In Pittsburgh, Westinghouse had not only begun producing home radio sets but had also launched America's first licensed radio station—KDKA. Through a series of well-managed publicity stunts, including the broadcast of the 1920 presidential election returns, Westinghouse had taken the lead in bringing news and music programs into America's homes. The success of Westinghouse and the others who followed came as a bitter blow to Sarnoff, the prophet of radio in the living room. Eager to get in the game, Sarnoff dusted off his "Radio Music Box" memo and took it to his superiors, receiving only a token budget of $2,500 to develop a radio prototype. Undeterred by the meager show of support, Sarnoff pushed ahead and enlisted RCA's director of research, Dr. Alfred Goldsmith, to create an RCA music box, called the Radiola.

At the same time, Sarnoff moved to shore up his status at RCA. The formation of the company had left him in a precarious position, severing his ties to the British Marconi organization and also to Guglielmo Marconi himself, who had long been his mentor and protector. Although Sarnoff had done his best to forge a relationship with Owen Young, RCA's chairman of the board, there were now many more executives in the expanded company's pantheon, and a great many of them stood between Sarnoff and Young in the corporate hierarchy. Once again, Sarnoff found himself isolated as the only Jew in the executive ranks, and whispers of his "money-grubbing" tendencies began to circulate through the company. Sarnoff began to notice that a subtle campaign of blackballing was underway. Busy work was funneled to his office. Invitations to company gatherings went astray in the interoffice mail. Indignant customers, many of them carrying faulty General Electric toasters, were directed to him. Sarnoff later recalled that "all the stray cat and dog problems of management were being dumped on my desk."

One night in the early months of 1921, Sarnoff rented a private dining room at the famed Delmonico's restaurant and invited Owen

Young to dinner. For two years, the chairman of the board had relied heavily on Sarnoff's technical expertise. Now, over the course of a lavish four-hour meal, Sarnoff moved to forge a personal relationship as well. In many ways the scene recalled Sarnoff's approach to Marconi outside the William Street wireless office fifteen years earlier. Once again he poured out his life story, from Russia to Hell's Kitchen and beyond. Then, having established his rags-to-riches pedigree, Sarnoff outlined his plans for the future of the wireless industry. By midnight, as the two men finished their cigars and coffee, Sarnoff had won another powerful ally.

Sarnoff would later recall the evening at Delmonico's as a turning point of his career. Young let it be known that Sarnoff was now his protégé, and the office hazing came to a sudden halt. Within weeks, Sarnoff was named general manager of RCA.

Having secured his home ground, Sarnoff now moved to neutralize the lead Westinghouse had established in the radio market. Although Westinghouse was a partner in the RCA patent pool, the language of the original agreement had not anticipated the emergence of potentially lucrative broadcasting stations. While Sarnoff had been sidetracked with meaningless paperwork, Westinghouse had secured broadcast licenses in New York, Chicago, and several other cities. Now, with the industry gearing up for a radio boom, RCA seemed likely to be left on the sidelines.

Sarnoff knew that he would have to take a gamble if he hoped to enter the market, and the Dempsey-Carpentier prize fight seemed to offer a prime opening. Though Sarnoff had little interest in sports, he knew that a successful radio broadcast would capture the nation's attention and generate a publicity bonanza. He moved quickly to make arrangements, allowing certain formalities, such as securing the approval of RCA's royalty partners, to fall between the cracks.

Working against the clock, Sarnoff managed to cobble together the equipment needed for the broadcast. He located a powerful General Electric transmitter bound for the Navy Department in Washington and managed to divert it to a railroad shed near the fight venue. A makeshift antenna was fashioned from wires strung along the railroad towers, linked by telephone to the RCA microphone at ringside. Specially amplified receiving sets were deployed throughout the broadcast area in Elks clubs, town halls, movie theaters, and school auditoriums so that the fight would reach the widest possible audience. Having no official authorization for the project, and therefore no budget, Sarnoff simply "plucked what I needed from whatever departments had a little cash in the till."

As the fight time approached, Sarnoff knew that if any link in the chain of equipment failed him, he would have a public relations disaster on his hands. Where possible, he arranged for backup systems. The same applied to the human element. Sarnoff drafted an RCA employee named Andrew White, an enthusiastic fight buff, to take the microphone for the blow-by-blow commentary. As a backup, in the event that White froze at the microphone, Sarnoff himself stood ready to step in.

As the opening bell sounded, White proved equal to the task—although his colorful account of the fight traveled no farther than the nearby railroad shed, where an RCA technician read an edited version over the airwaves in a comparatively flat and lifeless drone. Even so, the broadcast was an enormous success, reaching a record number of listeners and drawing newspaper headlines throughout America and Europe. Edward Nally, RCA's president, promptly fired off a congratulatory telegram to Sarnoff: "You have made history."

It had been a near thing. During the fourth round of the fight, as Dempsey finished Carpentier off with a flurry of blows to the head, the heat inside the RCA transmitter shed had climbed to a dangerous level. Moments after Carpentier hit the canvas, the transmitter blew out completely. Had the fight gone another round, the broadcast would have been a total flop. For the rest of his life, Sarnoff would express gratitude for Dempsey's amazing hand speed.

Overnight, it became clear that Sarnoff's gamble had paid off. RCA soon took a leading role in the radio boom, and the board of directors gave enthusiastic approval to an RCA broadcast transmitter in New York. "We were in the game at last," Sarnoff recalled.

Sarnoff had climbed aboard at the last possible moment. In 1921, the Department of Commerce issued thirty-two broadcast licenses; the following year, there were more than six hundred. The public, in

Sarnoff's phrase, "thought well of the new device," and demand soon exceeded supply. By 1922, RCA's first full year of radio sales, the company's gross income exceeded $11 million—a full $3 million in excess of Sarnoff's "Radio Music Box" predictions.

For Sarnoff, however, it wasn't enough simply to be in the game. The RCA patent pool, he believed, carried the power to set the rules. By 1923, more than two hundred radio manufacturers had sprung into being, along with an additional five thousand producers of individual components. Many of these were independent concerns, operating without regard to the patents on radio tubes, and some were little better than black market wholesalers, stripping down name-brand radio sets to assemble generic equivalents. Even major manufacturers such as the Zenith Radio Corporation, Sarnoff believed, were buying RCA radio tubes and plugging them into their branded models.

To Sarnoff, these activities represented millions of dollars in lost patent royalties. He resolved to clamp down on the offenders and assert the authority of the RCA patent pool. Otherwise, he concluded, the company would fumble away its greatest asset. Targeting suspect distributors, Sarnoff imposed severe restrictions on the flow of components, insisting that henceforth RCA tubes would be available only with complete radio sets. No single tubes would be sold; if a distributor wished to order a replacement for a damaged set, the burned-out tube would have to be returned.

Sarnoff now gained a reputation as the industry's enforcer, a role that would earn him many enemies. Among them was the president of Zenith, who charged that RCA had created an untenable situation by refusing to license its patents—competitors were forced to choose between infringement or bankruptcy. Soon, rumblings of antitrust action could be heard coming from Washington. Sarnoff offered a compromise. A package of RCA's essential patents would be made available to the leading manufacturers, in exchange for a percentage of sales revenues.

Even as this compromise went into effect, simmering charges of monopolistic practices gathered new force. In 1923, as the RCA patent pool expanded to nearly four thousand patents, the United States Justice Department geared up to challenge the company's legality. The irony was not lost on RCA's executive board: only four years earlier, the company had come into being under the aegis of the U.S. military; now the government was threatening antitrust action.

Even as he sprang to the defense, Sarnoff glimpsed an opportunity. The company's size had been an encumbrance as he moved to enter the radio market. "The system was just too sluggish," he lamented. Sarnoff began to sense that RCA would have to break free of its many layers of management to achieve true dominance of the market: "I was pretty much persuaded early on that if RCA was ever going to become a great company, it would have to do it on its own."

With that goal in mind, Sarnoff spent many late nights alone at his desk, with a cigar smoldering in the ashtray, plotting the future of the company. He had moved his family back into the city from Mount Vernon into a comfortable Manhattan apartment, and the time he saved commuting was usually spent at the office. "Somewhere down the road," he said of this period, "in some manner I couldn't then foresee, I felt that RCA was going to have to break loose, and I assumed I'd play a central role in accomplishing it."

Even as he prepared for this role, Sarnoff had already identified the next revolution in mass communication. "I believe that television, which is the technical name for seeing instead of hearing by radio, will come to pass in due course," he wrote in a 1923 memo. "Thus, it may well be expected that radio development will provide a situation whereby we shall be able actually to see as well as hear in New York, within an hour or so, the event taking place in London, Buenos Aires, or Tokyo."

Sarnoff expanded on these remarks in the pages of *The Saturday Evening Post* a few years later: "The greatest day of all will be reached when not only the human voice but the image of the speaker can be flashed through space in every direction. On that day, the whole country will join in every national procession. The backwoodsman will be able to follow the play of expression on the face of a leading artist. Mothers will attend child-welfare clinics in their own homes. Workers may go to night school in the same way. A scientist can demonstrate his latest discoveries to those of his profession even though they be scattered all over the world."

And, though Sarnoff was not so crass as to say so outright, these wonders would all take place under the auspices of the Radio Corporation of America.

Sarnoff's work on radio made him the obvious standard-bearer for television, though once again he arrived at the table long before his colleagues. Throughout the 1920s he would keep tabs on the progress of Charles Francis Jenkins and John Logie Baird, and he gave early support to the efforts of Ernst Alexanderson to explore mechanical transmission techniques. Very early on, however, Sarnoff became discouraged with the prospects for success along the lines Alexanderson proposed. "It's a great advance," he declared after one of Alexanderson's presentations, "but I can't sell it."

The Radiola had demonstrated that television would have to be compact and easily operated if it was to have any chance of commercial success. Alexanderson's proposed apparatus would be not only bulky but also difficult to use—General Electric's best engineers would have trouble operating the system. As time went on without any significant advances, Sarnoff grew increasingly certain that the future of television lay elsewhere. "There is a fortune to be made in television," he told a colleague. "If only we can find a man who can make it work."

Though Sarnoff did not know it at time time, that man was close at hand, working in relative obscurity for one of RCA's royalty partners.

/ / /

Vladimir Kosma Zworykin arrived in New York from Russia on New Year's Eve, 1919, aboard the luxury liner SS *Carmania*. He spent his first night in America at the Waldorf-Astoria on 34th Street. He was then twenty-nine years old.

Zworykin was the son of a wealthy businessman who ran a wholesale grain concern as well as a steamship line on the river Oka, a tributary of the Volga. He was one of twelve children, and the youngest of the seven who survived. The family estate in the thriving provincial town of Mourom featured a three-story stone mansion and extensive wooded grounds on which he and his brothers could hunt, fish, and ride horses. As a teenager Zworykin developed a passion for science, and he eagerly followed the work being done in Russia's major cities. "When I was a student," he would say in later years, "we suddenly underwent a sort of revolution in physics, which produced the new possibility of using technology and science for human welfare."

A promising student, Zworykin entered the St. Petersburg Institute of Technology in 1907 and threw himself into the study of physics. The professor in charge of the physics laboratory, Boris Rosing, took a particular interest in the eager young man's progress, noting that Zworykin often found time to help his fellow students with their assignments. By his third year of study, Zworykin had distinguished himself to such a degree that Rosing invited him to assist on a special project, housed in a private laboratory across the street from the institute.

This project proved to be something Rosing called "electrical telescopy," or seeing at a distance, a prospect that had intrigued him ever since he had learned of Karl Ferdinand Braun's progress with cathode-ray tubes in 1897. Rosing had even applied for a patent on a type of remote viewing system in 1907, and began to build it the following year. By the time Zworykin was shown the apparatus it had taken on massive proportions—a bewildering fusion of crackling electric motors, malodorous voltaic cells, pulsing dials, and sparking wires that threatened to overwhelm the laboratory.

On a bench at the center of the room sat a round glass tube supported by three leather straps. Several electrical wires fed into the tube's long, narrow neck, running off to form connections with various other pieces of apparatus. This was a Braun high-vacuum cathode-ray tube, a notoriously erratic and potentially explosive device that operated on 20,000 volts of electricity. Intended to display electrical wave forms, Rosing's tube had been modified with metal plates that could manipulate incoming signals. Used in conjunction with a camera pickup device housed in a wooden cabinet at the other end of the laboratory, the converted tube was intended to receive and display an electronic television signal.

Rosing's theories were well ahead of their time, and his apparatus could not keep pace. The equipment and techniques needed to realize his ideas were still many years in the future, and the means by which scientists of the day could approximate them were both time-consuming and impractical. Rosing and his eager new assistant spent many long hours lifting heavy bottles of mercury up and down, which was a laborious early method of creating a vacuum inside a glass tube. Very few of the resulting tubes survived their subsequent exposure to electrical charges, and fewer still could be successfully treated with a photoelectric chemical, such as potassium or cesium, so as to form a proper receiving surface.

Astonishingly, despite these limitations, Rosing appears to have achieved sporadic flashes of success. On May 9, 1911, he recorded in his laboratory notebook that a "distinct image was seen for the first time, consisting of four luminous bands." So far as is known, this was as close as Rosing ever came to achieving an electronic television transmission. For Zworykin, however, Rosing's seemingly modest results would provide the inspiration for a lifetime's work.

Upon graduating in 1912, Zworykin wanted to remain in St. Petersburg to work with Rosing, but his father had other plans. Faced with the prospect of returning home to enter the family shipping business, Zworykin elected to continue his studies abroad. In Paris, he joined the lab of the physicist Paul Langevin, a future Nobel laureate, where he conducted experiments involving X-rays. Moving on to Berlin, Zworykin immersed himself in advanced physics.

Zworykin was still in Berlin when war broke out in 1914. He hurried back to St. Petersburg—renamed Petrograd—and was immediately conscripted into the Russian army, eventually becoming a lieutenant in the Russian Signal Corps. Even in the army, Zworykin pursued his interest in electrical telescopy. While assigned to the Russian Wireless Telegraph and Telephone Company, a Russian subsidiary of the British Marconi organization, Zworykin made a close study of the latest radio vacuum tubes. He also found time to pursue a young woman named Tatiana Vasilieff, a student at a nearby dental school, whom he would marry in 1916.

Zworykin clung to the hope that at the end of the war he would be able to resume life as normal. To fellow officers he confided his hopes of continuing the work he had begun in Rosing's lab in St. Petersburg, and he even spoke of launching a television research team at the Russian Marconi factory. Not surprisingly, the revolution of 1917 forced him to abandon his plans. In spite of his service to the military, Zworykin's privileged background served to place him under suspicion as a potential enemy of the Bolsheviks. Hoping matters would improve, Zworykin remained behind while Tatiana fled to Germany. By now the family estate in Mourom had been requisitioned as a museum of natural sciences, with only a pair of small rooms allotted for the remaining family.

Matters took an ominous turn when Zworykin learned that the police were looking for him. He seized an opening to hook up with a departing geological expedition, and eventually he secured passage to America.

The New World proved difficult. Zworykin had trouble learning English and was nagged by doubt over his decision to leave Russia. When he received orders from the provisional Siberian government to return to Omsk as a radio specialist, he complied. Clearly he hoped that matters had improved in his absence. Instead, he found "hardship and despair as never before." At the end of 1919, he returned to New York.

At loose ends, Zworykin took a room in a Brooklyn boarding-house and set to work learning English. Ironically, the man who had witnessed the coming of electronic television now operated a mechanical adding machine for the Russian embassy. In time, Zworykin began to get a foothold in New York and was able to send for his wife. A daughter, Nina, was born in June of 1920.

As he settled into family life, Zworykin sought opportunities to work as an engineer. Shortly after his daughter's birth, he accepted a 50 percent pay cut in order to sign on with the Westinghouse Research Laboratory in Pittsburgh, where he helped to produce a new line of radio tubes. This brief stint came to an end when the company announced salary reductions; Zworykin, with a new baby, could not afford to stay on. He joined a small radio concern in Kansas City, and even designed a portable receiving set for use in automobiles. Before the new enterprise could get rolling, however, the local police put Zworykin out of business. The distractions of radio, they insisted, had no place in an automobile.

In 1923, word came from Pittsburgh that Westinghouse had undergone a major reorganization, partly the result of the internecine struggles with RCA. Zworykin was offered a new contract at a higher salary, along with job security. Apparently Zworykin had made a powerful impression on Otto Schairer, who managed the Westinghouse patent department. His new contract allowed him to retain the rights to any prior inventions, while Westinghouse reserved the exclusive option to purchase any future patents. Zworykin readily agreed to these terms, and by March 1923 he was back at work in Pittsburgh.

Within days of his return, Zworykin was summoned to the office of Samuel Kintner, the research division's new manager, to discuss future research projects. Seizing the opportunity, Zworykin outlined the work he had done with Rosing on electronic television and sketched out plans for a system that featured cathode-ray tubes at both the receiver and the transmitter. Intrigued, Kintner gave approval for Zworykin to devote a portion of his time to television research. His plans were turned over to Schairer at the patent department, who filed them with the U.S. Patent Office on December 29, 1923. It would be fifteen years before the application made its way through the legal system, by which time it would have touched off one of the bloodiest patent battles in corporate history.

For the moment, however, Zworykin threw himself into his new life in Pittsburgh. Over the coming months a second daughter would be born and Zworykin would become a naturalized American citizen. Along with his duties at Westinghouse, he also found time to enroll in the physics department of the University of Pittsburgh, receiving course credit toward a Ph.D for the work he had done in Russia and Paris.

Although Zworykin's television patent had been filed, Westinghouse showed little interest in "reduction to practice," the process of creating a working model to demonstrate the validity of the application. This would change in 1924, owing in part to an article that appeared in a technical journal called *Wireless World and Radio Review.* Entitled "The Possibilities of Television with Wire and Wireless," the article was an overview of the prospects for an all-electronic television system, and the author was none other than A. A. Campbell Swinton, the man who had first raised the possibility of a "kathode" apparatus in 1908. Once again Campbell Swinton emphasized that the notion was "an idea only," and he stressed the difficulties of producing a working system. He went on to say, however, that "if we could only get one of the big research laboratories" working on the problem, they would likely "solve a thing like this in six months and make a reasonable job of it."

The article provoked a great deal of comment, and seems to have been taken as something of a direct challenge by the RCA royalty partners. In Pittsburgh it gave fresh impetus to Zworykin's proposals, and in June 1924 he received authorization to move ahead with the plans he had drawn up the previous year. As materials and manpower were made available for the first time, Zworykin began work in earnest.

Zworykin's studies with Professor Rosing in Russia had shown him the possibility of receiving images electronically. The crucial factor, Zworykin believed, would be to discover a means of transmitting electronically as well. Unless both halves of the system were fully electronic, he reasoned, there could be no great advance over the limits of mechanical components. The conclusion was obvious: he would have to create an electronic camera tube, capable of performing a rapid scanning function.

The method by which Zworykin sought to accomplish this, and the degree to which it accorded with his original patent application, was to become a source of considerable legal and scientific debate. Initially Zworykin's ideas appeared to be similar to those of Campbell Swinton, but it is also clear that the process of trial and error in the laboratory produced many modifications and improvements, perhaps pushing his designs out of the realm of his original concept. While these revisions were a natural component of the inventive process, they would have serious implications for the success of his patent application.

Through the early months of 1925, Zworykin made enormous strides. He began working with a scientific glassblower to create modified cathode-ray tubes for transmitting and receiving, and he also experimented with different photoelectric chemicals and various methods of using those chemicals for effective scanning. He soon realized, however, that greater resources would be needed to take his researches to the next level. Hoping for a larger budget, Zworykin arranged a demonstration for a group of his superiors at Westinghouse in order to show them what he believed to be the future of television. Samuel Kintner, the general manager, was among those invited, as was Otto Schairer, the patent attorney who had been instrumental in bringing Zworykin back to Pittsburgh. Harry Davis, the general manager of Westinghouse, also planned to attend, and Zworykin was well aware that this was the man he would have to impress.

On the day before the demonstration, Zworykin made careful preparations to ensure that all went according to plan. Throughout the afternoon and well into the evening he checked and rechecked his equipment, fine-tuning the sensitive instruments for maximum efficiency. Just as he prepared to leave for the night, Zworykin made a final adjustment and inadvertently overloaded his circuits, blowing out several of the condenser tubes that focused light onto the display surface. Zworykin worked through the night in a state of mounting panic trying to repair the damage. By morning he had jury-rigged the condensers and restored the system to working order, but he could not be certain his hasty measures would hold.

As his superiors assembled for the demonstration, Zworykin offered a silent prayer and powered up the system. To his enormous relief, the apparatus buzzed and crackled but did not explode. Working quickly, so as not to tempt fate, Zworykin focused the image of a simple X mark onto the sensitive window area of his transmitting tube. A faint image of a "similar cross," as Zworykin later described it, appeared on the face of his receiving tube. By his own admission, the image offered only "low contrast and rather poor definition." Nevertheless, Zworykin was jubilant. In his view, this was a watershed moment in the history of television research.

Harry Davis did not appear to share Zworykin's elation. After studying the flickering lines for a moment, he asked Zworykin what the next step would be. Here, Zworykin later admitted, he made a crucial error and effectively "scotched" his own case. It seemed to him that the potential benefits of television development were obvious, so he did not trouble to elaborate on them. Davis clearly wanted to hear that a commercially viable form of the apparatus was within reach, along with the promise of a vast fortune for Westinghouse. Zworykin, realizing that he had a long road ahead, did not want to sully his reputation by making empty promises. Instead, he gave a précis of the research challenges that still had to be met, with a particular emphasis on the vast outlay of research materials and funding that would be needed before television might turn a profit.

It was not what his superiors wanted to hear. In fact, Zworykin had outlined the potential roadblocks so clearly that he effectively talked Davis out of any further involvement with electronic television. "Mr. Davis asked me a few questions," Zworykin later recalled, "mostly as to how much time I spent building the installation, and left after saying something to Mr. Kintner which I did not hear. Later, I found out that he had told him to put 'this guy' to work on something more useful."

Zworykin was duly instructed to put his television research aside and concentrate on something of more immediate benefit to Westinghouse. For the time being, the company's television researches would focus on mechanical methods of transmission. In hindsight, it is easy to ridicule this decision. In 1925, however, the potential value of Zworykin's device would have been difficult to apprehend. The RCA royalty partners had only recently persuaded the buying public of the virtues of an appliance that stored perishable foods—"Yes, folks," ran an advertisement of the time, "the electrical home refrigerator actually freezes your own favorite drinking water into cubes for table use." Against this background, a device that made a flickering X appear at the end of a foul-smelling glass tube cannot have seemed hugely promising.

Because Zworykin's work was terminated so abruptly, it is difficult to be certain exactly how far he had progressed. What is clear, however, is that his system cannot have been fully electronic, as he would later have occasion to claim, since at least some of the components would have required mechanical motors. For both Zworykin and Farnsworth, the goal of an all-electronic system, with "no moving parts," remained out of reach.

As for Zworykin, he had learned a costly lesson in corporate culture. Instead of telling his superiors what they wanted to hear, he had told them the literal truth.

It was not a mistake he would make again.

Seven

The Ideas in This Boy's Head

> *"What I plan on using in this new television*
> *is a double anode, high vacuum, cathode*
> *ray oscillograph tube and—"*
> *"That's enough!" interrupted Ned with a laugh.*
> *"I'll let you attend to the technical end of it.*
> *All I'm interested in is results."*
> —Tom Swift and His Television Detector,
> by Victor Appleton, 1933

Traveling west on the Southern Pacific Railroad's *City of Los Angeles* in the spring of 1926, Pem Farnsworth admitted to a certain feeling of uneasiness. Looking out at the farmhouses and hayfields flashing past the train window, the eighteen-year-old bride could not help but reflect on the many ways in which she differed from her new husband. For him, a row of fallen hay called to mind a revolutionary method of electronic image scanning. For her, it represented the life she was leaving behind. She had never been out of Utah before. The train porter was the first black man she had ever seen. Would there be a place for her in the new life her husband was rushing to meet? "Don't worry about it," Farnsworth assured her. "You'll do just fine."

It was a typical Farnsworth prediction—confident, intuitive, and completely accurate. In the months and years to come, Pem Farnsworth

Farnsworth, at age twenty-four, adjusts the controls on an early version of his television receiver. BETTMAN/CORBIS would become an indispensable part of her husband's work, with her practical intelligence providing a perfect complement to her husband's visionary abstraction. She had been raised to be the wife of a Mormon farmer. Now, along with her duties as a wife and helpmate, she would be given additional responsibilities as a spot welder, cable winder, and draftsman. The television project, she would say, marked her coming of age. Farnsworth himself left no room for equivocation: his wife's contributions, he insisted, were every bit as important as his own.

While the newlyweds made the two-day train journey to Los Angeles, George Everson and Leslie Gorrell remained behind to finish up the Community Chest campaign. Farnsworth was eager to get working as quickly as possible, so Everson instructed him to contact Harry Cartlidge, a fund-raising colleague, for advice as soon as he reached the city. Cartlidge invited Farnsworth to meet on the lot of MGM Studios, where he was raising money for a retired actors' fund. This was a heady experience for the new arrival; Farnsworth had not yet spent twenty-four hours in Los Angeles, but already he found himself shaking hands with Hollywood film stars such as Tom Mix. Pem would recall that Farnsworth felt "worshipful awe" upon meeting Bette Davis, though this seems unlikely, as the actress's film debut was still five years in the future. Nevertheless, it is undoubtedly true, as Pem would later write, that Farnsworth felt a growing conviction that television would "make a substantial mark" on Hollywood.

On Cartlidge's advice, the Farnsworths took a streetcar to Hollywood to search for convenient, affordable housing. Farnsworth's agreement with Everson and Gorrell allowed for only $150 per month in living expenses, so he and Pem hoped to find a place large enough to accommodate the television experiments, rather than renting separate laboratory space. After a brief search, they settled on a furnished ground-floor studio at 1339 North New Hampshire Street, available at $50 a month. Farnsworth immediately staked out the dining room for his experiments.

Even as they unpacked their cases, Farnsworth, mindful of the enormous job ahead, felt impatient to get started. "Farnsworth was conscious of the problems facing him," said George Everson, "but he did not let them trouble him. He attacked the whole assignment with no engineering experience and little engineering knowledge, but to compensate for these inadequacies he had courage and genius. The courage was not the foolhardy type born of ignorance. His was the real courage of the pioneer who knows the goal but has little knowledge of the intervening terrain."

Whether courageous or foolhardy, Farnsworth launched his research effort within two days of his arrival in California. While Pem set up housekeeping, he began gathering the materials he would need for his television laboratory—radio tubes, wires, crystals, resistors, and transformers. Like Boris Rosing before him, Farnsworth found that much of the equipment he needed simply did not exist. He would have to fashion his components—and even his tools, in some cases— out of apparatus designed for other purposes.

In much the same spirit, Farnsworth made a concerted effort to acquire the specialized knowledge he would need to get his ideas off the drawing board. He spent much of his time at the Los Angeles Public Library, giving himself a crash course with materials that had been unavailable in Idaho and Utah. He worked doggedly to correct his perceived weaknesses, studying up on advanced principles of chemistry and physics. At the same time, he boned up on the physiology of human vision, so that he would better understand the conditions under which the eye, seeing a rapid succession of images on a television receiving tube, would be fooled into a perception of continuous motion. Farnsworth understood that a phenomenon known as "persistence of vision," first identified in 1824, would allow the human retina to retain an image for approximately one-sixteenth of a second. If, in that brief fraction of a second, a second image were to replace the first, followed by a third and a fourth, the series of images would merge into an impression of normal motion.

In the case of motion pictures, this effect required a certain number of frames on a strip of film and a timed shutter system, such as the one designed by C. Francis Jenkins. With television, an added layer of complexity entered the equation. Not only would the eye need to register more than sixteen frames per second, but each of these frames would have to be composed of an undetermined number of individual picture elements. Other television experimenters had perceived of these elements as cubes or dots of light. Farnsworth, in his hayfield revelation, had envisioned them as rows, or scanning lines. The difficulty—and at times it would seem an insurmountable one—was that those lines would have to form an image in an almost unimaginably brief period of time. From the beginning, Farnsworth had understood that television would have to operate at speeds well beyond the limits of mechanical motion, which could never hope to outpace the human eye. He now realized that even certain photoelectric chemicals, many of which were being used by Baird and others, were also too slow for his purposes. Selenium, for instance, offered a chemical reaction that converted light to electricity, but it did not do so instantaneously, and would therefore never be suitable for television. Farnsworth would need to find a better, more suitable chemical.

Unfortunately, that was only one of his problems. Once he had found the proper light-reactive material, Farnsworth would have to find a way of distributing it evenly across a target area on the inside of a sealed vacuum tube—the television equivalent of getting a ship inside a bottle.

Farnsworth faced these problems with cheery confidence, and by the time Everson and Gorrell arrived in Los Angeles in mid-June, roughly two weeks later, the young inventor had his first television laboratory up and running. By this time, the apartment's small dining room was no longer big enough to contain the sprawling apparatus. A tube-making annex had been established in an adjoining closet, and an electrical generator could be heard pumping in the carport out back.

Everson and Gorrell were both eager to pitch in. At this early stage, the three partners had visions of cobbling together a crude but workable prototype in a few weeks' time, so as to be able to secure the crucial patent protection on Farnsworth's ideas. Toward that end, the two older men happily took on whatever menial tasks needed doing, in the hope of hurrying the process along. One of the more tedious jobs involved constructing the magnetic coils needed to manipulate and focus the electronic image. The process involved yards of copper wire and a manually operated coil-winding machine, along with a great deal of foul-smelling orange shellac and heavy insulation strips. It was a messy and disagreeable job, but Everson attacked it with a certain jaunty flair. Before long, his hand-tailored suits were dotted with orange shellac.

Everson also employed his talents in the kitchen, revealing a previously unsuspected culinary talent. Arriving one morning with a sack of groceries, he delighted the Farnsworths by whipping up a gourmet omelette with asparagus and hollandaise sauce on the side. Everson also proved to be a dab hand at pastry; when Pem's first attempt to bake a pie ended in ruin and despair, he stepped in with a badly needed tutorial.

Before long, the comings and goings at the Farnsworth apartment began to attract a fair amount of attention. "During the day the curtains in the dining room were drawn in order that Farnsworth could work under controlled light," Everson recalled. "From time to time my roadster would drive up with large bundles of material to be carried into the house. These strange activities excited the curiosity of the neighbors."

Soon that curiosity took a tangible form. "This was during the prohibition era," Everson explained. "When people became suspicious of anything unusual going on in a neighborhood, their first thought was that it might be the operation of a still." One afternoon, as Gorrell and Everson were having lunch with the Farnsworths, the front and rear doorbells of the apartment rang at the same time. Farnsworth went to the front door while Pem went to the back. "To their surprise," Everson said, "each faced a burly policeman. The policemen were polite but firm. They stated that they wanted to search the house because there had been a report from a neighbor that a still was probably being operated on the premises. The house was duly ransacked. Nothing of an alcoholic nature was found, but the police were greatly impressed and seemed to feel that maybe they had uncovered something more sinister than an alcohol plant. They guardedly asked what all the activity was, pointing to the assorted experimental apparatus around the dining room. When Phil told them he was working on a television system, one of the policemen said, 'Well, I'll be darned!' Then they both left, mumbling their mystification."

As it happened, there were other things in the immediate vicinity to interest the law. The beautiful starlet Hazel Keener, who had recently completed filming *The Freshman* opposite Harold Lloyd, was living in the apartment next door; the police carried on their investigation while Miss Keener reclined on her bed munching an apple. Not surprisingly, the search of her bedroom was especially thorough.

At this stage, at least, alcohol was the farthest thing from Farnsworth's mind. Already, however, he was having difficulty relaxing at night, and could not seem to shut off his mind from the technical problems that nagged at him during the day. Pem recalled that he would often go to sleep with his thoughts focused on a particular aspect of his work, only to jolt awake in the middle of the night when a solution came to him. At first, Farnsworth was grateful for the opportunity to "work in his sleep," as he described the process, but there would be times when he simply could not turn it off. "I felt he really needed his rest," Pem said. "I feared that working his brain all night, added to his long hours at the lab, would be his undoing."

Everson and Gorrell were acutely aware of the strain on Farnsworth, and both did their best to help ease his mind. One night, Everson loaned Farnsworth his roadster so that he could take Pem to the premiere of Rudolph Valentino's *The Son of the Sheik* at the newly opened Grauman's Chinese Theatre. On another occasion, Everson took the young couple to dinner at the famous Brown Derby restaurant, where Pem was delighted to find Boris Karloff entertaining a group of young starlets at the next table.

Pem also made an effort to help her husband relax through music. Farnsworth had rented a piano within days of their arrival in Los Angeles, so that they could continue the musical evenings they had enjoyed in Provo. It proved to be an emotional release for both of them. Pem often vented her feelings of homesickness through her piano playing, a fact that was not lost on her husband. One evening, as the two were playing a song called "There'll Be Some Changes Made," Farnsworth appeared dissatisfied with Pem's interpretation. "Play it as you do when you're angry," he said.

It took no great skill to sense Farnsworth's own preoccupation in the quavering strains of his violin. More and more his thoughts were absorbed by a series of technical hurdles he had encountered with his "image dissector," the fragile glass tube that was to serve as the brain of his television system. Everson described Farnsworth's conception as "a cylinder about the size of an ordinary Mason jar, with an optically clear window sealed into one end and a photosensitive plate at the other end." As Farnsworth attempted to construct the device, two major difficulties emerged. First, as he had expected, it proved extremely difficult to coat an area on the inside of an evacuated tube with the proper photoelectric chemical. Second, Farnsworth needed to devise a method of incorporating a flat, clear disk of glass at one end of the tube. The disk had to be large enough to display a visible picture, but not so large as to implode under a hard vacuum or extremes of temperature. This presented a formidable challenge. Round glass bulbs and cylindrical tubes were structurally sound; irregular, flat-ended image dissectors were not. Compounding the difficulty, as Everson reported, was the additional problem of "getting the right type of electrical leads in and out of the tube."

At the time, a radio vacuum tube represented the last word in scientific glassblowing. Farnsworth's image dissector, which added several layers of complexity to the process, was judged to be an impossibility by several technical consultants. Undeterred, Farnsworth began working with a professional glassblower. Soon, however, his brother-in-law Cliff Gardner would join him in California and—eager to make himself useful—would volunteer to learn the necessary glassblowing techniques. It was typical of Gardner, an amiable and industrious young man, to take on a job that several more experienced craftsmen had declared to be unworkable. Initially, at least, Gardner seemed an improbable candidate. "Gardner's total training," Everson declared, "was a high school education, a boldness comparable to Farnsworth's, dogged perseverance, and no knowledge of the subject."

Unlikely as it seemed, however, Gardner soon became a glassblowing expert. Within a matter of months, he would be producing tubes that the experts had judged to be unattainable. Gardner's talents soon made him indispensable, and his calming presence in the lab—with an air tube in one hand and an oxyhydrogen torch in the other—would be a steadying influence on Farnsworth for years to come. Over time, through a combination of innate skill and relentless effort, Gardner learned to produce exactly what Farnsworth required—a cathode-ray tube with a perfectly flat end. Having little in the way of professional equipment, Gardner improvised by combining a lens-grinding turntable with a small furnace. The arrangement allowed him to heat and rotate his tubes at the same time. By laying a disk of optically clear glass at one end of a heated tube, Gardner found, he could fuse them together in a smooth motion as the turntable revolved. "All the other glassblowers thought the tube would implode. I didn't know any better, so I went ahead."

With Farnsworth's help, Gardner brought the same ingenuity to bear on the problem of dispersing a light-reactive chemical inside the tube. "Potassium hydride was used as the photoelectric surface in the early dissector tubes," Everson recounted. "Since potassium combines with oxygen when exposed to air or water, the potassium pellets came from the suppliers submerged in kerosene. Gardner had to learn the art of distilling the pure potassium from the commercial pellets and sealing it in airtight glass tubes for future use." To form a photoelectric surface inside the image dissector, Farnsworth and Gardner devised a means of attaching the potassium containers to an electrical conduit that fed into the tube. The potassium could then be driven into the tube by the application of heat and, through practiced manipulation of the tube, spread across a plate at the rear of the device. Next, Gardner pumped hydrogen gas into the tube, which combined with the potassium to form potassium hydride, which was the desired photoelectric surface. "It was an intricate and exacting process," Everson declared, "better suited to the abilities and background of experienced chemical engineers than to the capacities of a boy fresh from high school."

At times, Gardner's inexperience proved costly. On one occasion, as he was sealing a potassium pellet into a glass receptacle, the materials gave way and sprayed hot chemicals across his face. Gardner lurched over to a sink and managed to wash out his eyes in time to prevent serious damage.

Along with potassium pellets, it was not uncommon for half-built image dissectors to explode in Gardner's face. "The first one I remember very well," he said. "I was standing there with the tube in my hands, and all at once—poof! It wasn't there anymore, and I had tiny slivers of glass in my eyes and face, as well as my hands. I was rushed to the hospital and got fixed up. Luckily there really wasn't much damage, but I had these little red dots all over my face." Gardner was making light of a fairly grave incident. The others spent an anxious day fearing for his vision, and Farnsworth would insist on safety equipment to prevent future accidents.

Through the summer of 1926, the apparatus on the dining-room table of the Hollywood apartment continued to expand, taking on added shadings of complexity as Farnsworth tinkered with the disparate components. Though Gardner had not yet begun producing tubes at this stage, Farnsworth managed to obtain a workable approximation of his design from a local glassblower. For Farnsworth, this first version of his image dissector tube was something of a holy object, the culmination of the dream that had begun in the Idaho hayfield. In late August, after carefully installing the tube into his crude transmitter setup and laboriously checking every circuit, he gathered his partners to witness the first concrete test of the Farnsworth television system. With Pem at his side, Farnsworth fired up the electrical generator and hurried forward to the lab table, expecting to see light collecting in the tube.

It promptly exploded. Farnsworth had not allowed for the power surge that occurred each time he fired up his electrical generator. Stricken, Farnsworth turned to face his partners through a cloud of black smoke. To Everson, he looked very much like a frightened boy.

Everson studied the charred remains for a moment, perhaps deliberating on the wisdom of having gambled his savings on a teenage inventor. Turning away from the dining-room table, he gave a shrug. "That's too bad, Phil," he said, laying a hand on Farnsworth's shoulder.

Gorrell nodded. "Of all the tough luck," he said.

"I should have known better!" Farnsworth cried, gesturing at the ruined image dissector. "I should have turned the power on before I connected the tubes. That's all I have to show you for your investment, George."

Everson appeared imperturbable. "I really didn't expect as much from it as you did, Phil," he said.

Everson may have put up a brave front for Farnsworth's benefit, but it was clear that the failed test marked the end of any hopes for a quick solution. At the same time, it became apparent that Everson's $6,000 grubstake would not be enough to get the job done. This did not seem to trouble either Everson or Gorrell, both of whom felt more comfortable raising money than winding magnetic coils. It was resolved that the two fund-raisers would go in search of additional backing for the project. In order to strengthen their hand, they planned to submit Farnsworth's designs to a review by technical experts, so as to gauge the possibility of obtaining patent protection for some of the work he had already done. Accordingly, Farnsworth wrote up a detailed description of the system, while Gorrell and Pem turned his rough sketches into finished drawings. Everson, meanwhile, contacted a lawyer named Leonard Lyon, a college friend of Gorrell's, who together with his brother Richard ran the firm of Lyon and Lyon, specializing in patent law. "If you have what you think you've got," Leonard Lyon told him, "you have the world by the tail; but if you haven't got it, the sooner you find it out the better, because you can waste a lot of money on a scheme of this kind."

Everson was instructed to "bring your young genius in here" so he could be grilled by Richard Lyon, the firm's technical expert, along with Dr. Mott Smith, a specialist from the California Institute of Technology.

Farnsworth, Everson, and Gorrell presented themselves at the firm's offices in early September 1926. The two technical experts, though courteous, were initially skeptical of the youthful inventor and approached the presentation with some impatience. As Farnsworth stood to explain his ideas, however, he underwent his customary metamorphosis from nervous schoolboy to compelling orator. "It became apparent that Farnsworth knew more about the subject in hand than either of the technical men," Everson recalled. "He completely overwhelmed them with the brilliance and originality of his conception. During the conference Richard Lyon often got up from his chair and walked the floor, pounding his hands together behind his back and exclaiming, 'This is a monstrous idea—a monstrous idea!'"

When Farnsworth had finished, Everson rose to speak. "Gentlemen," he said, "if we are to go any further with Farnsworth's idea it is necessary that we approach some people whom I respect, and whose good opinion I wish to retain, and ask them for financial help. I don't wish to do so unless I am completely sure of this proposition in my own mind. Therefore, I want to ask you three questions. First, is this thing scientifically sound?"

As Everson recalled it, Dr. Smith appeared "almost bemused" as he gave his answer: "Yes."

"Second," Everson continued, "is it original?"

Smith replied that he knew of nothing else like it, but added that a patent search would determine this for certain. Richard Lyon concurred, though he admitted that he would not necessarily know of any work being carried out in secret by the larger commercial laboratories.

Everson nodded. "Finally," he said, "is this thing feasible? Can it be worked out to make a practical operating unit?"

"You will have great difficulty in doing it," Lyon answered, "but we see no insuperable obstacles at this time."

This was exactly what Everson and Gorrell wanted to hear. The meeting broke up with an agreement to move ahead with a patent search. To the surprise of the legal representatives, the conference had lasted four hours. Clearly Farnsworth had exceeded all expectations, particularly those of Dr. Smith. Later, when Smith presented his bill for the consultation, he explained with considerable chagrin that his fee included the price of a parking ticket. "I left my car on the street," he said, "and came up here feeling sure I could throw this scheme into the discard in half an hour."

Smith would soon have even greater reason to be impressed. A week later, when Farnsworth visited the expert's laboratory to go over some details, the older scientist quizzed him on his plans to employ a particular type of crystal. "That dates back to Hamilton's work in Dublin," Farnsworth said, referring to Sir William Hamilton, the nineteenth-century mathematician. Reaching for a textbook on the properties of light, Farnsworth thumbed through and found a page of formulae. "There it is," Farnsworth said, pointing to an equation at the center of the page.

Once again, Smith had cause to appear bemused. "You're right," he said. "I should have seen it."

Everson and Gorrell felt greatly buoyed by Smith's favorable opinion. As they gathered themselves for a new campaign, making a transition from charity fund-raisers to venture capitalists, they asked Farnsworth to estimate the additional funds he would need to create a working prototype. Farnsworth felt certain he could do the job in six months, but wanted an additional six months to work out any bugs in the system. He calculated that the entire operation would require a total of $12,000—$1,000 a month for one year. Everson, mindful of the fact that Farnsworth had burned through the original $6,000 in only three months, concluded that the figure was far too low. He and Gorrell bumped it up to $25,000.

Everson's first thought was to contact some businessmen in Santa Barbara with whom he had worked in the past. His overtures were promptly rebuffed. "This is tougher than I thought it would be," he told Farnsworth. "It's a lot easier to raise money for social welfare than it is to find backing for a speculation." Seeking advice, Everson went to San Francisco for a consultation with Jesse McCargar, vice president of the Crocker First National Bank, who had chaired one of Everson's past campaigns. Apparently Everson had not bothered to phone ahead; he arrived to find that McCargar was away on vacation. As Everson turned to leave, his apparent irritation caught the attention of James Fagan, the bank's executive vice president.

Fagan was something of a legend in California banking circles. Considered to be the most conservative banker on the Pacific Coast, he had skillfully navigated the fiscal upheavals of both the petroleum boom of the 1890s and the earthquake of 1906. "He was the butt of many jokes," Everson said, most of them portraying him as a "cold-hearted, glassy-eyed guardian of the money bags. It was said that he could smell a bad investment when it came in the door."

Everson must have felt some trepidation, then, as Fagan asked him to "sit down and tell me about your scheme." Fagan listened attentively while Everson laid out the entire story. "Well, this is a damn fool idea," Fagan said when Everson had finished, "but somebody ought to put money into it. Someone who can afford to lose it." After consulting the bank's owner, Fagan decided to arrange a meeting with his technical adviser, Roy Bishop. Fearing that he would be out of his depth, Everson sent a telegram to Farnsworth telling him to drive up to San Francisco in the roadster.

When Farnsworth arrived a day prior to the meeting, Everson realized that his young partner's appearance needed work. By this time Farnsworth had grown an ill-considered caterpillar mustache in the hope of appearing older and more worldly, but the general impression fell well short of convincing. "Farnsworth, sartorially, was not a very well turned-out individual," Everson recalled. "His clothes were shabby and ill-fitting, and generally speaking he had the appearance of a poor inventor." Seeking to polish the image, Everson took Farnsworth to a tailor's shop and had him fitted out with a fashionable new suit of clothes, complete with hat and shoes.

A lunch appointment with Roy Bishop had been arranged for the following day at the elegant Palace Hotel. The concern over Farnsworth's appearance had apparently made him self-conscious about his table manners, so Everson took him for a practice run at a nearby hotel dining room. By the time of the lunch appointment Farnsworth had evidently plumbed the mysteries of the salad fork, and he managed to impress Bishop with yet another forceful presentation of his ideas. The meeting adjourned to the technical consultant's office for the remainder of the afternoon. After going over each detail of Farnsworth's plans and sketches, Bishop laid his cards on the table. "I am convinced that the idea is sound," he declared, "but doubt your ability to work it out commercially."

By this stage, along with table manners and dress sense, Farnsworth had picked up a great deal of salesmanship from Everson. He knew that Bishop was hooked, and decided to call his bluff. Farnsworth stood up, gathered his papers, and thanked Bishop for his time. Expressing regret that they had not seen eye to eye, Farnsworth turned and headed for the door with a worried Everson at his heels.

Farnsworth had his hand on the knob when Bishop called him back. As Farnsworth and Everson resumed their places, Bishop made a proposal. The Crocker banking family also ran a small research facility, he explained. If Farnsworth would agree to see one of their engineers—a man named Harlan Honn—Bishop would put aside his reservations. "Honn is a hard-boiled, competent engineer," Bishop said. "If you can convince him that your proposition is sound and can be worked out, I think we will find ways of backing you."

By the end of the day, Honn had rendered his verdict: "Why, sure, this system will work." Soon, Farnsworth and Everson found themselves summoned to the Crocker bank's boardroom. There James Fagan made a startling offer on behalf of the bank's directors. Not only would the Crocker group finance Farnsworth with $25,000, but it also would provide laboratory space through its research facility in San Francisco. In return, the bank would control 60 percent of the new Farnsworth research syndicate, with the remaining 40 percent to be divided among Everson, Gorrell, and Farnsworth himself. "Phil and I were elated," Everson said. For him, the fact that they had pried such a substantial investment from the conservative James Fagan seemed "even more miraculous . . . than Farnsworth's youthful genius."

"This is Farnsworth's show," declared Jesse McCargar, who was to assume a prominent role in the new syndicate. "We are betting on his ability. What he'll do would probably give an orthodox engineer heart failure. This isn't engineering we're backing, it's invention. If we back this boy we've got to go the whole way. He must be the boss of what he's doing."

There remained only one final hitch. As the legal documents were drawn up, it emerged that the boy genius was not of age to sign them. As Farnsworth's mother was still living in Utah, Everson arranged to have himself appointed Farnsworth's legal guardian.

"Well, Mr. Everson," said Roy Bishop as the agreement was finalized, "this is the first time anyone has ever come into this room and got anything out of us without laying something on the table for it. We are backing nothing here except the ideas in this boy's head. Believe me, we're going to treat him like a racehorse."

With that, George Everson's youthful ward climbed into the roadster and drove back to Hollywood. Presenting himself at the front door of the apartment in his new suit of clothes, Farnsworth snatched Pem up and waltzed her giddily around the living room as he told her of his success in San Francisco.

For the second time in only four months, Pem was informed of plans for a whirlwind move to another city. This time, Farnsworth wanted to be ready to depart the following morning, and he worked late into the night crating lab equipment for shipment. The couple rose at dawn and stuffed all of their clothes into one suitcase so that Farnsworth could use their only other bag for his books and papers. The two of them were so excited as they set off, Pem recalled, that they sang until their throats were raw.

By the time the Farnsworths reached San Francisco, their jubilant mood had darkened. The suitcase containing their clothes, which Farnsworth had tied to the fender of the car, had been lost or stolen somewhere along the way. Farnsworth's new suit was gone, along with Pem's wedding dress, leaving them with nothing but their traveling clothes. Farnsworth was distraught. "How can I ever face George?" he asked. He would be forced to borrow money to replace the lost items.

Farnsworth's spirits lifted at the sight of the Crocker Research Laboratories at 202 Green Street, not far from Chinatown. The facility was housed in a two-story gray stucco building, with a garage and carpenter's shop on the ground floor. Farnsworth had been allotted a loft space on the second floor, roughly twenty by thirty feet, with high ceilings and tall windows along two walls. The floor sagged and there was no plumbing of any kind. "The building was directly at the eastern foot of romantic Telegraph Hill," Everson recalled. "The rear windows of the loft faced the barren rocks of the precipitous side of the hill. It was not uncommon, after severe rainstorms, for loosened rocks to come tumbling down the hillside. On such occasions fragments of stone would sometimes hurtle through the windows or land on the roof with a great clatter."

In every way, the Green Street facility seemed ill suited to television development. Farnsworth knew that the encroachment of Telegraph Hill would be likely to interfere with his vital radio carrier waves. In addition, the building was nearly at sea level and was surrounded by electrical power lines, placing further limitations on broadcast experiments. Even so, Farnsworth was exhilarated. "Behold," he said, leading Pem and Cliff Gardner into the building, "the future home of television."

Farnsworth saw the empty loft space for the first time in late September 1926 and was determined to have his laboratory up and running by early October. To Everson, it seemed an unlikely prospect: "The initial equipment and personnel of the Farnsworth laboratories were just a few hundred dollars' worth of electrical equipment and experimental apparatus shipped up from Los Angeles, a long bench, a desk and a few chairs, and the inventor, Philo T. Farnsworth."

While Pem settled into a rented house in Oakland, Farnsworth and Gardner worked at setting up a better-equipped facility, beginning with the construction of workbenches, shelves, and a large, stable glassblowing table. Workers from the carpentry shop on the ground floor were hired to lay in plumbing. "Slowly," Pem said, "a working laboratory took shape."

Among Farnsworth's earliest concerns was the fact that traditional vacuum pumps, used to evacuate air from glass tubes, simply could not achieve the efficiency required to create an image dissector tube. Farnsworth and Gardner turned their attention to the creation of a new type of pump, a strange patchwork of hissing siphons and clanking motors. "It was fearfully and wonderfully made," said Everson. "Fantastic as it looked, it did the work."

As Gardner was still a complete novice in the art of glassblowing, he sought the counsel of local professionals. Some of these experts grew so intrigued by the goings-on at Green Street that they began to volunteer their time and equipment. Dr. Herbert Metcalf, a physicist and radio engineer, offered valuable advice on the use of cathode rays and photoelectric cells. Bill Cummings, head of the glassblowing lab at the University of California, supplied various pieces of apparatus and tutored Gardner in the difficult process of maintaining a tube's vacuum while sealing it off from the pump.

Though grateful for the help of these outside experts, Farnsworth initially restricted the lab's inner circle to himself, Gardner, and Pem—whose duties now ranged from stenography to the application of cooling pads to hot electrical leads during the manufacture of dissector tubes. According to Everson, Farnsworth's reliance on his wife and brother-in-law illustrated a guarded strain that would have lasting consequences: "First, his Mormon training made him cautious, and in getting Gardner to help him he was sure he had someone whom he could trust implicitly. Second, he was afraid to employ engineers or technicians who were better equipped technically than himself. Third, he always liked to have members of his own family associated with him in his work. All these traits were serious handicaps to Farnsworth in his development work. Often he and an inferior assistant spent months in solving problems that were at the fingertips of more fully trained engineers. This quality was a source of both strength and weakness. It contributed greatly to his originality of thought, but it retarded his ability to get things done in a practical way."

In addition, Farnsworth's unremitting budget worries were also a factor. Although the Crocker group had been generous, he knew from the first that he would have to watch every dime. Pem, in her capacity as bookkeeper, kept a running tally of the lab's expenditures for gas, electricity, coal, and telephone service—which, in the first week of operation, totalled $34.80. Initially it had seemed to Farnsworth that an operating budget of $1,000 per month would be more than adequate, but when he began laying out cash for radio parts, chemicals, batteries, and other lab essentials, he realized that he would soon be running in the red. "The result was that from the very first Phil never seemed to have all of the facilities the task required," Everson said. "He often spoke of this as an advantage, since it made for resourcefulness and invention and often led to a simplicity and directness of approach to a problem that might otherwise have become too deep."

It was Farnsworth's nature to make virtue of necessity, but the money worries soon took a toll at home as well as in the lab. The arrangement with the Crocker group provided Farnsworth with a monthly salary of $200, most of which went to housing, transportation, and groceries, along with a monthly check sent home to Utah to cover his mother's rent. By the end of the month, Farnsworth considered himself lucky if he still had enough money to take Pem to the movies. Occasionally, when the entertainment budget wouldn't stretch quite that far, Farnsworth improvised. One Sunday, as the lab workers were exploring the Berkeley area, they came across an outdoor theater built into a scenic hillside. Farnsworth promptly climbed onto the stage and began declaiming a lengthy passage from *The Taming of the Shrew*, a memento from his days at Brigham Young University. There is no reason to believe that his acting was any better than his violin playing, but his audience was forgiving.

In December 1926, when the lab had been operating for barely two months, Farnsworth became impatient to get some form of patent protection for his work. Everson brought the matter to the Crocker group, with the result that Farnsworth traveled back to Los Angeles to work with the patent attorneys at Lyon and Lyon. Farnsworth's application—the first of many—was officially filed with the U.S. Patent Office on January 7, 1927. It would be granted in August 1930, by which time it had attracted considerable notice from the legal department of the Radio Corporation of America. More than fifty years later, when an RCA patent attorney was asked for his thoughts on the Farnsworth case, he would be able to recite the seven-digit patent number from memory.

For the moment, Farnsworth believed his image dissector to be the only camera tube of its kind in the world, and he was determined, through the early months of 1927, to refine it to the point where he could transmit a "line picture"—a simple geometric shape drawn on a glass slide. One major problem was holding him back: the image dissector was nowhere near as light-sensitive as it would need to be to achieve practical results. In its present form, the tube would never be able to produce a viable signal. Farnsworth tried various methods of amplifying the signal, including a row of De Forest audion tubes hooked up in a series. The tubes boosted the signal, but the benefits were drowned out by a "motorboating" effect of cascading distortion, as each tube magnified the incidental noise from the previous one. After weeks of fruitless experimentation, Farnsworth decided that he would have to design an entirely new type of amplifying tube. Once again, he had to start from scratch, as there was nothing even remotely similar to his idea available at the time. "It was a little like making one's own automobile tires," Pem observed.

Pem had reason to know. To expedite the process, Farnsworth taught her to use a precision spot-welding tool, so that she could assemble some of the components. With her assistance, Farnsworth managed to create a "shielded grid tube," which provided superior amplification and frequency response, with greatly reduced distortion.

Spurred on by this advance, Farnsworth felt a growing impatience to make his first official television transmission.

Toward that end, Farnsworth adopted a punishing work schedule. His Mormon upbringing precluded working on Sundays, but he made up for it during the rest of the week, working at least twelve hours a day, Saturdays included. As the schedule intensified in the push toward an actual transmission, he found that he begrudged the two hours spent commuting to the rented house in Oakland each day. With the help of Leslie Gorrell, he found an apartment on the other side of Telegraph Hill, and he bought a dilapidated Maxwell touring car to shorten the travel time still further. Though Farnsworth enjoyed owning his own car, his engineering skills were sorely tested by the Maxwell's temperamental engine. He began carrying spare parts along with him so that he could make repairs on the road. One night, after a particularly late session in the lab, Farnsworth emerged to find that he had no gas in the car. As the filling stations were shut for the night, he went back upstairs and mixed a potent brew of alcohol and ether, which he then poured into the Maxwell's tank. The makeshift fuel, Pem reported, had the car virtually flying up Telegraph Hill.

George Everson and Leslie Gorrell no longer came to the lab on a daily basis, but they continued to check in whenever possible. "Hi, Phil!" Everson would invariably say as he breezed into the room. "Got the damned thing working yet?" When business took them out of town, Pem wrote frequent letters to keep them apprised of her husband's efforts. Farnsworth himself was not terribly communicative, and Everson "learned how deficient he was in this respect" during the early days on Green Street. "After my procuring his heart's desire in the way of financial backing, it never occurred to him that I might like to have occasional reports on how he was getting on," Everson recalled. "So the first news I had from him came from Cartlidge, who wrote me that he had loaned Phil a hundred dollars to replenish his wardrobe after the theft."

"I guess you think I'm a mighty poor correspondent," Farnsworth wrote at one stage. "Well, I'm not much to boast about. I have a habit of putting things off as long as I can get by. I want to get over it, though, and I hope you'll be indulgent with me. . . . I certainly appreciate the turn of fate that has meant so much to me lately—and don't you think for a minute that I don't recognize the personal element in it—the boost you and Les have given me."

As the work advanced, Farnsworth made a greater effort to keep Everson in the loop. In February 1927, he wrote to say that he "had everything set up to show a line picture," but had not done so because the Crocker group wanted to delay until he could transmit an actual photograph. "It's really about the same size job either way—line picture or photograph—I just hadn't prepared for the latter . . . television will then be the next step."

Farnsworth expected to be ready in another week or ten days, but in fact several more months would elapse without any significant advances. By this time Farnsworth had come to understand that his staff of three could no longer carry the load by themselves. In the early months on Green Street they had relied heavily on free advice from friendly engineers such as Cummings and Metcalf. During the long struggle to create the shielded grid tube, however, it became apparent that Farnsworth would have to overcome his misgivings about working with strangers. Though his budget was already stretched to the limit, he reluctantly brought in a pair of better-qualified engineers, Carl Christensen and Robert Humphries. To Farnsworth's relief, both proved to be diligent workers, as evidenced by their willingness to keep to Farnsworth's long hours, and both were full of suggestions to help refine the troublesome apparatus.

Throughout the summer of 1927, Farnsworth and his team continued to have trouble with the magnetic coils that were to be used to manipulate and focus his electronic image. Although Farnsworth's backers had wanted him to transmit a photograph, he had not yet been able to overcome the limitations imposed by the coils. Until he resolved the problem, he would not be able to experiment with two-dimensional images. Impatient to show results, Farnsworth pressed ahead with his original plan to transmit a simple, one-dimensional straight line.

At the end of August, Farnsworth and Gardner sealed off their latest image dissector tube and hooked it up to their transmitting apparatus. While his colleagues gathered around an oscillating receiver unit, Farnsworth fired up the dissector. The results were inconclusive, as Farnsworth noted in his lab journal: "Although lines appeared across the tube and the image would go bright and dark with changes in the illumination of the object, still I did not believe it to be a transmission, but only due to other currents on the input of the amplifier."

The team went back to work. Feeling that a breakthrough was close at hand, Farnsworth incorporated a few final adjustments into the design of the image dissector. While the new tube was being constructed, he combed through every inch of his equipment, searching for any possible means of improving its design.

On the following Wednesday—September 7, 1927—the Farnsworths drove to the lab in a mood of high expectation. While Pem finished up some technical drawings, Farnsworth and Gardner spent several hours making final adjustments. At last, Pem recalled, Farnsworth called her into the lab. Humphries and Christensen were gathered around the receiver unit while Gardner waited in an adjoining room with the image dissector. Squaring his shoulders, Farnsworth took his place at the controls and flicked a series of switches. A small, bluish patch of light appeared at the end of the receiving tube. Farnsworth lifted his head and began calling out instructions to Gardner in the next room.

"Put in the slide, Cliff," Farnsworth said.

"Okay, it's in," Gardner answered. "Can you see it?"

A faint but unmistakable line appeared across the receiving end of the tube. As Farnsworth made some adjustments, the line became more distinct.

"Turn the slide a quarter turn, Cliff," Farnsworth called. Seconds later, the line on the receiving tube rotated ninety degrees.

Farnsworth looked up from the tube. "That's it, folks," he announced, with a tremor in his voice. "We've done it—there you have electronic television."

"Everyone stood glued to the spot," Pem recalled, "the import of what we were seeing slowly sinking in." After a moment, Farnsworth went to switch places with Gardner, so that his brother-in-law could see for himself. "Well," said Gardner, "I'll be damned."

"What do you know," added Christensen. "If I wasn't seeing it with my own two eyes, I wouldn't believe it."

At that moment, George Everson arrived to find his boy genius hovering near the receiving tube in a sort of incredulous stupor. Pem Farnsworth, meanwhile, was literally jumping up and down. Seeing Everson, Farnsworth went to the controls to give a second demonstration. Everson stared blankly at the receiving unit for a moment. Then, as the significance of what had been accomplished washed over him, he gave a cry of delight and began pounding Farnsworth on the back.

In his journal entry that day, Farnsworth managed to preserve a sense of scientific decorum: "The received line picture was evident this time," he noted. "Lines of various widths could be transmitted and any movement at right angles to the line was easily recognized. This was experiment #12."

In a telegram to Leslie Gorrell, however, Farnsworth gave voice to his true feelings. It read simply: "The damned thing works!"

Eight

Photographs Come to Life

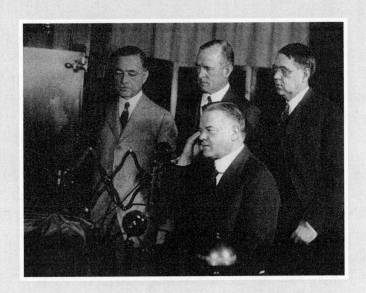

Time as well as space was eliminated.

—*New York Times*

on the Hoover broadcast, 1927

"There has been a lot in the papers lately about Television," Farnsworth wrote to George Everson shortly after his breakthrough transmission, "but that just means we're going to make a million out of this. We have them all scooped by a mile, as I believe they themselves would agree."

In fact, very few of Farnsworth's competitors would have agreed. His electronic achievement, however significant, had come in the midst of a fresh surge of interest in mechanical methods of television transmission, leaving Farnsworth and his backers uncertain of how to capitalize on their advance.

A few months earlier, on April 7, 1927, no less a figure than Secretary of Commerce Herbert Hoover had participated in a headline-grabbing demonstration of the American Telephone and Telegraph Company's new mechanical television system, sparking a major groundswell of enthusiasm. "Like a photograph come to life, Herbert Hoover makes a speech in Washington and an audience in New York watches him in action on a screen as they hear him speak," wrote Orrin Dunlap, the radio editor of the *New York Times*. "This is a triumph for television."

Pressing a telephone receiver to his ear, Secretary of Commerce Herbert Hoover, seated, prepares to have his image beamed to New York in April 1927. BETTMANN/CORBIS

Hoover himself, standing in front of a Nipkow disk transmitter in Washington, hailed the mechanical technology in terms seemingly calculated to infuriate Farnsworth. "This invention again emphasizes a new era in approach to scientific discovery," Hoover declared. "It is the result of organized, planned and definitely directed scientific research, magnificently coordinated in a cumulative group of highly skilled scientists, loyally supported by a great corporation devoted to the advancement of the art. The intricate processes of this invention could never have been developed under any conditions of isolated individual effort. I always find in these occasions a great stimulation to confidence in the future."

If Farnsworth was surprised by the AT&T demonstration, he was in good company. Dr. Herbert Ives and his research team had carried out a three-year television research program with a minimum of publicity, even within the company itself. Their results promised not only to establish a new standard for mechanical television but also to trump the competition.

"This is a day that will long be remembered in the annals of scientific advancement," declared *Radio-Craft* magazine, and the gathering of scientists, politicians, and academics who came together in the offices of the Bell Telephone Laboratories, AT&T's New York subsidiary, would undoubtedly have agreed. Though the system centered on a fairly standard set of fifteen-inch Nipkow disks, Ives and his team had made dramatic improvements. Ordinarily, mechanical television relied on the use of blindingly hot lights; Ives had engineered a means of playing a thin beam over the surface of his subject, through the holes in the revolving scanner disk.

As the demonstration proceeded, the advantages of this technique became readily apparent. The visiting group's attention was directed to a large display screen at the center of the room. There a glaring white patch appeared that slowly resolved itself into the forehead of Hoover, who had been leaning too close to the transmitter. With a telephone pressed to his ear, the secretary began to speak. "It is a matter of just pride to have a part in this historic occasion," he declared. "We have long been familiar with the electrical transmission of sound. Today we have, in a sense, the transmission of sight, for the first time in the world's history. Human genius has now destroyed the impediment of distance in a new respect, and in a manner hitherto unknown. What its uses may finally be no one can tell, any more than man could fore-see in past years the modern developments of the telegraph or tele-phone. All we can say today is that there has been created a marvelous agency for whatever use the future may find, with full realization that every great and fundamental discovery of the past has been followed by use far beyond the vision of its creator. Every schoolchild is aware of the dramatic beginnings of the telegraph and the telephone and the radio, and this evolution in electrical communications has perhaps an importance as vital as any of these."

As Hoover concluded his remarks, he yielded the floor to his wife. "What will you invent next?" asked Mrs. Hoover of her audience in New York. "I hope you won't invent anything that reads our thoughts."

Though New York and Washington had been linked by cable, the AT&T demonstrators now proceeded to show what they had accom-plished with radio wave transmission. From a studio in New Jersey, images of a vaudeville act were beamed to New York. "It is a historic performance," noted Orrin Dunlap "A. Dolan first appears. He is a comedian. He does a monologue in brogue. The audience sees him as an Irishman with side whiskers and a broken pipe. Then he disappears. But in a minute he is back on the screen, this time blackfaced with a new line of jokes in negro dialect."

If Dolan's material is badly dated by today's standards, the appara-tus that broadcast it now seems archaic. At the time, however, the AT&T demonstration appeared to signal a revolution in television sci-ence. While Philo T. Farnsworth labored in what Herbert Hoover might have called "conditions of isolated individual effort," a full-scale boom in mechanical television got underway. "The floodgates have opened," declared an editorial in Radio News. "We are now in the midst of a great race to realize the dream of television in the home."

Once again, the Radio Corporation of America appeared to have missed the starting gun. Worse yet, in David Sarnoff's view, was the prospect of watching helplessly as years of careful planning were swept aside by a hated rival.

Sarnoff had been predicting a new revolution in mass communication for some time. Years earlier, in June 1922, he had laid the groundwork in a memo calling for a centralized system of broadcasting. Sarnoff anticipated that the experimental novelty of early radio would soon fade, requiring manufacturers to "entertain a nation" with programs of "substance and quality." He proposed to establish a "separate and distinct company" for this purpose, to be called the National Broadcasting Company.

Given Sarnoff's reputation as a profit monger, it is illuminating to note that he envisioned this company as a "public service," not unlike a public library, with the costs to be shouldered by the radio manufacturers. The airwaves, he insisted, should be kept free of commercialization.

It was an idea that had strong advocates in Washington, including Herbert Hoover. At a radio industry conference in 1922, the secretary of commerce declared: "If a speech by the President is to be used as the meat in a sandwich of two patent medicine advertisements, there will be no radio left." Sarnoff himself drafted a resolution that direct advertising by radio be "absolutely prohibited."

To his lasting regret, Sarnoff would have to scuttle these plans to fend off aggressive competition from AT&T. Though the telephone company was a member of the RCA patent pool, the original agreement had not anticipated the explosive growth of the radio market, with the result that AT&T had not received a full share of the profits. Bristling over the inequity, AT&T sold off its RCA stock and its executives resigned from the corporation's board. By the end of 1922, AT&T had launched its own radio network, funded by "toll broadcasting" similar to that of its existing telephone service. At the same time, AT&T pushed ahead with the manufacture of a home radio set, cunningly designed to avoid the use of any RCA patents. To emphasize its grand ambitions, the company presented an early model to President Coolidge at the White House.

For Sarnoff and RCA, this amounted to an open declaration of war, and a rapid counterstrike was prepared. RCA would step up production of its own home radio set—the Radiola—and establish a network of nine radio stations, with a powerful 50,000-watt transmitter at its hub. Before the plan could be realized, however, Sarnoff's reputation as the industry's enforcer came back to haunt him. The company's rivals complained that the proposed powerhouse transmitter would give an unfair advantage to RCA. Sarnoff, they claimed, was trying to smother the competition. While the arguments raged, Sarnoff moved to an alternate plan—linking the radio stations by telephone cable. Predictably, AT&T refused to lease its circuits for this purpose. "Transmission by wire is ours," Sarnoff was told. "Stay out of it."

By this time, the face-off between the two companies had degenerated into personal attacks. Walter Gifford, the rising young executive who engineered the AT&T strategy, is said to have objected to Sarnoff, whom he considered to be an "abrasive Jew," and appealed to Owen Young, RCA's chairman of the board, to have the young general manager removed. Sarnoff, who freely confessed to being both abrasive and Jewish, responded with characteristic resolve. First, he approached Young and volunteered to step aside for the good of the company. When Young refused the offer, a compromise emerged: the question of AT&T's right to enter the radio market would be taken to independent legal arbitration, based on the terms of the original cross-licensing agreement.

It was an enormous risk. RCA derived the lion's share of its income from radio sales. If RCA lost the arbitration, AT&T could very well take control of the market, rendering RCA and its patent pool insignificant. Months elapsed while the arbitration proceeded under conditions of high secrecy. Technical briefs were scrutinized. Testimony was recorded. The language of the original agreement between the warring parties was studied, weighed, and parsed. At length, RCA was a handed a victory so complete that even Sarnoff could scarcely credit it.

In the end, however, RCA would effectively set aside the judgment. The Federal Trade Commission had now raised charges that RCA constituted a monopoly, with the "power to stifle competition" in the sale and manufacture of radio components. Neither RCA nor AT&T wished to invite further inquiries along these lines, so the two companies sought a middle ground. "It was like a dam breaking," Sarnoff said of the new round of negotiations. Within weeks, an agreement was reached. The resources of both organizations would join in a "self-supporting and probably revenue-producing" new enterprise. AT&T would sell its principal radio holdings to RCA and cease the manufacture of receiving sets. In return, RCA would lease the connecting cables from AT&T at a rate of $1 million per year. With that, AT&T withdrew from the radio business.

The AT&T deal left RCA in control of two major transmitting facilities in New York. Accordingly, the company decided to launch two broadcast chains—to be called the Red Network and Blue Network—under the control of its newly created National Broadcasting Company. The Red Network consisted largely of stations that had belonged to AT&T, while the Blue Network consisted of facilities belonging to RCA, General Electric, and Westinghouse. The names were drawn from the colors of the grease pencils used to map out the paths of the cables that linked the stations.

The battle had been costly. Among the casualties were Sarnoff's hopes that the networks would constitute, as one of his superiors had stated, a "sacred public trust." When the National Broadcasting Company was finally incorporated in September 1926, it was a fully commercial, revenue-producing enterprise. Still, as a limousine carried Sarnoff and his wife to the networks' inaugural celebrations at the Waldorf-Astoria, it was clear that the conflict had done him no lasting harm. In his tailored dinner jacket and with Lizette at his side in a floor-length Fifth Avenue ball gown, Sarnoff moved easily among New York's rich and powerful. At a time when Philo T. Farnsworth's annual salary was $2,400, Sarnoff earned $60,000, augmented by a generous expense account. "I may not be a millionaire yet," he declared, "but I'm beginning to live like one."

Even so, the firefight with AT&T had brought a hard lesson, and one can imagine Sarnoff's displeasure, less than one year later, when his old adversary reemerged to challenge RCA in the nascent television industry. Having gone to the battlements to defend RCA's radio holdings, Sarnoff now saw an entirely new arena of conflict stretching before him. It was clear, as *Radio News* had reported, that AT&T's Hoover broadcast had "thrown down the gauntlet to the entire industry." Though Sarnoff had serious reservations about the practicality of

AT&T's technology, RCA and its partners could not afford to let a competitor take the lead.

Ernst Alexanderson, RCA's foremost proponent of mechanical television, was ideally positioned to spearhead the response. In January 1927, even as Farnsworth filed his first patent for an all-electronic television system, Alexanderson had given a lecture before the Institute of Radio Engineers in New York City, at the conclusion of which he displayed the transmission of a film strip from RCA's General Electric lab in Schenectady. "It was a crude reproduction," reported Orrin Dunlap in the *New York Times,* "but it moved."

However crude, the demonstration was sufficient to propel Alexanderson into the headlines in both *Radio-Craft* and the *New York Times*—as the "First and True Father of Television." Alexanderson always took care to disavow the title, claiming only to have been one of many contributors, but his growing prominence drew international attention to his next major demonstration, in January 1928. Speaking before some two dozen reporters in Schenectady, Alexanderson explained that he had now abandoned the Nipkow disk in favor of a more efficient mirrored drum—an advancement which, he believed, marked "the starting point of practical and popular television."

Sarnoff himself was on hand to underscore the point. "The greatest significance of the present demonstration is in the fact that the radio art has bridged the gap between the laboratory and the home," he told the press. "Television has been demonstrated both in this country and abroad prior to this event, but it did not seem possible within so short a time to so simplify the elaborate and costly apparatus of television reception, that the first step might be taken towards the development of television receivers for the home."

Sarnoff's statement was intended to tout Alexanderson's achievement while emphasizing that television was not yet ready for commercial development. Even so, expectations were high as the reporters were directed to two small receiver cabinets, each with a three-inch-square screen. The face of Leslie Wilkins, a member of the research team, appeared on the screens. "Now I will take off my spectacles and put them on again," Wilkins announced, suiting action to word. The picture wavered slightly, but the movements were plainly visible.

"Here is a cigarette," Wilkins continued. "You can see the smoke." He sent a smoke ring drifting upward across the screen. Having made a strong impression on the audience, Wilkins yielded the floor to Louis Dean, a local radio announcer, who stepped forward to play "Ain't She Sweet?" on the ukulele.

The press responded favorably, with the ever-enthusiastic Orrin Dunlap declaring "another human conquest of space." Though the achievements of Philo Farnsworth had not yet received any press coverage at all, his transmission of a straight line would have seemed fairly modest when set against the ukulele stylings of Louis Dean. Farnsworth had superior technology but, for the moment, inferior results. For the time being, the advocates of mechanical television had the upper hand.

Among industry professionals, Sarnoff was one of the few who did not seem convinced. Publicly, it suited him to heap accolades on Alexanderson, whom he praised as the "Marconi of television." Privately, Sarnoff doubted that the Alexanderson system could ever be made practical for the home. Moreover, the success of RCA, and Sarnoff himself, rested largely on the thriving radio industry. If handled properly, Sarnoff believed, radio would gradually give way to television, solidifying RCA's position for decades to come. If an inferior product was rushed to the market, however, RCA ran the risk of losing the television race and eroding its own profitable radio empire. For the present, it suited Sarnoff to take a cautious approach.

Ernst Alexanderson had different ideas. He had spent his entire career as a corporate employee and, unlike Farnsworth, had a firm understanding of the difference between an invention and a commodity. Throughout 1928, even as he worked to refine his television apparatus, he also took steps to demonstrate its value as a commercial product. In May, General Electric launched the country's first regular television broadcasting schedule—Tuesday, Thursday, and Friday afternoons from 1:30 to 2:00. The broadcasts were intended primarily to allow Alexanderson a chance to experiment, but a GE press release offered the hope that amateurs, a small number of whom had managed to acquire or build receiving units, might "pick up the signals and carry on independent investigations." If so, it is to be hoped that these amateurs enjoyed ukulele music, which formed the cornerstone of Alexanderson's schedule.

In August, as Governor Alfred E. Smith of New York accepted the Democratic nomination for president of the United States, an Alexanderson television transmitter was on hand to relay his remarks throughout the greater New York area—to an audience of perhaps two dozen viewers. Governor Smith gamely submitted to rehearsals beforehand, a procedure that involved placing a 1,000-watt light bulb within three feet of his face. Although the GE press release anticipated "another great advance in the fascinating art of television," the reality fell short. Newsreel cameras were also on hand to capture the governor's speech; their lights bleached out Alexanderson's transmission.

Alexanderson pressed ahead. In September 1928, he mounted a groundbreaking broadcast of an "artfully televised" one-act melodrama. "For the first time in history," wrote Orrin Dunlap, "a dramatic performance is broadcast simultaneously by radio and television. Science is pushing asunder still further the curtains behind which man catches a glimpse of nature's secrets on the stage of Time." Under the circumstances, curtains being pushed asunder would have qualified as an expensive special effect. Given the constraints of his apparatus, Alexanderson had selected an 1899 play called *The Queen's Messenger*, by J. Hartley Manners, which featured only two characters and precious little movement. Three stationary cameras were used, one for each of the actors and a third to show the hands of a pair of doubles, who gestured with props such as glasses, cigarettes and—at the climactic moment—a revolver. Hoping to reach the widest possible viewership, Alexanderson arranged to have the play performed twice, first in the afternoon and then again at night, when it was hoped that the signal might travel farther.

It is difficult to say how many people actually received Alexanderson's historic broadcast, though some estimates have placed the figure in the single digits. What is clear, however, is that the efforts of Alexanderson and others in the field had now fostered a spirit of open participation, much as was the case in the early days of radio. Amateurs were encouraged to build their own home receivers so that they might participate, and many of them did so with a set of schematics published in *Radio News*. "This issue contains the first clear directions as to how to build a television set," wrote editor Hugo Gernsback in a 1928 issue. "As with radio, however, the home enthusiast must be cautious of working with resistors and battery voltages. For the experienced constructor, the schematic diagram is his servant; while for the neophyte the pictorial diagram is a master who must be obeyed literally."

Gernsback had launched *All About Television,* a magazine intended to rally these early "televisioneers," in the summer of 1927. The cover of the inaugural issue showed a family of the future gathered around their television to enjoy a football game, a scene that would not have seemed out of place in the magazine's sister publication *Amazing Stories.* In August 1928, Gernsback was on the air with his own experimental broadcast schedule, complete with program listings in the New York daily newspapers. The first day of programming featured a fitness instructor, a cooking demonstration, several concerts, and, perhaps not surprisingly, a lecture by Gernsback himself. Gernsback did not have the facilities to transmit picture and sound simultaneously, so he alternated between the two. A radio broadcast of a violin concerto, for instance, was followed by a televised image of the performer.

While televisioneers in New York tuned in for Gernsback's bifurcated transmissions, those in Washington, D.C., were receiving "radio movies" with such titles as *Little Girl Bouncing a Ball*. Like Alexanderson, Charles Francis Jenkins was also now working with a mirrored scanning drum, having temporarily abandoned the prismatic rings of his earlier efforts. Eager to capitalize on the publicity surrounding the AT&T demonstration, Jenkins brought an ingenious "Radiovisor" into production, so that "Pantomime Pictures by Radio" could be received in the home. In 1927 the Federal Radio Commission granted its first television license to station W3XK of the Jenkins Laboratories, and the station went on the air in July of the following year, just a few weeks after Alexanderson and GE. Though Jenkins promised "entertaining stories for the whole family," his early efforts offered little improvement over his "Windmill Broadcast" of 1925. Flickering silhouettes could be seen skipping rope, sniffing flowers, and pumping water. In time, when Jenkins added sound to his broadcasts, the range of his offerings expanded. Soon he was able to provide three hours of daily programming, including music, poetry readings, and short skits. A pair of singers opened each day's broadcast with a robust rendition of "The Television Song," written especially for the Jenkins station, which began: "Conjured up in sound and sight, by magic rays of light. . . ."

The investment community took notice. In December 1928, the Jenkins Television Corporation issued $10 million in common stock, with the De Forest Radio Company signaling its allegiance as the majority stockholder. At the time there were nearly two dozen stations broadcasting original television programs, usually in conjunction with a specific manufacturer of receiver kits. Among the most successful was Chicago's station WCFL, which began broadcasting in June 1928, using equipment designed by an inventive engineer named Ulysis Sanabria. Many others followed, including the newly formed Columbia Broadcasting System, which would shortly take to the air using Jenkins equipment.

A certain Barnumesque atmosphere of promotions and publicity stunts now entered the proceedings, with the press devoting a great deal of speculation to such matters as which type of woman would be best suited to television's harsh lighting. "Red-Heads Best for Television," announced one headline, "Blondes Poorest." Readers of the *New York Herald Tribune* were informed that a Miss Maxine Brown had been chosen "Sweetheart of the Air" for having the legs which registered best on camera. In Chicago, Northwestern University coeds vied for the title of "Television Girl," while in Pittsburgh, a man promised to "add eight inches to his height" for the amusement of home viewers. At the Sixth Annual Radio World's Fair at Madison Square Garden in September 1929, television was represented by a line of dancing girls bedecked with cardboard antennae, tuner knobs, and Nipkow disks. "If 'visual radio' needed anything to help put it over," observed an industry reporter, "a few dancing choruses like this would be just the ticket." The four-year-old *New Yorker* magazine weighed in with a "Talk of the Town" piece: "A prankish bond broker, who got the idea from a short story he read somewhere, visited an office on Pine Street and looked out of the window and saw several men he knew at work in their various offices across the narrow way. He immediately dropped the business of the moment and called them all in turn over the telephone, announcing that he had just taken an option on a new, simple and amazingly effective television device. He would demonstrate it, he said. He then proceeded to describe what the gentlemen were wearing that day and exactly what they were doing. One had on a bow tie with green polka dots, had nicked the left side of his chin while shaving that morning, and had half smoked a cigar. Another had a corkscrew and two glasses on his desk and was twirling a keyring with his left hand. Within ten minutes the joker had over $2,000,000 subscribed to buy all rights. He is wondering now if he ought not tell them to send the money to the telephone company."

Not surprisingly, the promise of easy money soon brought John Logie Baird and his representatives to New York. Baird had been very much in the headlines following a successful transatlantic transmission, and his arrival in Manhattan warranted a police motorcycle escort and a Scottish pipe band. In December 1929, representatives of Baird's new television corporation demonstrated their latest equipment for Mayor Jimmy Walker, who was invited to hold a televised conversation with the actress Betty Compton. Upon receiving an assurance that he "looked beautiful" on the receiving screen, the mayor retorted, "Huh? Then I resign right now!" According to an account in the *New York World,* the mayor then "essayed a conversation with the lovely Miss Compton, who, it may be and hereby is authoritatively stated, is admirably adapted to experiments in 'tele' or any other sort of vision."

Back in San Francisco, Farnsworth kept track of these developments by means of a stack of newspaper articles provided by a clipping service. Pem carefully pasted each story into a large scrapbook, creating a mosaic of strange and often conflicting information: "Weird Machine Projects Images and Voices Without Any Wires—Would Be Most Secret of War-Time Message Transmitters—Ray Penetrates Fog, Smoke and Darkness." "It's Here! You Will Soon Have a Television in Your Home!" "Television by Radio Is and Always Will Be Impossible, Declares Federal Radio Commissioner."

Perhaps the most resonant of all, as far as Farnsworth was concerned, was a headline in New York's *Daily News*. It read simply: "Fame Awaits Genius Who Solves Problems."

It was a sentiment echoed by A. A. Campbell Swinton, the longtime advocate of electronic television. Though he had initially been an enthusiastic supporter of John Logie Baird, Campbell Swinton now recanted. At the height of the mechanical television craze, he wrote to the London *Times* to protest the "absurd prognostications" appearing in the press. "The public are being led to expect, in the near future, that, sitting at home in their armchairs, they will be able, with comparatively inexpensive apparatus, to witness moving pictures approximating in quality to those of the cinematograph." This contention, Campbell Swinton insisted, was "obviously beyond the possible capacity of any mechanism with material moving parts. . . . The only way it can ever be accomplished is by . . . using the vastly superior agency of electrons."

Though Campbell Swinton was unaware of the work being done on Green Street in San Francisco, he had been keeping a careful watch on the larger American research efforts. At one stage, having been made aware of Vladimir Zworykin's experiments, he wrote to Ernst Alexanderson to express his hope that General Electric would explore the potential of cathode rays. Alexanderson, however, could not be lured away from his mechanical system. *The Queen's Messenger* had showed him the possibilities of the new medium; in his view, all that remained was to broaden his audience. "In my opinion," he told Sarnoff, "the time has come when we should take the public into our confidence by giving a short television act regularly in a New York theater." Toward that end, Alexanderson spent much of his time and resources developing a large receiving screen that would be suitable for use in movie theaters. Beginning in May 1930, audiences at the Proctor Theater in Schenectady were treated to a series of live performances by a full orchestra. The conductor, John Gamble, was not actually present in the theater—he was two miles away at the GE laboratory, visible to the audience at Proctor's on an impressive six-by-seven-foot screen. Alexanderson went on to offer several variations on the theme: "Vaudeville teams banter back and forth," reported Orrin

Dunlap of the *New York Times*. "One member performs and jokes before the televisor, while the other replies from the stage. Duets are sung by vocalists two miles apart. . . . Alexanderson, like a magician, waves aside the veils of secrecy and shows television performing tricks that astound the audience."

Alexanderson's demonstrations were hugely successful, presenting the very latest technology in a manner that captured the public's imagination. So far as Sarnoff was concerned, however, the effort had come far too late. "I can't sell it," Sarnoff had said of an earlier Alexanderson display. By then, however, he had met a man with something he could sell.

Following his inconclusive television demonstration in 1925, Vladimir Zworykin had been moved on to other research projects at Westinghouse. Unwilling to give up on his ideas, Zworykin continued to experiment on his own time, using Westinghouse laboratory facilities without official authorization. It is unlikely that his superiors would have begrudged these efforts, as Zworykin had now become one of the company's most valued and productive scientists.

In November 1928, Zworykin was sent to Europe to inspect the work being done by various electrical laboratories working under contract with the RCA partners. Zworykin, who was fluent in both French and German, was a natural choice for the mission, and he undoubtedly looked forward to a pleasant, if not especially demanding, research junket.

In fact, as Zworykin later acknowledged, the trip marked a decisive turning point in his career. In Paris, he visited the workshop of Edouard Belin, the French experimenter who had done innovative work sending photographs via radio wave transmissions. Belin's latest work in this arena had resulted in a new type of cathode-ray picture tube that offered a distinct advantage over the type of work Zworykin had been doing. One of Zworykin's fundamental challenges had been to devise a means of controlling the flow of electrons through his tube—the very same problem that had limited Farnsworth to the transmission of a simple straight line. Though there were several methods available, both Zworykin and Farnsworth had been using magnetic coils to manipulate the electrons. By contrast, Belin and his team were using electrostatic fields—the force resulting from an electrical charge at rest, in this case within a vacuum tube.

Two of Belin's colleagues, Fernand Holweck and Pierre Chevallier, had engineered a means of pumping out a cathode-ray tube to a very high vacuum, in the hope of improving the efficiency of electrostatic focusing. Their early tests, however, had shown no great improvement over the magnetic method. As an added complication, their technique required a continual pumping of the tube to maintain the high vacuum, a process that would never be practical in a home television unit.

In spite of the indifferent lab results, the Belin tube produced an image of startling clarity in Zworykin's mind. He saw at once how Belin's results dovetailed with his own, and how various elements of the French system could be incorporated into a new and better tube. All at once, the researches and experiments of nearly two decades came into focus.

Fired with renewed confidence, Zworykin promptly struck a deal on behalf of Westinghouse to make use of the Belin tube. Although he had not yet been authorized to resume his television work, Zworykin also made arrangements with Gregory Ogloblinsky, one of Belin's chief engineers, to come to the United States to join any future Zworykin initiative. Zworykin returned to Westinghouse in December 1928 with a Belin tube and one of Holweck and Chevallier's high-efficiency vacuum pumps.

In Pittsburgh, Zworykin's superiors remained unimpressed with the prospects for electronic television. Zworykin's ideas, one researcher would write, appeared to be "chiefly talk," and his notions about the potential market seemed "quite wild." Sam Kintner, the Westinghouse vice president who had supported Zworykin's earlier efforts, offered a piece of helpful advice. Zworykin might find a receptive ear, Kintner said, if he traveled to New York and presented his ideas to RCA's new executive vice president, David Sarnoff.

As it happened, Kintner's advice could not have been better timed. Sarnoff, fresh from his battles against AT&T, was ascending to new heights. The 1927 release of *The Jazz Singer,* the "world's first talking motion picture," had created a powerful new market for RCA's sound technology. In October of the following year, Sarnoff arranged to have RCA purchase a major interest in the Keith-Albee-Orpheum vaudeville theaters, which were to be wired for sound using RCA equipment. At the Oyster Bar in Grand Central Station, Sarnoff hammered out a deal with a rising Irish-American businessman, Joseph P. Kennedy, to create a new venture called Radio Keith Orpheum, or RKO, which was to become a familiar presence on the Hollywood scene.

Three months later, in January 1929, Sarnoff persuaded the board of RCA to authorize the purchase of the Victor Talking Machine Company for $154 million. By the end of the year, a new entity known as RCA Victor would come into being, and Sarnoff would add "Director of Research Activities" to his growing list of titles. Though Sarnoff had little interest in the "talking machine," or phonograph, the deal gave RCA a vast manufacturing and research facility in Camden, New Jersey, along with a far-reaching distribution network. Though RCA had originally been conceived as little more than a holding company for the royalty partners, it would now have a powerful manufacturing division of its own.

It was at this moment, just as the Victor purchase was being authorized in January 1929, that Vladimir Zworykin appeared in Sarnoff's office to discuss electronic television. Though the two men had met previously, this was probably the first time they had spoken at any length. Over the years, much has been made of the fact that Sarnoff and Zworykin were both Russian immigrants making their way in the New World—two men who literally spoke the same language. In reality, Sarnoff was a boy from the shtetl and Zworykin had been heir to a country estate; it is unlikely that they swapped stories from home.

If Sarnoff felt no particular kinship to Zworykin, however, he did know a born scientist when he saw one. "Zworykin had the spark in his eye," a colleague later recalled. "Sarnoff immediately saw in him the man he wanted."

Sarnoff sat at his desk smoking a cigar as Zworykin spoke of his findings in Paris. Next, Zworykin sketched out the details of a television system that would do away with Nipkow disks and mirrored drums. The receiving unit that Zworykin had in mind would be inexpensive to produce, small enough to sit in the living room of the average American family, and no more difficult to operate than a Radiola. "Sarnoff listened without interrupting," Zworykin would recall. "He asked a few questions to clear some points that I didn't make sufficiently clear, and then asked how long it would take—and how much it would cost—to build an electronic system."

Zworykin paused. Very likely his mind reached back to the demonstration at Westinghouse in 1925, when he had been asked much the same question. In that case he had given a cautious and literal answer, only to find himself cut off from television research for four years. He had no wish to repeat the mistake. "I had learned by this time that it is impossible to work on an idea in commercial research without camouflaging it," he recalled, "unless you can convince commercial people of its immediate profitableness."

Zworykin considered the problem for a moment longer, then gave an answer that he hoped would not blunt Sarnoff's interest. In order to bring an electronic television system to the public, he said, he would need two years and $100,000.

Sarnoff considered the figure. "All right," he said after a moment. "It's worth it."

In fact, RCA would spend ten years and more than $50 million before it saw its first profits from television. Even more costly, in Sarnoff's view, would be an obstacle he and Zworykin had not foreseen. Before any revenues could roll in, they would have to come to terms with Philo T. Farnsworth.

Nine

Dollars in the Thing

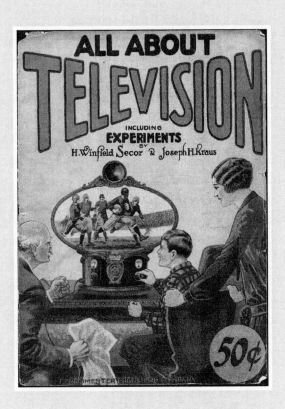

The difficult we do right away;
the impossible takes slightly longer.
—Philo T. Farnsworth

"Who Will Be the Television Moses?" asked a headline in the *Washington Post* in the early months of 1928. The question was posed by J. E. Smith, the president of the National Radio Institute, during a survey of the various technologies on the horizon. "Somewhere, somehow, sometime, a certain man is going to come across the idea for a practical system," Smith declared. "Just as Dr. Lee de Forest, in the dark ages of radio, came through with the audion, or vacuum tube, in place of the tricky crystal detector, some bright man, with a fundamental knowledge of radio, is going to stumble across the correct television principle, and, if he exploits his discovery or invention properly, he is going to earn both fame and fortune. Like all other industries, television officials are looking for 'that chap in torn trousers, faded tie, and unshaven face' who will give us the answer to the television problem. And you can be sure we are overlooking no bets! We will make it worth his while."

On Green Street in San Francisco, there was no doubt as to who that chap would be. "In view of all that has been published with regard to the work on Television in the east," Farnsworth told a colleague, "which we judge to be with the means of rotating disks, etc., for scan-

A 1927 magazine was aimed at early television experimenters, known as "televisioneers." ALL ABOUT TELEVISION MAGAZINE

ning and transmitting, we feel rather optimistic with our accomplishments, using no moving elements."

Privately, Farnsworth admitted to Everson that he felt impatient to give a public demonstration and stake his claim. "Now George," he wrote in one of his infrequent letters, "we cannot be damaged by what other workers are doing—our patent situation tells us that—so long as we hold up our end of it. Holding up our end of it seems to me to mean keeping a jump ahead of everyone else. We certainly are so far, in spite of the fact that we haven't made any spectacular demonstrations. I certainly wish that we could organize to transmit a picture from the Lab here and have the picture received by several small receiving sets in the locality. That is not a big step right now—I don't see why we can't do it, do you?"

Everson was delighted with Farnsworth's enthusiasm, but the Crocker syndicate had developed a severe case of jitters. The original agreement had called for a $25,000 budget over a period of one year. By the spring of 1928—a full eighteen months later—the bank directors had put up a total of $40,000. For all of Farnsworth's optimism, it seemed to his patrons that he had produced nothing that could compete against the Jenkins and Alexanderson systems. "It had been my chore to keep Mr. McCargar, Mr. Fagan, and the other backers of the venture informed," Everson recalled, "since all thought it best not to visit Phil until he had some definite progress to show them. Very often I would be greeted by Mr. Fagan, who would make rings around his eyes with his forefingers and thumbs. Peering through them he would ask, 'Have you seen any dollar signs in that Farnsworth tube yet?' "

For the moment, Everson had to stall. Though Farnsworth radiated confidence, he offered a more cautious assessment of his progress in his lab journals. "Line pictures can be transmitted with the amplifier system as it is," he noted, "but I always get practically negative results when I attempt to show variations in two dimensions." Though he had attacked the problem from every angle, he admitted that "I cannot discover anything wrong."

Meanwhile, Cliff Gardner's skills were improving. Eager to create a better receiving apparatus, Farnsworth ordered a supply of blank Pyrex glass tubes from the Corning Glass Company in New York and set Gardner to work. Gardner carefully heated each tube and re-formed it into an exaggerated pear shape, with a flat end on which to receive an image. As with the image dissector, the inside of the tube had to be coated with a special photoelectric chemical. After much trial and error, Farnsworth settled on a mineral compound called willemite, a substance that met his unique requirements: it glowed brightly when hit with an electron beam but shut off again instantly, so that there would be no overlap of received images. Farnsworth dubbed his tube the "oscillite," after the oscillating stream of electrons that coursed through it.

By the spring of 1928, Farnsworth had made dramatic improvements to his system, including the magnetic focusing coils. A few months earlier, the transmission of a straight line had shown the potential of his work. Now, Farnsworth believed, he could ascend to the next level—a two-dimensional image. With both the image dissector and the oscillite in a state of readiness, he had created what Everson called the "first edition of the Farnsworth television system." Once again, in early May 1928, the team assembled in the lab to make their final preparations. Everson arrived to find Farnsworth at his desk checking over the plans while Gardner tinkered with the image dissector. Pem busied herself with bookkeeping chores. "I think we will have a picture as soon as the boys get the new circuits wired up," Farnsworth said cautiously. "I don't know how good it will be."

Looking around, Everson admitted that he could sense "something of the historic importance of the occasion," however unlikely it would have seemed to a casual observer. With its ever-expanding array of jury-rigged electrical fittings and wooden braces, the Farnsworth lab appeared better suited to the efforts of Dr. Frankenstein. "In one room the dissector tube with its coils and amplifiers was placed on a small stand before a windowlike aperture in the room," Everson explained. "The dissector tube was hooked up to some panels containing the scanning generators. Leads were fed into a black box containing the amplifier. A copper tube led out of the amplifier into the receiving room, where the receiving tube and the necessary receiving set apparatus were mounted on an oblong box of imitation mahogany. Here was our first television receiving set. It was all very handmade and crude-looking."

Farnsworth had no illusions about the quality of the image his system could produce. His primary concern was to demonstrate that the apparatus could scan vertically as well as horizontally, so that actual pictures would someday be possible. Accordingly, he made up a glass slide that showed a simple black triangle.

With the slide in hand, Cliff Gardner took up his post by the image dissector. The others gathered around the oscillite's four-inch screen as Farnsworth switched on the power. "A square luminescent field of bluish cast appeared on the end of the receiving tube," said Everson. "A series of fairly sharp bright lines was unsteadily limned on the screen."

Farnsworth called to the other room for Gardner to position the slide in front of the image dissector. The bluish glow seemed to pulse for a moment, then resolved itself into a messy blur that in no way resembled a triangle. "Phil and I looked at the blur with a sickening sense of disappointment," Everson said. It appeared that the test had been a dismal failure.

For two hours Farnsworth and his team made frantic adjustments to the apparatus. Everson, feeling that his presence was making the men nervous, retired to a back room. "I didn't have the heart to leave the lab," he said, "Phil was so certain he was going to get results."

At last, Farnsworth appeared in the doorway. "I think we've got it now," he said. Once again the apparatus hummed and crackled as the bluish glow appeared at the end of the oscillite. Hovering over the tube, Farnsworth again called out his instructions to Gardner. "Cliff, is the arc light going okay?"

"Just fine, Phil," came the reply.

"All right." Farnsworth took a breath. "Put the slide in."

Almost at once, a blurry but distinctly recognizable black triangle appeared at the center of the blue screen. "There it is, folks," Farnsworth announced, "a two-dimensional television picture!"

"We gazed spellbound for a while," Everson recalled. Then, as the others shook hands and slapped each other on the back, Pem gave her husband a "very big, unbusinesslike hug."

Suddenly the revels were cut short. As Farnsworth tried to sharpen the focus on the oscillite, the triangle suddenly vanished from the screen. In its place was a strange swirling distortion. Farnsworth was crestfallen. He rushed into the transmitting room while the others stared at the malfunctioning tube in disbelief. A moment later, Farnsworth returned pulling a sheepish-looking Gardner behind him. "I was just trying something," Gardner explained. "First I put my face in sideways, between the arc light and the camera, but I got no response, and it was too hot anyway. Then I blew a cloud of smoke from my cigarette so it would rise up past the viewing area."

For Farnsworth, it was a revelation. He had expected to transmit nothing more than a static line drawing. Instead, he found that the system could televise continuous motion. "You realize, of course," he told Everson, "that our ability to see that smoke rising means we'll have no trouble transmitting moving objects, whether it's moving pictures, sporting events, or anything else that moves."

"This interlude of satisfaction endured but an instant," Everson recalled. "Then Phil burst forth with a shower of ideas, telling the boys in hurried, feverish words of changes to be made."

Before leaving Farnsworth to his modifications, Everson made arrangements to bring the principal trustees of the Crocker syndicate to Green Street to see what had been accomplished. Although Farnsworth still had grave reservations, he knew that the time had come. A date was set and Farnsworth promised to be ready.

In late May, a contingent of San Francisco's most prominent businessmen descended on Green Street. Along with James Fagan and Roy Bishop, the group included bank president William H. Crocker and R. J. Hanna, the vice president of Standard Oil of California, who had also put money into the enterprise. Farnsworth and his crew, aware that their future financing was on the line, were anxious to make a good impression. The lab had been tidied and the apparatus polished to a high gleam. The visitors appeared impressed as they wandered through the lab peering at the unfamiliar equipment.

The mood gave way to apprehension as Farnsworth made a transparent effort to scale back the group's high expectations. The apparatus was still in a primitive state, he explained, so there would be nothing more to see than basic geometric shapes. Indeed, he couldn't promise even that, given the temperamental nature of the system. As Farnsworth continued in this vein, the trustees grew restless. At length, James Fagan prodded the young inventor along with his familiar refrain: "When are we going to see some dollars in this thing, Farnsworth?"

Though Fagan couldn't have known it, he had just handed Farnsworth his cue. In the transmitter room, Cliff Gardner placed a glass slide in front of the image dissector. On the glowing blue screen of the oscillite, a distinct image came into view—a thick, black dollar sign.

Farnsworth's gag made a strong impression on the visitors, as did the series of demonstrations that followed. The group seemed especially gratified by Cliff Gardner's smoke-blowing display, which effectively illustrated the potential for the broadcast of moving images.

Fagan and the other backers were clearly impressed by Farnsworth's achievements, but their concerns remained. Roy Bishop, speaking on behalf of the group, pointed out that the total cash outlay for the Farnsworth lab had now exceeded $60,000—more than doubling the original estimate. "Phil," Bishop continued, "you've done what you set out to do and we feel that thus far you have fulfilled your contract. Speaking for the trustees, we feel that we, too, have lived up to our contract. Now it's a question of what shall be done with this development. It's my opinion that it will take a pile of money as high as Telegraph Hill to carry this thing on to a successful conclusion, and I feel that we should take immediate steps to place it with one of the large electrical companies where there will be adequate facilities for its development. I think it's time to incorporate this undertaking and then take steps to dispose of it in some way or other."

This was what Farnsworth had been dreading. He knew very well that disposing of the lab in "some way or other" would very likely involve a total buyout, stripping him of any future profits or patent rights. From his perspective, the timing would be disastrous. None of his patent applications had yet been granted, and a sale of the lab might well prevent him from filing any new ones. In its present form, his system appeared too crude and problematic to warrant more favorable terms, such as a licensing deal or cooperative research arrangement.

Though Farnsworth recognized the potential benefits of joining up with a major lab, his previous efforts along these lines had not been encouraging. Just a few weeks earlier he had given a demonstration for a pair of engineers from the California offices of General Electric, hoping to explore the possibility of an exchange of resources. The GE men had seen no great value in Farnsworth's image dissector. Farnsworth knew that he would probably get the same response from the other electrical laboratories. From the beginning, Farnsworth had gone to extraordinary lengths to retain control of his invention. Now, on the brink of success, he faced the very real prospect of seeing it handed over to a competitor.

Hoping to strengthen his bargaining position, Farnsworth offered a compromise. If the Crocker group could hold out for a short time longer, Farnsworth would be able to bring the system to a new plateau. Soon, he promised, he would be able to transmit still photos or, better yet, movie film. "Either one of these," he told the trustees, "could bring us to the point of realizing a much greater profit than we would realize if we sell out now." Bishop asked how much longer this would take. Farnsworth hesitated. One more month, he said. After a few moments of discussion, the backers agreed. The lab would continue to receive funding through the end of June.

Farnsworth had won a stay of execution, but even as the trustees filed out of the lab, he found himself wondering if he could possibly accomplish his ambitious goal in only one month. He had burned through a great many resources in a very short time. Around the lab, the cabinet that housed Farnsworth's tubes had been dubbed "Jonah," because it swallowed everything that came near it—time, light, and money. "I know I can perfect this invention and make it commercially viable," he told Pem later that evening, "but it's going to take some time. And Mr. Bishop was probably right; it will also take quite a bit of money. But if I can persuade the backers not to sell out now, then once television does become commercial, we'll have all the money we could ever dream of."

It may have seemed that way to Farnsworth, but the Crocker group was clearly getting ready to cut its losses. Within days of the meeting on Green Street, Roy Bishop contacted General Electric's

California representatives to inquire about selling off Farnsworth's patents. After the unimpressive demonstration earlier that year, General Electric showed only moderate interest, offering instead to hire Farnsworth under a "regular television engineering contract." The offer was refused and—so far as is known—word of Farnsworth's progress at that stage was not passed along to RCA.

Matters worsened as Farnsworth developed an adversarial relationship with Albert Mann, who handled some of the bookkeeping for the Crocker trustees. Mann, who had experience as an acoustical engineer, had solicited Farnsworth's advice when the organ at San Francisco's landmark Grace Cathedral began causing excessive vibration. Farnsworth spotted the problem immediately—although a cushion of felt padding had been laid down, Mann had secured the material with metal bolts. The bolts conducted the vibrations and rendered the padding useless. According to Pem, this struck Farnsworth as a fairly obvious mistake for an acoustical engineer to have made, and he "may have communicated some of his feelings" to Mann. Whatever the reason, Pem soon noticed that the lab's bills were not being paid on time, and relations with the Crocker group began to show signs of growing strain.

On Green Street, the one-month ultimatum had thrown matters into disarray. When Carl Christensen, one of the hired engineers, announced his decision to leave San Francisco, Farnsworth brought on a circuitry expert named Robert "Tobe" Rutherford, even though Rutherford's increased salary came out of Farnsworth's own pocket. Although Rutherford was filling a vacancy, the Crocker group objected to the hiring of a new member of staff at a time when expenses had to be reined in. Farnsworth was forced to let Rutherford go, leaving the lab understaffed. When Farnsworth brought two of his brothers to San Francisco to fill in, Mann protested the hiring of family members, though the new arrivals were working for little more than room and board.

Even with these new restrictions in place, Farnsworth managed to make steady progress over the next few weeks. Nevertheless, at the end of June, when the one-month deadline elapsed, he was not yet able to make good on his promise to broadcast photographs or motion picture film. When the time came to meet with the trustees to assess the lab's future prospects, Farnsworth feared the worst.

Help arrived from an unexpected quarter. Willie Crocker, the son of bank president William H. Crocker, had been spending a great deal of his free time in the Green Street lab. Having become fascinated by Farnsworth's work, the younger Crocker now argued passionately with the banking syndicate to allow the research to go forward. After a lengthy debate, the trustees reached another compromise. The Crocker syndicate would go on funding Farnsworth's work, but the search for a corporate buyer would continue. There was an additional condition: as a sign of good faith, Farnsworth, Everson, and Gorrell were to contribute capital to help make up the additional funds. For Farnsworth, who had been living on a beans-and-toast budget for two years, this meant selling off some of the shares he owned in the syndicate and further reducing the degree to which he controlled his own invention. Seeing no alternative, he reluctantly agreed.

Having bought himself some breathing room, Farnsworth pushed ahead with his experiments with motion picture film. From the beginning, Farnsworth's work had been hampered by the fact that his image dissector was not as sensitive to light as it would need to be—a fatal flaw in a device intended to convert light into electricity. By moving ahead with motion picture transmission, Farnsworth was sidestepping the problem. He bought a secondhand movie projector and replaced its lamp with a high-intensity carbon arc light. This provided all the illumination he needed, as opposed to the lighting challenges presented by still photographs or live action scenes. Although the problem of light sensitivity remained crucial, he was now able to move forward with other aspects of the system.

At first, Farnsworth worked with transmissions of a short strip of film showing a hockey game in progress. At the receiving end, he found that the action was blurred and the puck completely bleached out, but after some tinkering he was soon able to pick out the individual players. Encouraged, he went to a local film exchange to find clips that offered a high contrast of black and white values, so as to be more suitable for television experimentation. A bootleg film of the famous "long count" in the Jack Dempsey vs. Gene Tunney boxing match gave strong results. Even better was an excerpt from a recent film of *The Taming of the Shrew,* starring Mary Pickford and Douglas Fairbanks. One particular scene, in which Miss Pickford sat combing her hair at a dressing table, drew special attention. The clip was played over and over as Farnsworth made minute adjustments to the transmitter and regulated the receiver. Piece by piece, the various elements of the scene came into focus—the shine of Miss Pickford's hair, the delicate braiding on her costume, a glimpse of the casement window in the background. As George Everson recalled, "Mary Pickford combed her hair at least a million times for the benefit of science and the development of television."

Though Farnsworth was getting strong results—"The picture was improved (again) tenfold," he noted in his journal—mounting expenses caused a further erosion in his relations with the backing syndicate. On at least one occasion the Crocker trustees shut the lab down completely, only to be persuaded by an irate Farnsworth that a thriving lab would be easier to sell than a mothballed one. He received a grudging authorization to resume work, but it was clear that time was running out. As the summer of 1928 drew to a close, Farnsworth knew that he needed to take a dramatic step.

Up to this stage, Farnsworth had shied away from newspaper publicity. Although he had filed his first patent applications more than a year earlier, none of the patents had yet been granted, and he was wary of tipping off his competitors before he could secure adequate protection for his ideas. Up to this point, it had suited him to let Baird and Jenkins grab the headlines while he worked to render their mechanical systems obsolete. Now, however, he could no longer afford to maintain his silence. Hoping to reinvigorate his supporters, Farnsworth arranged a press conference on September 1, 1928.

Pem, who had not accompanied her husband to the lab that day, waited anxiously at home to hear the result. Farnsworth arrived in high spirits, but he would say little of the day's events. The following night, as they returned from a movie, he stopped to pick up an early edition of the *San Francisco Chronicle* from a newsboy. He handed the paper to Pem, who opened it to find a large picture of her husband on the front of the second section.

"S.F. Man's Invention to Revolutionize Television," read the headline. Below, Farnsworth was seen holding an image dissector in one hand and an oscillite tube in the other. The accompanying article gave a breathless description of the "young genius" who had been "quietly working away in his laboratory" to perfect a new method of television. "Farnsworth's system employs no moving parts whatever," noted the reporter. "The system is thus simple in the extreme, and one of the major mechanical obstacles to the perfection of television is thereby removed."

As for the picture produced by the Farnsworth system, the reporter admitted that "it is a queer looking little image in bluish light now, one that frequently smudges and blurs, but the basic principle is achieved and perfection is now a matter of engineering."

With this perfection imminent, the article concluded, readers could soon look forward to having a Farnsworth television in their homes: "Farnsworth estimates the receiving apparatus could easily be attached to an ordinary radio set and can be manufactured to retail at $100 or less."

The story caught on. By the end of the month, articles describing Farnsworth and his "miracle box" were appearing in newspapers around the world. Many of the stories played up Farnsworth's humble beginnings, marveling over the manner in which a young and relatively inexperienced farm boy had succeeded where the established electrical laboratories had failed.

Some of this coverage took on a decidedly fanciful tone: "Out of the West like the realization of a prophet's dream has come the greatest magic of the civilized day," ran one account. "The thrilling news that the Pandora's box of science had opened at last to release this greatest of all electrical gifts to the human race came only this week. . . . One stands amazed before the perfected miracle of the new plaything of the world's millions, the newest pet of science and the god-child of Edison's electric light."

Farnsworth, who was no longer the naive farm boy that the press made him out to be, took no great pleasure from his growing celebrity. Although the Crocker trustees were momentarily appeased by the favorable attention, Farnsworth looked ahead to what would happen next. The publicity, he reasoned, was certain to draw some of the larger research outfits into the television arena. Farnsworth's limited budget would make it difficult to maintain a competitive edge. "Our small size and method of operating allows us to maneuver like a speedboat alongside their juggernauts," he said. "But speedboats eventually run out of gas."

It would happen even sooner than Farnsworth had foreseen. Despite all the positive press, most of the big research firms were still in the thrall of the spinning Nipkow disk. In the fall of 1928, when no serious buyers had come forward, the Crocker group voted to withdraw its support.

On Green Street, Farnsworth gathered the lab team to break the grim news. The money had stopped, he explained, but he would do whatever he could to keep going on his own, even though it meant paying the bills out of his own pocket. In the meantime, however, he would be unable to pay anyone's salary, and he didn't expect them to stay on. Farnsworth promised that he would try to hire everyone back when his fortunes improved.

To Farnsworth's delight, the lab team held fast. By unanimous agreement, they decided to soldier on at subsistence wages. Along with the normal workload, they also decided to take on whatever odd jobs they could manage in order to raise some working capital. "That was what it was like working for Phil," said Tobe Rutherford, who had recently returned to the lab. "He never asked us to do anything he couldn't or wouldn't do. You worked with Phil, not for him."

Before long, the Green Street lab had started up a profitable sideline in manufacturing radio control units. At the same time, as Hollywood made the transition to talking pictures, Farnsworth and Gardner hired themselves out to install sound systems in a number of local theaters. In the meantime, George Everson continued to plead Farnsworth's case to the Crocker group, eventually winning a limited reinstatement of their backing.

Though Farnsworth had managed to hold the lab together, Pem

was growing ever more concerned for his health. With the financial pressures heaped on top of his grueling lab schedule, Farnsworth was finding it increasingly hard to relax. He slept poorly and sometimes found it difficult to eat, leaving his features gray and haggard. At Pem's urging, Farnsworth decided to take up an outdoor sport. Everson suggested that he try his hand at golf, but Farnsworth felt he couldn't afford the time or money. Instead, he and Pem learned to play tennis. Cliff Gardner had recently married his longtime girlfriend, Lola Buker, and the newlyweds agreed to meet the Farnsworths several times a week for an early game of doubles.

One morning in the late fall of 1928, the arrival of a police cruiser interrupted their match. "Are you Farnsworth?" asked the officer behind the wheel. "You might want to get down to your laboratory right away. The place is on fire."

Farnsworth jumped into his car and followed as the police cruiser, with its siren blaring, led him back to Green Street. Firefighters were spraying the building with their hoses, but each jet of water seemed to touch off an explosion or a column of flame. Farnsworth waded in, found the fire chief, and hastily explained that the lab was filled with potassium and other chemicals that reacted violently with water. By the time the firefighters managed to bring the explosions under control, the lab had all but collapsed.

As he surveyed the damage, Farnsworth realized that this was likely to be the end. He had no reason to believe that the quarrelsome Albert Mann, who had been so negligent in paying the lab's other bills, had troubled to maintain its insurance. Farnsworth spent a restless night, but in the morning he discovered to his relief that his losses were indeed covered. It would take time, but the lab would be restored.

In fact, things would be better than before. Farnsworth took advantage of the opportunity to update his equipment and iron out some troublesome technical hitches. At the same time, while the lab was being reconstructed, Farnsworth worked with his new attorney, Donald Lippincott, to bring his portfolio of patent applications up to date.

Lippincott, who had taken over Farnsworth's patent business shortly after the move to San Francisco, was fast becoming one of

Farnsworth's closest confidants. Along with his legal training, Lippincott also had a degree in electrical engineering and had recently been chief engineer of the Magnavox Corporation. As a result, he had a unique ability to understand and isolate the elements of Farnsworth's work that qualified for patent protection. For Farnsworth, a conference with Lippincott was a pleasure—he had finally found a lawyer who spoke his language. Early in their association, Lippincott was able to tutor Farnsworth in advanced mathematics. Soon enough, he ruefully admitted, Farnsworth had moved "so far beyond me that I could scarcely understand what language he was speaking."

Much of that rarefied language was directed toward the problem of television's wave band requirements. For some time, Farnsworth had been troubled by the nagging realization that a television signal, which contained far more information than a radio signal, would require a very wide wave band—or range of frequencies—to be successful. "The electrical engineering profession as a whole was quietly skeptical of television because of the breadth of wave band needed," explained George Everson. "It became apparent that in order to transmit a picture of sufficient detail and clarity to give entertainment value, the wide range of variations involved would require space in the radio spectrum comparable to that used by a hundred commercial radio stations for sound." Since there were only a limited number of wave bands available within the radio spectrum, it was by no means certain that television's requirements could be accommodated. Already the Federal Radio Commission had balked at assigning experimental frequencies for television research. If television had any hope of progressing to the commercial stage, the problem would have to be addressed. Farnsworth believed that the difficulty could be resolved by narrowing or compressing television's wave band requirements, and he threw himself into a bewildering morass of higher mathematics in the hope of finding a means of doing so. The problem would absorb him for several months.

By December 1928, the Green Street lab was up and running with a renewed sense of mission. Over the coming year, Farnsworth would strip his system down and put it back together, refining each element so that the total package would be better than ever before. The oscillite tube was enlarged to accommodate a seven-inch screen, giving a much improved picture. More important, Farnsworth had devised an "electron multiplier"—also known as the "multipactor"—to address the problem of light sensitivity. By August 1929, Farnsworth was able to abandon his high-intensity illumination and transmit an image by the light of a simple room lamp. "This marks an important step," he noted in his lab journal.

For all of these refinements, Farnsworth was not yet satisfied. The enlarged picture on the oscillite showed a dark smudge running down the center, and the transmissions were usually shadowed by a double image. After much study, Farnsworth traced the problem to the electrical waves he was using to scan the scene. The natural wave form of the electric current—the sine wave—scanned the images in two directions, as though a human eye were reading a line of type both forward and backward. Farnsworth's ingenious solution was to change the shape of the scanning wave. With a device called a vacuum-tube pulse generator, he found that he could produce a sharper "sawtooth" scanning wave instead of the sloping sine wave. This wave provided a crisp line-by-line scan, resulting in a clearer transmission and better picture.

Along with new equipment, the lab fire had brought about a strengthened commitment from the Crocker syndicate. Bolstered by Farnsworth's progress and by the continuing publicity his efforts were receiving, the group made a decision to go public. "This was the era of wonderful nonsense in the financial world," declared George Everson. "On March 27, 1929, the venture was incorporated as Television Laboratories, Inc., under the laws of the state of California, with an authorized capitalization of twenty thousand shares. Ten thousand shares were issued to the trustees and the original partnership of Everson, Farnsworth, and Gorrell." Jesse McCargar, who had recently resigned from the Crocker Bank to become an independent financial consultant, was named president of the new company, vowing to serve as the liaison between the lab and its backers. Farnsworth became vice president in charge of research, and Everson took on the role of secretary-treasurer.

As the largest single shareholder in the new enterprise, Farnsworth slowly realized that he no longer needed to drive a rust bucket and wear shabby clothes. Leslie Gorrell had already splashed out on a sporty new car, and Everson would shortly dispose of one-fortieth of his holdings for an impressive $2,500—which placed the value of Farnsworth's shares at over $100,000. At age twenty-two, Farnsworth had suddenly become a man of means. His sister Laura had occasion to ask if Farnsworth's success might possibly bring her a new pair of shoes. Some time later, when Farnsworth gave her television shares as a wedding gift, she recalled that early flush of excitement: "I've got my new shoes," she told her brother.

For Farnsworth, the shares in the company represented far more than money. For three years he had worried that the Crocker group might trade away control of his invention to a competitor. Now, as the largest individual shareholder, he had a strong voice in the future disposition of the company. There would be few extravagances; Farnsworth was far more concerned with protecting his interests.

Soon, however, he would have reason to dip into his capital. As the number of technicians in the lab rose to seven, Pem found that her role in her husband's work had diminished. Feeling isolated from the excitement of the lab, she joked to Farnsworth that she had half a mind to seek out new employment prospects. A short time later, Pem greeted her husband at the door with the news that she had, in fact, found a new job, scheduled to begin in nine months' time with the birth of their first child. An elated Farnsworth picked her up and whirled her around the living room. "The weight of his problems had begun to rob him of much of his old way," Pem recalled, "but for the moment he was the same lighthearted Phil I had met five years before in Provo."

Insisting that "no child of mine is going to be raised in an apartment," Farnsworth arranged to buy a new row house in San Francisco's Marina District, and joked that he had "high hopes of paying the mortgage" when television brought him the promised windfall. At the top of the house, the so-called "airplane room"—which afforded a view of passing flights—served as Farnsworth's study. Farnsworth's mother, who had recently arrived from Utah, helped Pem to furnish the house with handmade curtains and a lace trim for the bassinet. All was in readiness for the arrival of Philo Taylor Farnsworth III on September 23, 1929. A second child, Kenneth Gardner Farnsworth, would follow less than sixteen months later.

Throughout 1929 and 1930, Farnsworth's activities continued to draw newspaper coverage, and the Green Street lab came to be known as the "Kitty Hawk of television." As a result, Farnsworth received a steady flow of distinguished callers, and he came to enjoy taking on the role of the eccentric young inventor. "When visitors came to the lab," Everson recalled, "Farnsworth took boyish pleasure in removing the cap of the liquid air container and inserting a piece of rubber hose for instant freezing. Pulling it out, he would break the brittle frozen rubber. Igniting pellets of crude potassium by throwing them into water was another of his favorite stunts." Undoubtedly Farnsworth put these parlor tricks aside for the visits of Lee de Forest and Guglielmo Marconi, both of whom came to Green Street to witness demonstrations of the system. Little is known of their reactions, but Farnsworth was undoubtedly pleased to host his boyhood idols.

In the early months of 1930, Farnsworth received a call to arrange a demonstration for none other than the celebrated Mary Pickford, known to movie fans throughout the world as "America's Sweetheart." For the lab crew, who had so often mooned over the clip of the actress combing her hair, this was a source of considerable excitement. Better still, Pickford was to be accompanied by her husband, screen idol Douglas Fairbanks, the star of such swashbuckling action films as *Robin Hood* and *The Mark of Zorro.* Pickford and Fairbanks were not only among the most popular film stars in the world, they were also founding partners, along with Charlie Chaplin, of the United Artists Film Corporation. As such, they were said to be curious about the potential of television and its possible effect on the motion picture industry.

Farnsworth was aware that Hollywood viewed the coming of television with some alarm. "Hollywood Sees Television Ahead as Next Bugaboo," declared a headline in the *Hollywood Reporter.* "Fears New Upset Before Terror of Talkies Has Subsided." If Fairbanks and Pickford shared in these fears, what they saw in Farnsworth's lab would not have given them any particular cause for concern. Ever the perfectionist, Farnsworth had spent the previous evening making final adjustments, only to have the entire system break down without warning just as he was preparing to leave for the night. The lab crew worked through the night trying to get the image back, but by the time the Hollywood stars arrived on Green Street, Farnsworth had only managed to restore the picture to a rudimentary state, much as it had been two years earlier.

Farnsworth was bitterly disappointed. "He had the awe and adoration of a picture star common to all those of his age," said Everson. "To have failed to put his best foot forward was a tough experience for him." Later that night, a faulty wire was discovered to have caused the disruption. When it was corrected, the oscillite gave its best image yet—too late to make an impression on the emissaries from Hollywood.

For Farnsworth, the episode had been an embarrassment. To his backers, the matter was more serious. "This probably has cost us the completion of a transaction with United Artists Studios," an angry investor told Roy Bishop, "and it is traceable quite directly to the work done at the laboratory." Farnsworth resolved to do better for his next demonstration.

The opportunity came barely four weeks later, in April 1930. "One morning when I dropped in at the lab I found Farnsworth in a most jubilant mood," Everson reported. It emerged that another distinguished scientist was expected at the lab, and Farnsworth had been instructed by Albert Mann to extend every courtesy.

Farnsworth insisted that "there was no engineer in the country he would rather have view his results," Everson recalled. "Phil felt that here at last would be someone from the outside who understood the language he spoke and who had the proper appreciation of what he had accomplished."

This was undoubtedly true, but the results would be far different from what Farnsworth might have hoped. The visitor was none other than Vladimir Zworykin, who had traveled to California at the behest of his new boss, David Sarnoff.

Ten

A Beautiful Instrument

I don't get ulcers; I give them.
　　　　　　　　　　　　　　　—David Sarnoff

"How near is television to the home?" Orrin Dunlap would ask in the pages of the *New York Times* in June 1931. "Discussion of that subject is usually prefaced with the general statement that it is just around the corner. No one seems to have discovered what corner; whether it is where Zworykin Avenue crosses Ives Street, where Baird Avenue meets Alexanderson Boulevard, or where Farnsworth Road crosses Sanabria Lane."

Dunlap anticipated that the successful resolution of television's problems would require the blending of various innovations, but in the earliest days, the innovators themselves seldom crossed paths. When they did—as when Zworykin visited Edouard Belin's lab in Paris—there were often dramatic results and far-reaching consequences. This was never more true than in the case of Vladimir Zworykin's visit to Farnsworth's Green Street laboratory in April 1930. In the world of television research, the episode has assumed a status roughly analogous to that of the Yalta Conference.

For more than two years, Zworykin's name had been known to the Farnsworth team, owing in part to the 1923 patent filed by Zworykin's superiors at Westinghouse. Of greater interest to Farnsworth was the work Zworykin had done since, chronicled in the

Vladimir Zworykin, the Russian immigrant who headed RCA's television research juggernaut, poses with a kinescope receiving tube in 1929. BETTMANN/CORBIS

newspaper clippings that continued to arrive from New York. Five months prior to the Zworykin visit, in late November 1929, Pem Farnsworth had pasted an especially significant article into the scrapbook. "Scientist Shows Televisor," announced the headline. "New System Drops Disk and Uses Cathode Ray Tube." The accompanying photograph showed a stiff and uncomfortable-looking Zworykin explaining the fundamentals of his new television tube to a young fashion model, who was doing her best to appear interested. "The use of a cathode ray tube in place of the usual scanning disk and neon lamp as the heart of a television machine was demonstrated last night before the convention of Radio Engineers in Rochester, New York, by Dr. Vladimir Zworykin," reported the *New York Times.* "The cathode ray television receiver has no mechanical moving parts."

Though this announcement can only have alarmed Farnsworth, for the moment he believed that his portfolio of patent applications, once granted, would protect his interests. It was clear, however, that Zworykin's new tube had marked something of an official public debut for electronic television. Zworykin had traveled to Rochester to deliver a paper entitled "Television with Cathode-Ray Tube for Receiver," and it would mark the first time that he described his new receiving tube—the "kinescope"—by name. Though Zworykin and Farnsworth had been only distantly acquainted with each other's work, Zworykin's address made it clear that their efforts had proceeded along parallel lines. Like Farnsworth's oscillite, Zworykin's kinescope could display a picture on a seven-inch screen coated with willemite. Unlike the oscillite, however, the kinescope made use of the electrostatic focusing Zworykin had observed in Belin's experiments. In addition, Zworykin claimed, the kinescope could be easily operated by a layperson and, more important, it was bright enough to be viewed in normal household lighting.

Zworykin could easily have said a great deal more about his kinescope—at the time, he had a working unit operating in his own living room—but in the midst of his presentation he received an urgent message from the Westinghouse patent department ordering him to give no further details. His supervisors had apparently gotten cold feet at the last instant, forcing Zworykin to cut his remarks short. It was a curious piece of timing. Had Zworykin been allowed to lay his cards on the table, he might have established a position that would have been unassailable by anyone apart from Farnsworth. Instead, RCA's upper management decided to play their hand closer to the vest, creating an air of uncertainty over exactly what had been accomplished at the new television laboratories in Camden. It proved to be the beginning of an information blackout that would remain in force for four years.

The gag order had come too late to prevent Zworykin from revealing the existence of the kinescope, or its basic function. Though he had not yet created anything to approximate Farnsworth's image dissector camera tube, the announcement of the electronic receiving tube sent a tremor through the industry. Rival companies, many of which had bet heavily on mechanical television, greeted the news with skeptical caution. Others, such as AT&T, dismissed Zworykin's achievement as showing "very little promise." When journalists sought clarification from RCA and Westinghouse, they were brushed aside with assurances that work was "proceeding in a promising and orderly fashion."

Some of the mixed signals were coming directly from David Sarnoff. In February 1929, just one month after giving Zworykin his authorization to begin work, Sarnoff described television as "far from practical" in an interview with the *New York Times*. "It may be tapping at the window," he said, "but it is still in the laboratory stage of development. Its proud parents have labored hard to bring it into the world. A vast assemblage of relations and friends stand ready to greet it; it carries the highest fulfillment of radio communication—the transmission and reception of both sound and sight. But the fact remains that the infant is far too delicate for any but laboratory treatment. Its future is bright with promise. The regular exchange of broadcasting services between nation and nation is certain to bring about a more solid understanding between peoples—the spectacle as well as the sounds of life broadcast to our firesides by radio television—the scenes and sights of the world reproduced on much larger screens in natural colors—three dimensional or stereoscopic projection, if you please, which with color and speech would make the fleeting visions on the screen palpitate with the reality and expression of life—new education and cultural services which such facilities are bound to call into being; all these, I am confident, will come to pass."

The enthusiastic if uniformative statement had been crafted to reflect RCA's slow and steady approach to television development. With the Zworykin effort under way, Sarnoff felt confident that he would eventually have a viable system for the home market. In the meantime, the public could rest assured—and potential competitors could consider themselves warned—that RCA was hard at work on the problem. Until then, America was encouraged to enjoy its Radiolas.

For the moment, Sarnoff had other things on his plate. That same month—February 1929—he was asked to accompany RCA's chairman of the board, Owen Young, to Paris for a high-level conference on the matter of Germany's foundering economy and its potentially destabilizing effect on Europe. The wartime reparations imposed on Germany by the Treaty of Versailles at the close of World War I had now brought its government to the point of collapse, opening the door to the emerging National Socialist German Workers Party under Adolf Hitler. As one of America's best-known businessmen, Owen Young was selected to lead an American mission to examine the problem and, together with representatives of the leading European governments, suggest a possible revision of Germany's schedule of payments. Along with Young and Sarnoff, the American team included banker J. P. Morgan and lawyer Thomas Perkins.

In Paris, at the newly opened Hotel George V, the delegates convened for what promised to be a difficult negotiation. The German representatives offered compelling evidence that their government could no longer afford the level of reparations it had been paying, but the European Allies declared themselves unwilling to reduce the burden. The negotiations went on for weeks, often continuing long into the night, without any sign of progress. Initially Sarnoff was not present in the conference room, and he jokingly referred to himself as little more than a glorified bellhop. Over time, however, as Young attempted to forge personal relationships with the principal negotiators, Sarnoff's skills came to the fore. Dr. Hjalmar Schacht, Germany's leading delegate, had taken a liking to Sarnoff over the course of the talks. Unlikely as it seemed, the German banker—a future Nuremberg defendant—held a doctoral degree in Hebrew, a language Sarnoff still dimly recalled from his early rabbinical training. Over the course of a series of private dinners, the two men built a relationship that laid the groundwork for a resolution to the stalled talks. The "Young Plan," as it came to be known, linked a revised schedule of German payments to the performance of the country's economy, giving both sides a face-saving concession.

The successful conclusion received an ecstatic reception in the American press. Young was named *Time* magazine's "Man of the Year" for 1930. A telegram from Adolph Ochs, publisher of the *New York Times,* predicted that Young would shortly be in the White House. Young, for his part, was careful to share credit with Sarnoff. "David did the job of his life," he told Lizette Sarnoff, and in a *Saturday Evening Post* interview, Young declared that "there came a time when only one man could save the situation, and that arose toward the end with Sarnoff and the German delegation." J. P. Morgan expressed his appreciation with characteristic flair by dispatching an aide to London aboard a chartered plane to fetch a particular type of meerschaum pipe admired by Sarnoff. As the Paris mission disbanded, Morgan drew Sarnoff aside to sound him out on the possibility of becoming a partner at J. P. Morgan & Co. Had Sarnoff been motivated by money alone the offer would have been enormously tempting, as it would have increased his income many times over. For Sarnoff, however, money had always been of secondary importance to power, and he believed that the evolving structure of RCA would shortly offer him power in abundance.

Back in New York, however, Sarnoff immediately found his plans in jeopardy. In his absence, rivals within the company had moved to loosen the rivets on his plan for the consolidation of RCA and the Victor Talking Machine Company. Sarnoff's blueprint, which had been approved when he departed for Europe, called for the transfer of all radio manufacturing and television research to the Victor plants in Camden, New Jersey—under the control of RCA. The revised plan, engineered by lawyers representing the interests of the individual royalty partners, would restore control of the manufacturing facilities to the separate electrical companies—primarily General Electric and Westinghouse—and push RCA into a minor supporting role.

Once again, Sarnoff girded for battle. At a hastily called meeting of the RCA board, Sarnoff presented his case and demanded that the original agreement be restored. Otherwise, he announced, he would resign on the spot and make his reasons public. Andrew Robertson, the chairman of Westinghouse, and Gerard Swope, the president of General Electric, had both traveled to New York for the meeting, and neither man was accustomed to being addressed in the blunt language Sarnoff employed. Technically, Sarnoff was an underling, but he had the unequivocal backing of Owen Young, and in the end he got exactly what he wanted: the consolidation plan went through as originally drafted.

Though RCA had been in existence for barely ten years, its revenue had risen from $2 million in 1919 to more than $180 million in 1929, with more than 90 percent coming from radio sales and patent royalties. In 1928 alone, the value of RCA's stock rose from 80 to 420, and it would soon split five for one. Needless to say, the events of "Black Tuesday"—October 29, 1929—put an end to what George Everson had called the "wonderful nonsense" of the financial world. RCA's stock fell from a post-split peak of 110 to less than 10.

Miraculously, Sarnoff emerged unscathed. The previous June, just a few days after his return from Germany, he had sold off every stock he owned. Pressed for a reason, he would only say that he had acted on a hunch. Others were not so fortunate. The crash left Owen Young with a personal debt of $3 million. Any presidential ambitions he might have entertained came to a precipitous end. Young's financial straits, coupled with his wife's debilitating heart ailment, led him to withdraw from his position as the chairman of RCA in favor of a less demanding post on its executive committee. In the resulting shake-up, Sarnoff finally attained the goal he had pursued for a decade. On January 3, 1930, by unanimous vote of the board of directors, Sarnoff was named president of the Radio Corporation of America. Nearly twenty-five years had passed since he had buttonholed Guglielmo Marconi on William Street, but Sarnoff was still only thirty-nine years old and expected to remain at the helm for many years to come. When a newspaper reporter appeared to chronicle his rags-to-riches ascent, Sarnoff preferred to look forward. "Forget the sob stuff," he said. "The Alger stories are out of date." He may have taken that line with the press, but his origins still mattered a great deal to him. Each year he marked the anniversary of his start with the Marconi company by holding a lunch with the RCA telegraph delivery boys.

Throughout this period of upheaval, Sarnoff continued to give his unwavering support to Zworykin's research. It would be difficult to exaggerate the importance of Sarnoff's commitment, weighed against what would have seemed a distant and perhaps unattainable objective. Across America, banks were failing and factories were shutting down in the aftermath of Black Tuesday. At RCA, profits fell and board members scattered for cover. Sarnoff himself had only narrowly survived the challenge to his consolidation plan. Nevertheless, while the ground shook beneath him, Sarnoff kept eyes on the horizon. He continued to pump money into television research even as his financial officers counseled him to fortify the company's position in radio. More important, only Sarnoff had the breadth of vision to see that control of television would rely on more than the creation of the best camera tube. He knew that it would entail what he called "the whole ball of wax," meaning not only equipment, but also content—a role that would be filled by the National Broadcasting Company. "Sarnoff was a genius," one of his vice presidents would recall. "He wasn't given credit for much of what he did. He convinced the public who owned RCA stock to put up the money to develop this project alone against the rest of the world. And this was during the heart of the depression."

First, he would need a man who could "get it all in one box," as he often described the problem, and he had now pinned his hopes on Zworykin. Sarnoff would serve as Zworykin's protector for the next ten years. As the electronic research effort transferred to Camden, Sarnoff was often found in the lab, sleeves rolled up and a cigar clamped in his teeth, wandering from bench to bench to check on the stages of progress. "We always knew someone up there understood us," said one member of the team. "We felt we were doing the most important job in the world. That's how Sarnoff made us feel."

Zworykin had assembled an extraordinary team of engineers at Westinghouse, and most of them came along with him to Camden. Harley Iams, a recent graduate in physics from Stanford University, worked with Zworykin on the receiving unit, while engineers John Batchelor, Arthur Vance, and Gregory Ogloblinsky, who had recently arrived from the Belin lab in Paris, concentrated on various aspects of the cathode-ray camera tube. Though Zworykin's team had achieved its breakthrough kinescope prototype in a matter of a few months, little progress had been made on a camera tube.

By contrast, Philo T. Farnsworth and his team had made enormous strides with their image dissector camera tube, but were lagging behind in the development of their receiving tube. The situation appeared to offer the possibility of a mutually beneficial exchange of ideas and resources, at a time when Farnsworth desperately needed to shore up his support. The stock market crash had rattled his backers. Although the principals would hold firm, some of the more recent investors were anxious to sell out. As the economy worsened, the television industry appeared to be a risky, if not foolish, speculation. Most of the smaller research firms were going broke, while others, among them the Jenkins Television Laboratories, were on the point of being swallowed up by larger concerns. With RCA gearing up its electronic initiative, the time appeared right for Farnsworth to strike a deal, and various members of the syndicate had begun making overtures to RCA. Jesse McCargar, the new president of Farnsworth's Television Laboratories, expressed his conviction that RCA would have to "get aboard" sooner or later, adding that "if they waited long enough, they might wake up to find themselves just another radio manufacturer."

Zworykin cannot have been entirely surprised at being dispatched to San Francisco. As with his trip to the Belin laboratory in Paris, Zworykin was charged with assessing the state of Farnsworth's progress and suggesting a course of action to his superiors. Although he was reluctant to leave his own lab at a time when important advancements were being made, Zworykin had long been curious about the young man whom the press had dubbed "the Genius of Green Street."

For Farnsworth, Zworykin's visit held the promise of an end to all of his financial worries. Farnsworth had read a great deal about the older scientist, and already their patent applications had come into minor contention in the form of interferences, in which the claims of one applicant appear to conflict with those of another. Nevertheless, although Farnsworth was generally suspicious of competitors and protective of his work, he recognized Zworykin as a kindred spirit. The two men had been plowing the same field for several years, and Zworykin carried the backing and unlimited resources of RCA. If Farnsworth could impress Zworykin with what he had accomplished with his comparatively limited advantages, perhaps RCA would be inspired to underwrite the final stages of his work.

"Farnsworth and all of us recognized that we were courting competition of the keenest sort," George Everson noted. "Farnsworth knew enough through published reports and through interferences he had encountered in the Patent Office to appreciate that a great risk was being taken by making complete disclosures to the eminent scientist. It was not fear that Farnsworth's ideas would be stolen, but that it would spur Dr. Zworykin on to intensive work that would be highly competitive. Yet, we reasoned, if television was ever to become a commercial reality, it was felt that RCA, one of the leaders in the radio industry, must have a hand in it."

Just what form RCA's involvement would take remained very much open to debate, as each of the players had a different agenda. Farnsworth, who had been treading water for four years, thought Zworykin might throw him a lifeline. His backers, meanwhile, were hoping for an outright sale of the lab and Farnsworth's patents, an outcome that Farnsworth was prepared to fight tooth and nail. Zworykin, though curious about Farnsworth's advances, was largely doing the bidding of Sarnoff, who wanted to see if the young inventor was likely to cause trouble down the road.

For the moment, these conflicting motives and hidden intentions were pushed to the background. Zworykin arrived in San Francisco on April 16, 1930, and was received in a spirit of goodwill and open communication. As his backers had instructed, Farnsworth extended every courtesy, even inviting Zworykin home for a family meal.

"Dr. Zworykin spent three days in the laboratory," Farnsworth recorded in his lab journal. Demonstrations were arranged to display all phases of the system, including the transmission of moving pictures. "The demonstrations were all successful," Farnsworth noted. According to everyone present, Zworykin was unfailingly gracious throughout his visit and expressed keen admiration for what the Farnsworth team had accomplished. Not surprisingly, given the state of Zworykin's own research, Farnsworth's image dissector made an especially strong impression. The tube's construction, with its flat, optically clear end, struck Zworykin as a wonder of scientific glassblowing. Any number of experts had told him unequivocally that such a thing couldn't be done. "That's what they told us," Cliff Gardner declared, "but Phil wouldn't believe it."

At the visitor's request, Gardner built a dissector tube while Zworykin observed, carefully illustrating the various stages of its construction with a special emphasis on the sealing off of the Pyrex viewing surface. Afterward, Zworykin sat behind Farnsworth's desk and studied the finished tube. "This is a beautiful instrument," he is reported to have said. "I wish that I might have invented it."

Zworykin's praise, to Farnsworth's way of thinking, indicated that the visit had been a roaring success. As Zworykin departed at the end of the third day, Farnsworth had reason to believe that he had won a powerful ally. Already, however, the Crocker syndicate was having second thoughts. While Zworykin was still on the scene, Albert Mann had dashed off a curt note to Farnsworth: "I wish you would make a report, sending me duplicate copies, of all time spent with Dr. Zworykin, both at the laboratory and elsewhere, mentioning subjects discussed generally and the tests and observations made at the laboratory. We want your signature witnessed by a notary." Clearly, Mann and the other backers had begun to suspect that Zworykin's motives were not entirely pure.

As matters developed, the Zworykin visit marked the opening round of a series of negotiations that would ultimately end up in court, in a patent dispute that would last more than ten years. As a consequence, the details of Zworykin's visit have been subjected to much analysis and scrutiny, with conclusions that vary in accordance with the objectives of those concerned. It has been suggested by some that

Zworykin presented himself under false colors, leaving Farnsworth to assume that he had come on behalf of Westinghouse, rather than RCA, which might have been judged to be a more direct competitor. While it is true that the details of Zworykin's transfer to RCA were not widely known, the implications are perhaps not as grave as the Farnsworth partisans would suggest. Not only had the Crocker syndicate already made direct contact with RCA at this stage, but RCA and Westinghouse had been royalty partners for nearly ten years. Farnsworth would have assumed at least some sharing of information between the two companies.

Others have implied that Farnsworth was a naive dupe who was so overawed and flattered by the presence of Zworykin that he essentially gave away the store. "Phil was quite verbal in answering questions he shouldn't have answered," declared Farnsworth's brother Lincoln. "Phil good-naturedly talked too much to one whom he considered a scientific colleague." Such statements are easily made in hindsight, but while it is certainly true that Farnsworth was a scientist first and a businessman second, he could not have been called gullible. It would perhaps be more accurate to say that Farnsworth was overly confident in the strength of his patent protection. At the time of Zworykin's visit, Farnsworth had filed more than a dozen patent applications, covering every aspect of his work. In later years, Farnsworth gave the impression that he found nothing surprising in the fact that he and Zworykin had simultaneously done such similar work. "I have no doubt," he said in 1970, "that God could inspire two scientists at the same time and in different places with similar ideas." The essential difference, in Farnsworth's view, was that he had done it first, as he believed the patent applications would undoubtedly prove. He had pressed himself to the limit to get the documents filed three years earlier; now he was convinced he would reap the rewards.

Pem Farnsworth would later write that it was "a few years later" that they realized that Zworykin had been acting on behalf of RCA, although this seems at odds with her own recollection that further representatives of the company, including a patent lawyer, followed within the next few weeks for further scrutiny of the lab. Much had happened in the interim. On leaving San Francisco, Zworykin stopped in Los Angeles for a few days. While there, he sent a wire to the Westinghouse tube laboratory containing a set of highly specialized instructions. On his way back to the new facilities in Camden, Zworykin stopped off in Pittsburgh to pick up a very exceptional package. It contained several duplicates of the Farnsworth image dissector.

Farnsworth's advocates have made it plain that they regard this action as nothing less than outright theft. The truth is perhaps somewhat less ominous, though the consequences would be equally grave. Zworykin made no secret of what he had done, and his defenders maintain that the duplicates were the inevitable result of Gardner's demonstration—as Farnsworth would have realized. RCA would insist that the copies of the image dissector were made for testing purposes only, to verify that the Farnsworth system did, in fact, work as claimed. No offer of support or licensing could possibly have been made, the company declared, without taking this step.

This may be so, but the tests on the Farnsworth image dissectors would soon progress beyond simple verification. Initially, however, Zworykin was chiefly interested in producing a report on what he had seen on Green Street. The report has not survived, but it is known that Zworykin had a great deal of praise for Farnsworth's transmitting setup, though he recognized that for all of Farnsworth's innovations, the image dissector offered only limited sensitivity to light. Zworykin was less impressed with Farnsworth's oscillite, which he judged to be primitive when compared with his own kinescope. On the whole, however, there is little doubt that Zworykin's report was extremely positive. Having made his conclusions, Zworykin forwarded the report to his superiors for evaluation.

As fate would have it, the shifting power structure at RCA placed Zworykin's report in the hands of the man least likely to give it a fair reading—Ernst Alexanderson, the champion of mechanical television. Fresh from his triumphant demonstrations at the Proctor Theater in Schenectady, Alexanderson remained firm in his conviction that the future of television rested with the spinning mirrored drum, not the cathode-ray tube. Farnsworth, he admitted, had "evidently done some very clever work, but I do not think that television is going to develop along these lines." Alexanderson advised against making any sort of financial offer, insisting that "Farnsworth can do greater service as a competitor," and adding that "if we buy his patents now, it involves a moral obligation to bring this situation to a conclusion by experimentation at a high rate of expenditure."

In reality, such "moral obligation" had seldom troubled the new president of RCA, and Farnsworth's would not have been the first patents that were bought for no other reason than to eliminate competition. A prime example would be the Jenkins Television Corporation, which fell into decline as the economy worsened following the stock market crash. The company would be absorbed by RCA in 1932, and the hundreds of patents issued to Charles Francis Jenkins would never again see the light of day. Heartsick over the failure of his company, Jenkins would die in poverty two years later.

Though Alexanderson saw little value in the Farnsworth system, Sarnoff wasn't ready to dismiss it out of hand. Over the next few months he would continue to send technical and legal experts to Green Street while he decided on a course of action. In the meantime, Zworykin returned to his own work. As George Everson had foreseen, the visit to Green Street had spurred Zworykin on to a period of intense effort. On May 1, 1930, just two weeks after leaving San Francisco, Zworykin applied for a patent on a new type of camera tube—his first in five years. Though the timing is highly suggestive, Zworykin's new design was notable for the manner in which it differed from the Farnsworth image dissector. It made use of an electrostatic focusing technique similar to that used in the kinescope, as opposed to Farnsworth's troublesome magnetic focusing. At the same time, Zworykin's new design also made mention of a key advance known as the "storage principle"—a process which made it possible for the photoelectric chemicals inside the tube to store up an electrical charge, increasing the brightness of the tube.

It would be some time before Zworykin would manage to perfect this new type of camera tube. In the interim, he and his lab team were getting far better results from their duplicates of the Farnsworth image dissector. Over time, the Zworykin team would modify and improve the Farnsworth blueprint, and elements of the image dissector would be folded into the evolving Zworykin design. The degree to which Zworykin's advances relied on Farnsworth's innovations is difficult to assess. It is clear, however, that in the months following Zworykin's trip to San Francisco, the Farnsworth image dissector got a thorough workout in Camden.

Zworykin's latest advances, along with the backing he received from Sarnoff, had begun to create further stresses among the RCA royalty partners. With the success of Alexanderson's large-screen television demonstrations in Schenectady, General Electric remained convinced that the future of television lay in mechanical technology. In spite of Zworykin's progress with his electronic system, Sarnoff could not entirely dismiss Alexanderson and his adherents. Sarnoff was now chairman of the board of Radio-Keith-Orpheum, and it seemed possible that the Alexanderson system might give him a tool to strengthen RCA's presence in the motion picture industry. Previously, it had suited Sarnoff to hedge his bets by funding both initiatives. Now, as the two sides came into direct conflict, Sarnoff realized that he would have to make a decision.

Seeking to resolve the debate once and for all, Sarnoff decided to stage a decisive competition between the mechanical and electronic systems at a neutral facility in Collingswood, New Jersey, in July 1930. At face value, the Alexanderson equipment appeared more impressive, giving the same reliable, if flickering, results it had produced for more than a year. By contrast, Zworykin's apparatus was still at a primitive stage. Although his kinescope gave a fair indication of things to come, he had not yet produced a working camera tube and was obliged to fall back on a mechanical Nipkow disk transmitter for purposes of the competition.

Even so, the Zworykin team emerged with a clear victory. Although the electronic system was still in a primitive stage, its potential was obvious. Sarnoff and his panel of engineers were looking for a television system that would become a fixture in the living rooms of millions of American homes, eventually supplanting radio as a source of home entertainment. The Zworykin system, though far from perfect, seemed to offer infinite possibilities. The Alexanderson setup, impressive as it was, appeared to have found its limits. Though Zworykin could not yet transmit a live picture, RCA decided that electronic television was the horse to back.

RCA's game plan would be spelled out in its 1930 Annual Report: "Television must develop to the stage where broadcasting stations will be able to broadcast regularly visible objects in the studio, or scenes occurring at other places through remote control; where reception devices shall be developed that will make these objects and scenes clearly discernible in millions of homes; where such devices can be built upon a principle that will eliminate rotary scanning discs, delicate hand controls and other movable parts." Philo T. Farnsworth had reached much the same conclusion in Idaho nearly ten years earlier: for television to succeed, he concluded, it must have no moving parts.

Because of Alexanderson's prominence and the protests of his supporters at General Electric, the mechanical research effort would limp along for a while longer. From that point forward, however, the RCA television research budget would reflect the new reality—90 percent of the available funds went to the Zworykin system, 10 percent to Alexanderson. By the end of the year, a number of prominent General Electric engineers would be working in Zworykin's lab.

Three months later, Alexanderson sent a memo to Sarnoff requesting additional funds to develop a system that would be "new in several essential respects." Sarnoff waited five weeks to reply: "I regret I cannot authorize the expenditure to which you refer." At long last, it came home to Alexanderson that he had been left standing at the platform while the train pulled away. Writing to Sarnoff later that year, Alexanderson expressed regret over this "financial embarrassment" and offered a sad acknowledgment of his reduced status: "I have many friends in the RCA with whom I wish to continue my contract, even if it must be only 'for the love of the art.' "

Alexanderson was at pains to stress that others were also affected by the "present crisis," a reference not only to the economic depression but also to a fresh round of government antitrust charges. In May 1930, as Sarnoff arrived at a dinner party in celebration of his installation as president of RCA, a United States marshal served him with a formal summons from the Justice Department. The monopoly charges that had been simmering for years had at last come to a boil. Sarnoff pocketed the complaint and managed to carry on through the evening as though nothing had happened. As the dinner party drew to a close, however, he asked several RCA executives to accompany him back to the office. There Sarnoff held a war council that would last through the night.

For years, RCA had been regularly accused of exerting unfair control over the communications industry. The patent pool, critics said, allowed the company to impose high-handed restrictions on the manufacturing rights of competitors, while wetting its beak with the revenues of hardworking independent concerns. Sarnoff's actions as he pushed through the RCA Victor deal had served to reinforce the charges. He had moved to buy back controlling shares of NBC and the Victor Talking Machine Company from General Electric and Westinghouse, further solidifying RCA's power. In the aftermath of the stock market crash, however, the prevailing mood in Washington, and across the country, had turned against big business. Eleven years earlier, the government had endorsed the creation of RCA's patent pool. Now it appeared politically expedient to dismantle it.

The Justice Department had charged that the original patent pool on which RCA had been founded constituted an illegal restraint of trade, in direct violation of the nation's antitrust laws. RCA, General Electric, Westinghouse, and AT&T were all listed as defendants, along with more recent signatories such as the GM Radio Corporation. As Sarnoff studied the charges in detail, it became clear that the survival of RCA was at stake. If the government won its case, the patent pool would be disbanded and the licensing agreements, from which RCA continued to draw much of its income, would be nullified. RCA's new manufacturing and research divisions would be broken up, effectively reducing the company to little more than a minor radio manufacturing concern.

Attorney General William Mitchell later described the case as perhaps the most complex in the history of antitrust law. The depositions and hearings and negotiations would absorb most of Sarnoff's time and energy for the next two and a half years. During that time, RCA posted the first losses in its history. Even as the company hit its lowest point, however, Sarnoff caught sight of another opportunity. For years he had dreamed of engineering total independence for RCA. Now, under the cover of incoming fire from the government, he saw a means of achieving it. The antitrust suit stipulated that the original partners divest themselves of RCA and enter into direct competition. Sarnoff countered with a carefully crafted proposition that appeared to give the government what it wanted while maintaining RCA as an "effective unit."

The negotiations would conclude on November 11, 1932—four days before the case was set to go to trial, and three days after the election of Franklin D. Roosevelt as president of the United States. The agreement, which was hailed as a government victory, decreed that General Electric and Westinghouse would surrender their interests in RCA, but would agree not to enter into radio manufacturing for two and a half years. The patent pool would remain largely intact under RCA control, but the communal licensing agreement was abandoned—the patents were now available to be licensed by anyone, without restriction.

Incredibly, RCA had emerged as an independent and self-supporting entity, and it would soon be stronger than ever before. Though the stock market responded with a heavy sell-off, Sarnoff had achieved nearly everything he wanted. RCA controlled two networks, several broadcasting stations, the Camden manufacturing and research facilities, and a vast network of other communications operations. More important, the company had broken free of its many layers of upper management. "They gave me a lemon," declared a victorious Sarnoff, "and I made lemonade of it."

As a result, there would be a further shifting of power on the RCA board of directors as the representatives of General Electric and Westinghouse resigned their positions. Owen Young, who held a spot on RCA's executive board, now faced an agonizing decision. He could remain with RCA, perhaps regaining his former position as chairman of the board, and help the company find its feet in the new circumstances, or he could choose the infinitely safer option of remaining with General Electric as chairman of the board. Weighed down by his financial losses, Young could not afford the risk of siding with RCA. In May 1933, he resigned from the company he had helped to create.

Sarnoff remained loyal. RCA petitioned the Justice Department for a waiver that would have permitted Young to remain an RCA director during the two-and-a-half-year period of noncompetition with General Electric. The request was promptly denied. In truth, though the effort satisfied Sarnoff's sense of duty, he cannot have been entirely devastated. Young's departure had effectively placed the total control of RCA and its board in his hands. He would hold that power for the next thirty years.

One of Young's unfinished tasks had been a negotiation with the Rockefeller organization for a new headquarters for RCA and NBC. For some time, the Rockefellers had been creating a vast plaza of office buildings in midtown Manhattan, originally intended to include the new home of the Metropolitan Opera. In the wake of the stock market crash the opera withdrew and RCA took over, transforming the centerpiece of the new Rockefeller Center into a complex to be known as Radio City.

With the departure of Young, it fell to Sarnoff to complete the transaction with the Rockefellers, who complained of the new man's hardheaded tactics—described with the now familiar term "abrasive." Among the concessions Sarnoff demanded was the naming of the centerpiece building at 30 Rockefeller Center, then the largest office structure in the world. It was to be called the RCA Building, with the bold neon initials "RCA" shining across the Manhattan skyline.

One month after the withdrawal of Young, Sarnoff moved RCA and NBC into the new headquarters. In the lobby, a photographic mural by Margaret Bourke-White celebrated the development of radio, emphasizing RCA's new focus on blending art and science. "Now comes a city sired by science, mothered by art, dedicated to enlightenment and entertainment," declared Dr. Alfred Goldsmith, RCA's chief broadcast engineer. "It exists not for an immediate trade territory but for the world. Its drama and its dreams will be flung across oceans and continents. It will share its conceptions of beauty and culture with the farmer, the village store, and the schoolrooms as well as with aristocratic foyers."

Be that as it may, Sarnoff made certain to establish himself in an appropriately aristocratic foyer. Though he had voluntarily slashed his own salary to reflect RCA's diminished profits, his perquisites did not appear to have suffered. His massive, oak-paneled corner office on the fifty-third floor featured a sweeping view of the city and the Hudson River beyond. A photograph of Guglielmo Marconi, inscribed "with sincere friendship," offered a reminder of his hardscrabble beginnings, as did the telegraph key he had used at the Wanamaker's message post more than twenty years earlier, which now rested on a marble mantelpiece above the fireplace. Though that key was merely for show, a specially constructed drawer of his gleaming leather-topped desk held a working telegraph key, allowing him to communicate with the head of RCA Communications by direct link. A hidden panel in the interior wall opened onto a private barber's chair, dressing area, and lavatory.

Sarnoff's family also moved into lavish new quarters that year. The Sarnoffs had been living in an apartment on East 68th Street, but now, on the advice of his friend Bernard Baruch, the Wall Street wizard, Sarnoff purchased a townhouse on East 71st. It had thirty rooms and six stories, complete with servants' quarters, a solarium, and a private elevator. Sarnoff found little time to make use of the amenities of his new home. For more than two years, while he battled the Justice Department, he had virtually lived at the office. The pattern would continue for some years to come. As a result, the man who complained of having been "hermetically sealed off" from his own childhood would not participate fully in the childhood of his own sons. "I did not find sufficient time to spend with my children when they were young," he would admit with regret in later years. His marriage, too, began to suffer the consequences as Sarnoff allowed himself further emoluments of his high office. To all outward appearances, Lizette Sarnoff remained a devoted wife, but privately she could not ignore the fact that her husband had begun to seek the company of other women. In later years he would maintain a hotel suite for this purpose.

In time Sarnoff would have cause to regret his negligence and move to repair some of the damage. For the moment, he had more pressing concerns. "A separate theater for every home—although the stage may be only a cabinet and the curtain a screen—is, I believe, the distinct promise of a new era of electrical entertainment," Sarnoff told the *New York Times* as the Radio City deal took shape. "The stage, the concert hall and the opera first entered the average home with the phonograph. It is true that musical instruments in some form have existed since the dawn of civilization, but with the exception of the first crude piano rolls, it required the creative artist or the amateur to make them vibrant with music. The phonograph reproduced music and speech wherever it entered. It gave to the home the recorded art of the concert performer, the operatic star, the stage favorite. Now comes the promise of television as applied to the theater of the home. Important as has been our progress in the development of sight transmission, great technical problems still remain to be solved before such a service can be established upon a practical basis."

The crucial difference, Sarnoff omitted to say, was that he himself intended to dictate exactly when that service would be established. "Finally," Sarnoff would later say, "I had the authority to move television at my own pace. No executive layers above, no electric committees to question expenditures." This total control had come at a crucial juncture. Zworykin had originally promised to produce a commercial system in two years, at an expenditure of $100,000. It was now abundantly clear these estimates had been wildly optimistic. Sarnoff had always known better, and in later years he often joked about it. "Zworykin is the greatest salesman in history," he would say. "He put a price tag of one hundred thousand dollars on television, and I bought it." With expenses mounting, however, Sarnoff needed to protect his investment. This meant, as it always had, keeping an eye on the competition. The economic depression, coupled with the demise of mechanical technology, had put many of his potential competitors out of business. Others, such as Allen DuMont and William Paley, had not yet mounted their challenges. Now, as he surveyed the prospects from the fifty-third floor, there seemed to be only one man left standing— Philo T. Farnsworth of San Francisco.

For more than two years, even through the worst of the turbulence at RCA, Sarnoff had taken an unusually close and direct interest in Farnsworth's progress. In the months following Zworykin's visit to Green Street in 1930, however, the reports Sarnoff had received from San Francisco had been inconclusive. His envoys had high praise for Farnsworth's technical achievements but doubted whether he would ever have the resources to bring them to fruition. On the one hand, it appeared to make perfect sense to buy Farnsworth's work outright and fold his advances into the Zworykin effort. On the other, several of Sarnoff's advisers were assuring him that RCA could do the job without Farnsworth, while still others felt that it would be more practical to let Farnsworth find his own research funding, since RCA could always buy him out at a later stage.

Sarnoff knew perfectly well that Zworykin and his well-funded research team would eventually produce an acceptable electronic television system. Farnsworth, however, now had something that RCA did not—key patents on the technology underlying the electronic camera tube. One of these patents, issued under the disturbingly broad heading "Television System," had been issued in August 1930, shortly after Zworykin's visit. It had been one of Farnsworth's first applications and had already weathered some initial legal interference from the RCA patent attorneys. The importance of this was not lost on Sarnoff. His entire career at RCA had been built on one simple principle—he who controls the patents controls the industry. As Sarnoff and RCA pressed forward toward a commercial television system, they were confronted with the prospect that someone outside of the company controlled the patents. Accordingly, barely one year after Zworykin's trip to San Francisco, Sarnoff had made an extraordinary decision. In the face of conflicting reports and recommendations, he decided to go to Green Street and see Farnsworth's lab for himself. It is a measure of Sarnoff's concern over Farnsworth that he made the trip in May 1931, when the outcome of the Justice Department suit was still very much in doubt.

Much had changed on Green Street since Vladimir Zworykin's visit the previous year. With all phases of the system working well, the Farnsworth team now felt ready to come out of the lab and attempt television transmission over a distance. Farnsworth began by testing the possibilities of transmission over phone lines, but was discouraged by the poor results. Turning his focus to transmitting over the airwaves, he established a receiving apparatus at the Merchants Exchange Building, about a mile from the lab. The early results were poor, but Farnsworth believed that improvements would not be long in coming.

He was eager to set up an experimental television studio for further experimentation, but continuing financial battles with Jesse McCargar and the backing syndicate pushed these plans to the background.

In many other respects, Farnsworth's work had continued to run parallel to Zworykin's. The RCA annual report for the previous year had touched on the problem of television's heavy wave band requirements and spoken of the need to develop a method of transmission "that would not interfere with the use of the already overcrowded channels in space." This problem had also been a prime concern of Farnsworth's for some time. "No one ever approached a problem more earnestly or with more sincerity, or spent more intensive effort to find a successful conclusion, than did Farnsworth," reported George Everson. One morning Farnsworth called Everson to the lab and displayed two sheets of paper on which he had plotted two simple curves, representing thousands of mathematical equations that he had worked out over a period of months. "George," he said, throwing the pages on his desk, "there is your narrowed wave band."

Initial tests of Farnsworth's plan for compressed signals gave promising results, and the calculations were submitted to outside engineers for confirmation. Though the final verification proved elusive, several attempts were made to prove Farnsworth's calculations by means of an actual transmission over the airwaves. Though the transmissions failed, Farnsworth remained confident. "We have succeeded in narrowing the wave band for sure this time," he wrote to McCargar in October 1930. "I have not been able to grasp the full import of this idea yet; it has us all gasping for breath, since, as you will realize, it permits television to be transmitted over all existing broadcast networks." The following month he sent a second enthusiastic bulletin. "I am quite anxious to make an announcement of this development," he declared.

The opportunity came in December, when the Federal Radio Commission conducted a series of informal hearings concerning television and the possible allocation of wave bands. The subject had recently received a fair amount of attention in the press, drawing comment from a number of prominent experimenters. "The progress of television should be very much more rapid than was that of broadcasting," insisted Lee de Forest, urging the government to take prompt action, "because broadcasting had only a few thousand potential listeners while television has millions of potential 'lookers.' " Farnsworth, whom de Forest had somewhat misleadingly praised as "one of the coming men in radio," was invited to Washington to give his views.

Farnsworth was energized by this opportunity. It seemed to him that he was finally being asked to join the grown-ups, and he planned to make the most of the chance. Better still, the trip would give him a chance to indulge a new enthusiasm for flying. Delighted at the prospect of making a cross-country flight, Farnsworth made arrangements to buy a seat on an airmail plane. Pem would clearly have preferred to see her husband board a train. She had already seen enough flying some weeks earlier, when an investor offered Farnsworth a ride in his private plane, a two-seater with an open cockpit. Farnsworth was so enthusiastic that he arranged to take Pem along for his next flight, and even encouraged the pilot to try out some stunt flying, complete with a nose-down freefall. "If you don't make him land," Pem shouted to her husband over the roar of rushing wind, "I'll jump."

It was with some trepidation, then, that Pem watched as Farnsworth and Donald Lippincott, his patent attorney, departed for Washington in late November 1930. She would hear nothing from her husband for three days. When bad weather forced the plane down in Kansas City, Farnsworth sent a reassuring telegram, but the message never reached San Francisco. The travelers took off again but only made it as far as St. Louis, where stormy conditions forced them to continue by train to Indianapolis. From there they boarded another plane to Washington, saving barely twenty-four hours over the transcontinental train ride from California.

The difficult journey had done nothing to diminish Farnsworth's zeal. Writing to McCargar, he insisted that the Farnsworth television system was "fully commercial in its present state of development." Returning to the subject of wave band compression, he added, "I am quite anxious to make an announcement of this development, and I believe that we should not announce it in pieces, since this will destroy the effectiveness of the publicity." McCargar urged caution, but Farnsworth was determined not to waste his moment in the spotlight.

Farnsworth appeared before the Federal Radio Commission on December 3, 1930, delivering a paper in which he described recent developments on Green Street. In the past, the "earnestness and conviction" that George Everson had described had served to make Farnsworth a compelling and almost hypnotic speaker, sweeping aside whatever doubts his listeners may have had. Now, however, before an audience of industry professionals, the bar had been raised. In reviewing Farnsworth's performance, Everson could not bring himself to be quite so lavish in his praise. "This marked Phil's first important public appearance," Everson noted. "He made a very favorable impression as an authority on television."

In fact, the twenty-four-year-old Farnsworth had stumbled badly, allowing himself to get carried away on the matter of wave band compression. Farnsworth had long been accustomed to exaggerating his progress to keep his investors on the hook. Now, before a vastly more knowledgeable crowd, he indulged the same instinct. Farnsworth genuinely believed that his basic principle had been verified in the lab and confirmed by outside authorities. This gave him the confidence to speak at length about the matter, causing considerable consternation in Washington. According to Herbert Ives, the architect of the Hoover broadcast three years earlier, Farnsworth appeared to be "an ingenious and sincere experimenter," but he added, "If Mr. Farnsworth is doing what he says he is doing, we simply do not know how he does it."

No one would ever know whether he had done it, or how. Farnsworth's calculations would never be verified, and though sincere efforts were made to give a practical demonstration, it was never achieved. However well-intentioned, the gaffe would have serious consequences. "It was an unfortunate disclosure," Everson noted, "because later, when his findings were found to be inoperative, despite their checking and approval by experienced outside engineers, it did Farnsworth a great deal of harm among the radio engineers." Indeed, the episode made Farnsworth appear to be an impetuous young blowhard and threw doubt on the equally audacious, if more fully justified, claims he made for his television system. For years, Everson claimed, some communications engineers would "speak slightingly" of Farnsworth over the affair. "It was one of the big failures in Farnsworth's development work," Everson admitted, "and it later became a source of considerable embarrassment. The theory worked in a test demonstration over wires, but somewhere along the line Phil felt there was a fundamental fallacy which prevented his getting results in sending the signal through the ether. It was a bitter disappointment to him." This single misjudgment, weighed against his extraordinary catalog of achievements, would cast a pall over his reputation for many years.

It would be some while, however, before the effects of Farnsworth's mistake would be felt. He left Washington in a mood of great optimism and traveled to New York, where a press reception was waiting. Farnsworth gave them good copy. He announced that the Farnsworth receiving apparatus would be only slightly larger than one foot square and could be easily attached to existing radio sets. "If the delicate tube burns out," he added, "the owner releases a catch, unscrews the tube like changing a light bulb, and inserts the new one." He added: "The entire device and tube should cost less than a hundred dollars."

Farnsworth had now become a newspaper fixture in the way that Baird, Alexanderson, and Jenkins had been five years earlier, and his backers recognized that his new prominence could be used to advantage. Though the stock of Farnsworth's Television Laboratories, Inc., had been stalled for some time, McCargar and the others in the backing syndicate began to find renewed interest from electrical and research firms. In the spring of 1931, the Crocker group took out ads in newspapers and magazines across the country looking for a buyer, and exploratory meetings were held with both the International Telephone and Telegraph Company and the Philadelphia Storage Battery Company. In May 1931, Farnsworth made a sweep of several East Coast cities for discussions with the interested parties. Joining him on the trip was Jesse McCargar, who had now grown desperate to sell the Farnsworth holdings.

In New York, Farnsworth and McCargar met with a promoter named Cox, who was attempting to forge a partnership of various radio, television, and motion picture concerns. By the time Farnsworth came on the scene, Cox's plans had fallen apart and several of the other players had withdrawn. When Farnsworth backed away from the proceedings, Cox slapped him with a lawsuit. It would take more than a month to untangle the mess, during which time Farnsworth was served with a court order that prevented him from leaving New York. After cooling his heels for three weeks, he called Pem and invited her to join him in New York to celebrate their fifth wedding anniversary.

Leaving her two young sons with relatives, Pem made the four-day train journey to New York, where Farnsworth took her on a giddy shopping spree at Lord & Taylor. "I felt like Cinderella," Pem said—which is perhaps not surprising, since Farnsworth had fitted her out in a flowing chiffon ball gown with silver slippers. No longer reliant on George Everson for his own attire, Farnsworth selected a dinner jacket and full regalia for himself. As the couple dressed for an evening of dancing at the St. Regis Hotel, it emerged that the man who could control electrons could not manage his own bow tie. Pem slipped downstairs to a haberdashery shop, where a salesman offered a quick lesson.

As with her early date at Bridal Veil, however, Pem soon found herself compromised by an ill-mannered horse. As the couple hailed a cab and made their way along in slow-moving theater traffic, a team of dray horses pulling a freight wagon drew alongside. One of the horses turned as if to admire Pem's finery, then gave a mighty sneeze, effectively dousing her in greenish phlegm. Farnsworth was amused; his wife was not.

It was typical of Farnsworth that it required a legal injunction to make him take a vacation. Over the next few days he and Pem followed the usual tourist tracks through New York, visiting the Statue of Liberty and the newly constructed Empire State Building, and even trekking to Yankee Stadium to see Babe Ruth knock out a pair of home runs. Unfortunately, the enforced holiday had come at the most inopportune time imaginable. It was during this period, in May 1931, that David Sarnoff made his way to San Francisco to see the Green Street lab.

The arrival of a corporation president, especially one as prominent as Sarnoff, was a noteworthy occasion for the Farnsworth team. That

Sarnoff had troubled to visit the lab personally, after reviewing the findings of Zworykin and his various other representatives, was unusual in the extreme, and suggested a serious interest on the part of RCA.

In Farnsworth's absence, the job of showing Sarnoff around the lab fell to George Everson. Sarnoff spent only "about an hour at the laboratory," according to a letter Everson sent to Farnsworth in New York. He was shown transmitted images first on a small oscillite and then on a larger screen the crew had recently perfected. Typically, Sarnoff showed impatience when Everson tried to demonstrate the degree of the lab's progress. He wanted only the very latest results. "Now that you have the large picture," he asked irritably, "why did you show me the small one?"

For the most part, however, Sarnoff was cordial and seemed genuinely fascinated by the work. As the meeting progressed, however, Everson could not be certain what form that interest would take. At the time, Everson was in the midst of discussions with representatives of the newly created International Telephone and Telegraph Company, which had recently expanded into overseas communications through a deal with AT&T, brokered by Sarnoff's old adversary Walter Gifford. The prospect of squaring off against his old rival seemed irksome to Sarnoff. "The most outstanding feature of the conference," Everson told Farnsworth, "was the seeming anxiety of his over the possibility of our having anything to do with IT&T. He said, 'You know the IT&T and the Radio Corporation are like the proverbial "cat and dog," and it will be difficult to deal with both of us.'"

At the same time, Sarnoff seemed ambivalent as to whether he wanted to deal with Farnsworth at all. "Sarnoff seemed impressed with what he saw at our laboratories," Everson would write some years later, "but told me that he felt Dr. Zworykin's work on the receiver made it possible for RCA to avoid the Farnsworth patents, and that at the transmitter they were using a mechanical mirror device that he thought would equal the results which we could obtain by our dissector-tube camera."

Not surprisingly, Sarnoff had not been entirely candid. At that stage Zworykin's experiments relied heavily on Farnsworth's image dissector, though the primary thrust of his research lay elsewhere. At the time, however, RCA was keeping a tight lid on its television project, and Sarnoff would have been unlikely to share any news of its progress with Everson.

Still, though Everson could not have fully appreciated it at the time, Sarnoff had essentially laid his cards on the table. He was certain that Zworykin would eventually produce a system that was as good as Farnsworth's or better. More important, Zworykin's system would not rely on any Farnsworth patents. At the same time, though he didn't want it himself, Sarnoff didn't want anyone else to have Farnsworth's work, either. Farnsworth's lab would not have been the first to have been bought up by RCA for no other reason than to spike a competitor. For these reasons, and to avoid possible legal trouble in the future, Sarnoff would eventually make an offer for Television Laboratories—$100,000, including the services of Farnsworth himself.

Things might have developed differently if Farnsworth had been present to show his apparatus to Sarnoff personally. Eighteen months earlier, Sarnoff had recognized in Zworykin a certain "spark in the eye" that suggested a man who could get the job done. Farnsworth also had that spark, as anyone who ever met him has attested. Sarnoff might well have warmed to the young man who, like himself, had come a long way on sheer determination. More to the point, despite Sarnoff's statements to the contrary, Farnsworth had something that Sarnoff could use. Zworykin's kinescope, according to a *New York Times* article published that month, had allowed Sarnoff to "clip four years" off his estimate of when television would be ready for the home. For all his promising early results, however, Zworykin had not yet produced anything to compare with Farnsworth's image dissector.

It is doubtful that Farnsworth gave even a moment's consideration to Sarnoff's offer. Though it was generous, especially given the fragile state of the American economy, the figure of $100,000 was considerably less than the amount of money his backers had invested over the years. At the same time, the offer amounted to a complete buyout. Farnsworth would not only have lost control of his designs, his patents, and his laboratory, he would also have lost control of his future—he would have become a contract engineer at RCA. While

Ernst Alexanderson and Vladimir Zworykin had done very well for themselves as employees of RCA, Farnsworth had patterned himself after Marconi and the young Edison, the staunch independents of a bygone era. For five years he had expended as much effort in preserving control over his television system as he had in creating the system itself. He did not want to sell his company at any price; he wanted a licensing deal that would oblige RCA to pay royalties for the use of his patents. He knew full well that the royalties would be worth millions, and he refused to settle for anything less.

Here the two men had misjudged one another badly. RCA had been founded on the buying and controlling of patents. There had never been a single instance in which the company had paid a royalty—not even to Sarnoff's friend Howard Armstrong. For Farnsworth, however, this was the crux of the matter. He had invented television and no one was going to take it away from him. He promptly rejected the offer.

By all accounts, Sarnoff was surprised. He was the head of a multi-million-dollar corporation; Farnsworth was running a dog-and-pony show. He had made a magnanimous offer, and to his way of thinking, Farnsworth's insistence on receiving a royalty was absurd. The RCA patent department didn't think much of the strength of Farnsworth's position, and Sarnoff was certain that he would be able to avoid using any disputed patents, just as AT&T had done with its home radio set nine years earlier. Farnsworth was free to turn down the offer, but he would have to live with the consequences.

Farnsworth had no way of knowing what he had unleashed. His lawyers and Zworykin's had been skirmishing for years at this point; now they would bring out the big guns. Sarnoff, for his part, could not have troubled himself much over the outcome. Though he was barely forty, he was an experienced fighter. He had fought two bloody campaigns against AT&T, he had gone toe to toe with European diplomats, he had survived attempted coups within his own company, and at that very moment he was crossing swords with the United States Justice Department. Set against those challenges, Philo T. Farnsworth and his image dissector cannot have seemed much of a threat.

Given the chance, it is unlikely that either man would have done anything differently. As Sarnoff finished his tour of the Green Street lab, however, he did not yet know for certain how Farnsworth would respond to his offer. Everson, knowing Farnsworth as he did, had not been encouraging, but Sarnoff assumed a posture of indifference.

The mogul took one more look around before taking his leave. "Well," he said, "there's nothing here we'll need."

Eleven

Priority of Invention

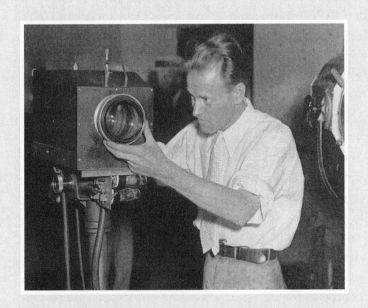

> *How the Gods must have laughed that day when
> they set the impecunious ex-soldier of the
> Czar and a child in kneepants at each other.*
>
> —Frank Waldrop and Joseph Barkin, 1938

Within days of Sarnoff's appearance on Green Street, RCA prepared a press release intended to blow a hole in the favorable publicity Farnsworth had been receiving, perhaps leaving him more amenable to a buyout. As Everson reported to Farnsworth—and contrary to what Sarnoff had said in San Francisco—RCA was now claiming that their television system "was entirely electrical." In addition, the press release insisted, RCA had produced an apparatus that was "much better than the Farnsworth system."

The relative merits of the two systems at this stage remained very much open to debate. However, it was patently untrue that RCA's system was "entirely electrical," nor would it be for some time. The Zworykin transmitting system still relied on various forms of mechanical equipment and had not yet achieved the company's stated goal of eliminating "delicate hand controls and other movable parts." It is unlikely that the distinction would have mattered a great deal to the public at large. The fact remained that RCA's powerful publicity machine was gearing up to attack Farnsworth, and he lacked the resources to mount an effective defense.

Farnsworth, age twenty-seven, adjusts a camera during a demonstration of his television equipment at Philadelphia's Franklin Institute in 1934. BETTMANN/CORBIS

Nevertheless, Everson resolved to do what he could. "The Associated Press are here taking pictures," he reported to Farnsworth. "I thought it would be a good idea to spike their campaign of misrepresentation of our system." Everson realized, however, that press coverage would only carry them so far. "Money is awfully tight," he admitted to Farnsworth, "and we are having a devil of a time selling any of our interests."

In his dealings with Jesse McCargar, Everson's concerns came to the fore: "I am not getting 'panicky,' " he wrote a few days later, "but I am naturally a little nervous and concerned; however I feel confident that things are coming out as we want them to." For Farnsworth's sake, he kept up a cheery front. "We are broke but enthusiastic," he wrote at the end of the month.

By June 1931, salvation appeared to be at hand. With the resolution of the bothersome legal injunction that had kept them tied up in New York, Farnsworth and McCargar headed to Philadelphia for discussions with the Philadelphia Storage Battery Company, better known as Philco. The company, which was then the nation's largest manufacturer of radio sets, had established a small television laboratory three years earlier. Walter Holland, the vice president in charge of engineering, had been to Green Street in the early months of 1931 and come away convinced that Farnsworth would give Philco a competitive edge against RCA.

Within days, an agreement was finalized between the Philco Corporation and Television Laboratories, Inc. The two-year contract would bring Farnsworth to Philadelphia, along with most of his lab equipment and staff, to set up operations at the Philco manufacturing plant. The deal offered strong incentives for both Farnsworth and his Crocker syndicate backers. Though it was not the total buyout that McCargar and the others had originally sought, the burden of funding Farnsworth's lab would now transfer to Philco. The Crocker group would maintain its interests, though in a reduced role, while Philco provided the resources to push Farnsworth's work into profitability.

For Farnsworth himself, the deal seemed an auspicious validation of his work on Green Street. Philco would not only provide the working capital he desperately needed, it would also enter a nonexclusive agreement to pay royalties on his patents. In addition, it would finance the move from California and provide funds to keep the Green Street lab running, with a skeleton staff of two, to provide backup development work. Some of these expenses were to be charged against future royalties, and as a further consideration of the company's backing, the first 22,500 television sets produced by Philco were to be exempt from royalty payments. These details aside, Farnsworth believed he had made the deal of a lifetime. There was even talk of establishing an experimental television station, as RCA had recently done.

"It was the first substantial recognition by a major radio or electrical company of the Farnsworth system," wrote Everson. "Naturally Farnsworth was elated." Better still, in Philadelphia Farnsworth would no longer be isolated from the work of the other major electrical companies and the government agencies that regulated them. Even the company's name—a shortening of Philadelphia Storage Battery Company—seemed to augur well for its new resident genius. With Philco behind him, Farnsworth believed he could trump RCA and bring commercial television to the home market inside of two years.

Philco was perhaps even more eager to beat out RCA. Although the company was running a thriving radio business, for years it had been paying its rival patent royalties on every set manufactured. If Farnsworth could place Philco on an equal or better standing in the emerging television market, Philco would no longer be held under RCA's thumb. With that goal in mind, the company went to great lengths to avoid drawing unwelcome attention from RCA as Farnsworth came on board. Only three of the top Philco executives would have access to the new lab.

Although Pem, in particular, felt reluctant to leave their home in San Francisco, she could see that her husband was delighted that "big boys" in the East were finally giving him his due. By mid-July the Green Street lab had been disassembled and crated for shipping. As the last details were finalized, Farnsworth chartered a Pullman railroad car to carry his staff and their families to Philadelphia in comfort. Unfortunately, the journey coincided with the onset of an oppressive heat wave, pushing the temperature inside the crowded compartment to well over one hundred degrees. Six-month-old Kenny Farnsworth grew miserable with a heat rash, while the others found themselves longing for the chill fogs of San Francisco.

Conditions were no better on arrival. Philco had allocated lab space on the top floor of its manufacturing plant at Ontario and C streets. Farnsworth, who had not seen the facilities prior to the move, found himself setting up his equipment in a chamber that was actually smaller than Green Street, though it was expected to accommodate a larger staff. Worse, the lab was unventilated, and the plant's flat asphalt roof acted as a heat conductor, transforming the new working space into a crucible. Farnsworth requested a set of exhaust fans, but Philco's management was slow to respond.

From the first, the Green Street crew had difficulty fitting in. Farnsworth and his men were accustomed to working in shirtsleeves, and given the oppressive conditions in their new lab, they were unwilling to conform to Philco's suit-and-tie culture. Soon, however, William Grimditch, Philco's director of research, let it be known that Farnsworth and his men were having a corrosive effect on office decorum. Farnsworth, who still liked to get his hands dirty with electrical cable and acids, saw no reason for formal attire in a working laboratory. Matters came to a head when Grimditch walked into the lab to find a shirtless Cliff Gardner sweltering over a glassblowing flame. Enraged by this breach of etiquette, Grimditch demanded that Gardner put on his shirt—only an "animal," it seemed, would handle molten glass in anything less than a jacket and tie. The normally even-tempered Gardner lost his composure and angrily threatened to quit if the promised exhaust fans were not delivered within the hour. That said, he turned his bare back and resumed his work. The fans arrived, but a chasm had opened between the Farnsworth team and the rest of the employees, to whom they became "those mavericks from the West."

Isolated from the rest of the company, the lab crew occasionally resorted to practical jokes to keep themselves amused. Russell Varian, who had joined the team shortly before the move from San Francisco, arrived one morning to find that his Tesla coil transformer had been rigged to give him an electric shock. Without a word, he set the coil down and looked around for the likely perpetrator, his assistant Joe Knouse, whom he found struggling to suppress a giggling fit. Varian, a powerful man, calmly lifted Knouse high in the air and deposited him on top of a cabinet filled with fragile tubes. Dusting off his hands, Varian turned away without comment, leaving Knouse stranded and unable to climb down for fear of shattering the glass inside. Varian suffered no further pranks.

Happily, these distractions had little effect on the lab's progress, and by the end of the summer Farnsworth had drafted an application for an experimental television station. Farnsworth traveled to Washington personally to apply, and in spite of protests from RCA, he soon received a broadcasting license under the call letters W3XE.

Establishing a broadcast facility had long been a dream of Farnsworth's. He had tried and failed to gather sufficient funding to do so in San Francisco, and the promise of getting on the air had been an attractive component of his agreement with Philco. While there was little pretense of providing consistent programming, the station would allow him to experiment with varied types of transmissions and refine his broadcast equipment. Perhaps more important, the initial broadcasts from W3XE would serve notice that Farnsworth had arrived on the broadcast spectrum to claim his share of the airwaves.

At first, Farnsworth's programming ran largely to cartoons such as "Steamboat Willy," the debut of Mickey Mouse. "These cartoons are going to be very popular over television," he predicted. "They are so easy to transmit that they come over perfectly—and are most entertaining." Given the nature of the broadcasts, it is not surprising that Farnsworth's older son was among the first viewers, becoming a "charter member" of the television generation.

It soon became clear that young Philo wasn't the only one watching. The Philco plant was within broadcast range of the RCA facility in Camden, New Jersey, across the Delaware River. For some time, Farnsworth had been able to monitor Zworykin's test broadcasts and keep track of his rival's progress. "At first they made Phil uneasy and nervous," Everson said, "but later he got in his stride and took advantage of Zworykin's broadcast to study it for checking and evaluating his own developments."

With W3XE on the air, however, Zworykin would be able to do the same. Philco had gone to great lengths to keep Farnsworth and his television project a secret; now Farnsworth was literally broadcasting his presence to the world. It now became standard procedure for each of the lab crews to watch what the other was doing, and a spirited sense of rivalry soon emerged. When Philco set up a camera at a swimming pool on the University of Pennsylvania campus, RCA engineers phoned to let them know that some of the undergraduates were swimming in the nude.

Zworykin, it seemed, had better things to do than watch naked swimmers. Although he had learned much from the Farnsworth image dissector, his efforts remained focused on his own camera tube, which he believed to be a more promising design. One of the major differences lay in the idea of storage, the process by which photoelectric chemicals inside the tube were able to store up an electrical charge, increasing the unit's efficiency. This process was centered on a plate inside the tube, covered with a sheet of light-sensitive chemicals formed into individual droplets, as opposed to a continuous surface. The image to be televised would be focused onto this plate, and then scanned with an electron beam. In order for the storage principle to be effective, however, the chemical droplets would have to be formed in such a way as to allow each one to be insulated from the next, forming a sheet of individual photoelectric cells. This would create a unique surface, called a mosaic, on which electrical charges could accumulate without the usual rapid dissipation.

Zworykin and his men had labored for months to find an appropriate chemical and a means of creating a workable mosaic of insulated droplets. For some time they had been experimenting with surfaces made of mica, a transparent, flaky material known for its insulating and heat-resistant properties. By depositing a silver compound onto a mica surface, the team hoped to resolve the storage problem.

The solution came in an unexpected manner when an engineer named Sanford Essing was baking one of the silver-covered mica sheets in a lab oven. Essing forgot about the sheet and left it in the oven far longer than normal. By the time he noticed his mistake, the silver had reacted in a surprising way, breaking into a uniform mosaic of insulated silver globules. For Zworykin, it proved to be a turning point. He and Essing repeated and refined the process until they could reproduce it flawlessly. In time, Essing would take out a patent on the procedure.

This happy accident, according to Zworykin, provided the "final link" in the chain of creating his all-electronic television camera tube. Through the summer of 1931, the Camden team produced one tube after another, each slightly better than the last. "Zworykin's tube was a great improvement over anything else that had been used, and that includes the Farnsworth tube, because it stored light," insisted Ted Smith, an RCA vice president. "However, it had some basic defects. The electrons that hit the plate were apt to bounce off and come back again. So you've got black and white areas all over the picture. So it was necessary to 'shade' the area in order to get a good picture. This took twenty-two knobs that had to be adjusted. But it started things off at least."

A twenty-two-knob tuning process did not bode well for television in the home, but it was now clear to everyone at RCA that Zworykin was on the right track. In October, he made a note in his lab notebook naming his new camera tube the "iconoscope"—from the Greek words *eikon,* meaning image, and *skopein,* to observe. The following month Zworykin achieved what he judged to be a "reasonably good picture," and four days later he filed for a patent on the new system.

While Zworykin worked to perfect his iconoscope in October 1931, RCA completed the construction of a transmitter and broadcast facility on the eighty-fifth floor of the Empire State Building, making a powerful statement of RCA's position in the broadcast world. It is said that when William Paley of CBS moved to enter the television market, he tried to ensure that his tower atop the Chrysler Building would be taller than Sarnoff's. When Sarnoff raised his still higher, Paley is said to have countered. Over the years, television historians have devoted much speculation to this topic.

RCA's television engineers delighted in the increased range afforded by the Empire State Building. Other, less constructive, advantages also suggested themselves, and it was not long before a group of engineers had formed a club of paper airplane enthusiasts called the "Top Notchers." To become a member, recalled Ted Smith, "you had to fly your paper airplane from the Empire State Building either to Brooklyn or New Jersey."

Though the very existence of the iconoscope camera remained a closely guarded secret, Sarnoff decided in May 1932 that it was time to inform the industry of RCA's continuing progress. At the transmitting station in the Empire State Building, Sarnoff stood before a Nipkow-disk mechanical camera and addressed a group of more than a hundred radio executives and engineers, representing some fifty companies, who watched on kinescope receivers at the RCA Victor recording studios on East 24th Street. "We have arranged this demonstration in the spirit of the greatest possible cooperation with our licensees," Sarnoff told his audience, "so that you might be kept abreast with the progress of our laboratory research work and might judge for yourself the extent of the technical progress we have made in television." Sarnoff was at pains to emphasize that some technical obstacles remained before "practical, feasible commercial television service" could be achieved, and that the lingering effects of the economic depression made it necessary to wait until "the business sun is shining"—perhaps sometime the following year.

This "spirit of the greatest possible cooperation" carried an unambiguous message for Philco and other potential rivals: RCA intended to dominate television just as it had dominated radio. Among those who received the message was Farnsworth himself, who was in the audience at the 24th Street studio. Reporting to Everson afterward, he declared it to be "the best television picture I have ever seen."

"I was afraid, when I went to the meeting, that RCA was ahead of us," he told Everson. "I still believe that they are in many respects, but in others we are miles ahead of them, particularly as regards detail and the amount of equipment which we require in our receiver. . . . There are various points of technique in which they have completely outstripped us, and other places where, I think, we are considerably ahead of them."

Returning to Philadelphia, Farnsworth resolved to push harder to overtake Zworykin. "Phil seemed to enjoy this rivalry," Everson noted. "When he found something in the Zworykin picture that showed his own to a disadvantage, he was always hot on the trail of something to surpass it."

At home, however, the Farnsworths were having trouble adjusting to life in Philadelphia. At the outset, they had moved with the other lab families into a somewhat shabby apartment building near the plant. Although this simplified the transition for the lab workers, it left the families in a state of grim quarantine. None of them had a car—Farnsworth had given his away to his brother rather than trouble to bring it east—so they were all more or less stranded in the musty building. Pem developed a serious case of asthma, and even with medication it soon reached a stage where she could only sleep in snatches while sitting upright in a chair. The condition eased only when the family moved to a home in Chestnut Hill, a picturesque suburb to the north.

Although the Philco deal had promised financial stability, Farnsworth continued to have difficulty making ends meet. Shortly after the move he sold off some of his stock and deposited a large check into a bank that promptly failed, leaving him and Pem with $1.57 between them. It would take months to resolve the matter, at the end of which Farnsworth considered himself lucky to get fifteen cents on the dollar.

Matters worsened in the spring of 1932 when their younger son, Kenny, who had turned one in January, had to be hospitalized with a strep infection in his throat. Then as now, this was a serious condition in an infant. With penicillin and other antibiotics not yet available, there were limited means of halting the spread of the infection. Fearful that the disease would close off the baby's airway and infect the lungs, doctors performed a preventive tracheotomy, cutting into the windpipe to insert a breathing tube. "The operation rendered our sweet little Kenny speechless," Pem would recall many years later. "It tore at our hearts to see him so sick and so frightened at being unable to make a sound."

In hindsight, it appears possible that the infant was actually suffering from diphtheria, a more aggressive infectious disease, which was difficult to distinguish from a more self-limiting strep infection at that time. In either case, the horrific course of treatment was soon made worse by frequent clogging of the breathing tube. More than once the Farnsworths' doctor had to snatch the baby from his hospital bed and sprint down the corridor to an operating theater in order to clear the airway.

Late on the night of March 6, the Farnsworths received the glad news that their son was out of danger. It was nearly midnight when their doctor left for the night, leaving the boy in the care of an intern. Pem, exhausted from her long vigil, was told that she should try to get some rest in an empty room down the hall. Farnsworth went along to get her settled, but found that he could not sleep himself. After an hour or so, he went back down the hall to check on his son.

He found the intern asleep in a chair. Kenny, his airway blocked, had turned blue and was near death. Farnsworth raised the alarm and ran for Pem as medical staff swarmed the room trying to revive the baby. "We had to stand helplessly by and watch his precious life slip away," said Pem. "Suddenly, unbelievably, our darling son was gone."

This devastating blow was immediately compounded by an almost incomprehensible display of insensitivity by Farnsworth's superiors at Philco. The grieving parents had made arrangements to take their son's body back to Provo to be buried with Farnsworth's father and Pem's mother. Philco let it be known that it couldn't spare Farnsworth for the trip; his presence in Philadelphia was too essential to its investment in television. Farnsworth was inclined to break his contract on the spot, but Everson and McCargar made him see the consequences that this would have for his employees. In the end, Farnsworth reluctantly stayed behind, and the unhappy duty of transporting their child's body to Utah fell to Pem. "It is hard to relate the agonizing loneliness and grief I suffered during those four seemingly endless days crossing the continent," she would write decades later, "knowing my baby lay cold and alone in a coffin in the baggage car ahead."

Back in Philadelphia, Farnsworth and Pem could not bring themselves to talk about the tragedy. "It seems so unfair to take our baby away," Pem had written to her husband from the train to Utah. "Phil, dear, please don't work like you have been doing for a while." For Farnsworth, however, there seemed to be no alternative but to seek consolation in his work. At home he appeared stiff and withdrawn, leaving Pem to conclude that he blamed her for their son's death.

Months passed as a frost settled over the marriage. "We lived together almost as strangers," Pem recalled. As the holidays arrived at the end of 1932, both parents struggled to make a show of warmth for the sake of their surviving son. On Christmas Eve, Farnsworth worked long into the night to set up an elaborate Lionel train set, only to watch with amusement as young Philo showed greater interest in the electrical transformer than the train. The boy, Pem noted, appeared to share his father's fascination with electricity.

In the new year, as Farnsworth retreated into his lab, the marriage reached a crisis. For some time, the couple had been attending a regular Saturday-night dance in Philadelphia, and they continued to do so even now by force of habit. To Pem's dismay, Farnsworth began paying attention to one of the other wives, a woman named Kay, with whom he appeared to be smitten. "I decided to show Phil that two could play this game," Pem declared, so she began giving most of her dances to Kay's husband, Hank.

For some weeks, the Saturday-night dances became a staging area for the Farnsworths' marital discord as each affected to be unconcerned with what the other did. Earlier they had made a point of sharing one or two dances for the sake of appearances, but even this pretense was now abandoned. "Our attitude toward each other by now might be called coldly civil," Pem admitted, "and I was actually thinking about running off to Reno for a divorce so I could marry Hank."

Matters came to a head one Saturday night when Pem had all but given up hope of a reconciliation. "About the fifth dance, the orchestra began to play 'Always,' " Pem recalled. Her mind drifted back to the day in Provo seven years earlier when Farnsworth had presented her with the song's sheet music: "From that day, it had always been our song."

Apparently Farnsworth's thoughts were running in the same direction. With an awkward expression on his face, he crossed the room to his wife. "I think this is our dance," he said. Pem allowed herself to be led out onto the dance floor. "At first it was like dancing with a stranger," she said, "because I was not at all sure we still loved each other." Suddenly, Farnsworth drew his wife close and whispered fiercely in her ear: "What's the matter with us? We must be crazy!"

They left the dance and talked through the night. "It took that long to talk out all the hurt and resentment we had been harboring," Pem recalled. "I felt that since I had blamed myself for not being able to prevent Kenny's death, Phil had also blamed me. It turned out that all this time, he was blaming himself." Though the process would be "very painful," Pem said, "from that night we gradually rebuilt our relationship."

Even as Farnsworth revived his marriage, however, his relationship with Philco had broken down irretrievably. Farnsworth had been inclined to quit over the company's insensitivity to his son's death, and matters had not improved to any great degree in the months since. In addition, he had come to suspect that Jesse McCargar, who still controlled a large share of Farnsworth's financial interests in San Francisco, was maneuvering behind his back. McCargar, Farnsworth believed, was seeking to make an outright sale of Farnsworth's assets, including his patents, to Philco. At a stroke, this would have undone everything that Farnsworth hoped to achieve in his competition with Zworykin and RCA. Not only would he be robbed of any future profits from his television innovations, but he would become little more than a contract engineer for Philco. Unwilling to let this happen, Farnsworth drew up plans to separate himself and his lab from Philco.

In hindsight, Farnsworth could easily see that he and Philco had different agendas. Farnsworth wished to carry his research forward to an extent that would allow him to establish ironclad patent protection on all phases of his system. Philco wanted only to get its manufacturing effort into gear. Since the company did not own Farnsworth's patents, it had no vested interest in the outcome of his competition with Zworykin. Though Philco hoped to produce its own televisions independently of RCA, the company was not willing to sacrifice short-term profits. As a last resort, Philco would even have been willing to take out licenses on RCA patents, which would have been unthinkable to Farnsworth.

Not surprisingly, David Sarnoff had a role in the widening chasm.

Farnsworth's agreement with Philco had followed on the heels of his rejection of the RCA offer, emphasizing the fact that Philco intended to compete directly with RCA. Though the two companies had a long history of hostility dating back to Sarnoff's days as RCA's patent enforcer, Philco still relied heavily on RCA patents to sustain its radio production. In the early months of 1933, as Philco maneuvered to beat RCA to the television market, RCA is said to have delivered an ultimatum: drop Farnsworth or forget about renewing the radio licenses.

It is not known to what degree Sarnoff's pressure contributed to Farnsworth's separation from Philco in the summer of 1933. What is clear, however, is that his withdrawal from the company left Farnsworth in a dramatically weakened position. Deprived of the resources and facilities of a major corporation, he feared that he would lose whatever edge he might have had over the Zworykin team. At the same time, the rupture very nearly led to a split between Farnsworth and his San Francisco backers, including Everson and McCargar. McCargar was inclined to bring the operation back to San Francisco, but Farnsworth was convinced that he needed to stay on the East Coast, where the important television work was being done. According to Pem, McCargar tried to "lay down the law," but Farnsworth would not be swayed. As the conflict deepened, McCargar and Everson boarded a train for Philadelphia, hoping to resolve their differences in person. At length, when it became clear that Farnsworth wouldn't budge, McCargar reluctantly agreed to establish a Philadelphia subsidiary of the California operation, with Farnsworth in charge. The new company would be called Farnsworth Television Inc., with an office near Farnsworth's new home in suburban Chestnut Hill.

Farnsworth's independence came at a price. McCargar insisted that expenses be cut to the bone, which required Farnsworth to pare the staff down to just three—himself, Cliff Gardner, and Tobe Rutherford. The decision marked a further souring of his relationship with McCargar. Farnsworth was deeply pained at having to fire several of his devoted lab workers, many of whom had stuck by him when the Crocker group cut off his funding in San Francisco. For the moment, he realized, he had no choice in the matter. Farnsworth had now come full circle. In the summer of 1933, he was once again a "speedboat among the juggernauts," working out of a tiny, underfunded lab with a devoted staff of two.

Once again, Farnsworth's reduced circumstances sparked his creativity. By the end of the year he had applied for several important new patents, including one entitled simply "Image Dissector," which demonstrated that he was catching up to Zworykin in designing a camera tube that made use of the principle of electrical storage. Farnsworth also improved his electron multiplier tube, or multipactor, which greatly increased the light sensitivity of his apparatus. Now that he was no longer constrained by Philco's corporate secrecy, Farnsworth's advances again began to be reported in the press, often as a result of Everson's public relations efforts. In August 1933, the *San Francisco Chronicle* gave a glowing report on Farnsworth's "magic box of science," assuring its readers that they would not have long to wait before the miracle came to their homes: "It works," the paper reported. "It is here."

According to Pem, Farnsworth also found a way during this period to channel his grief over their son's death into medical advances, which he hoped might prevent such tragedies in the future. Although difficult to verify, there is evidence that Farnsworth arranged for a team at the University of Pennsylvania medical school to carry out research toward a streptococcus vaccine, an effort that would have been soon overtaken by the advent of penicillin. Later, Pem would recount, Farnsworth did preliminary work on an early hospital incubator known as the "Isolette," although here again the extent of his advances has not been definitively established. What is clear, however, is that Farnsworth's concern for the welfare of children would have a profound influence on his work in years to come.

As his modest lab in Chestnut Hill began operations, Farnsworth took an opportunity to erase the embarrassment of his failed demonstration for Mary Pickford and Douglas Fairbanks four years earlier. When Pickford opened in a play on Broadway, Farnsworth invited her to Chestnut Hill to see his latest equipment. By this time the actress had heard and read a great deal about television and its likely importance in the entertainment industry, and she was glad of the chance to see how the technology had progressed. At their meeting in San Francisco, Farnsworth had struggled to transmit a segment of film from one of Pickford's movies. Now his image dissector had the ability to capture live objects, so Pickford herself was invited to step before the camera, though the blazing hot lights could not have made the experience pleasant. "Whew!" the star exclaimed. "This is hotter than color!"

Eager to demonstrate his advances to the widest possible audience, Farnsworth created a mobile version of his system so that he could give exhibitions outside of the lab. In the summer of 1934, the ideal showcase presented itself. Philadelphia's famed Franklin Institute had opened a new science museum earlier that year, featuring a large showcase of modern technology. Farnsworth had delivered a paper at the museum earlier that year, leading to an invitation to display his television apparatus to the public.

Farnsworth gladly accepted. He had every reason to believe that his system, which could now broadcast in natural sunlight, was every bit as good as anything being produced by Zworykin. The ten-day event at the Franklin Institute promised to draw national media coverage, and send a strong message to RCA that Farnsworth Television Inc. was still in the game.

The exhibition began on August 24, 1934, and is believed to have been the world's first public demonstration of a fully electronic television system. Farnsworth's greatest concern, apart from the fact that his enlarged oscillite tubes now had a tendency to implode, was in finding broadcast material that would hold the public's attention. In the lab, a simple smoke ring, hand gesture, or cartoon snippet would suffice. Here, Farnsworth knew, greater entertainment value would be required.

Farnsworth's ingenious solution was to position a television camera at the entrance of the exhibit. As the visitors filed past, their own images were televised on a small monitor near the camera. Today this simple gimmick is familiar to anyone who has ever walked past a department store security camera or electronics shop window. In 1934, however, the novelty of seeing one's own face on the twelve-inch oscillite screen made a powerful impression. Few, if any, of the many hundreds of visitors to the Franklin Institute had ever seen a television before, far less appeared on one.

If this sample pleased them, visitors were encouraged to pay seventy-five cents to enter a small auditorium where the main exhibition took place. Every fifteen minutes, from 2:00 p.m. to 10:00 p.m., Farnsworth and his crew would present whatever acts came to hand on a "greenish fluorescent screen," transmitted via cable from an adjacent room by means of the image dissector. The range of performers was truly astonishing—local politicians competed with trained dogs and monkeys for airtime. Davis Cup stars Frank Shields and Lester Stoefen demonstrated proper racquet grip. Chorus girls sang and danced. A cellist held the audience spellbound until the hot lights blistered the varnish on his instrument.

In good weather, Farnsworth would take the mobile camera outside and recruit neighborhood boys to spar in a makeshift boxing ring. Sometimes he dragged the apparatus up to the roof and swept it across the skyline and traffic below. On one particularly clear night, Farnsworth noticed that the moon was full and decided to turn his image dissector skyward. The next day's newspapers carried ecstatic reports: "Moon Makes Television Debut in Pose for Radio Snapshot," read a headline in the *Christian Science Monitor*.

Across the river in Camden, Zworykin and his team were more interested in the quality of Farnsworth's images than in their content. "Some of the scientists who watched," the *New York Times* said of Farnsworth's demonstration, "declared it the most sensitive apparatus yet developed." At a time when RCA's television initiative had again retreated behind a curtain of secrecy, the newly independent Farnsworth appeared to be gaining strength. The increased interest allowed him to sell off some of his stock, enabling him to expand his lab crew with new members and rehire some of the faithful old hands.

In the midst of the Franklin Institute exhibition, Farnsworth received an unexpected plea for help from a former rival—John Logie

Baird. The British pioneer of mechanical television, it emerged, could no longer ignore the electronic revolution. After a long struggle to get the British Broadcasting Corporation interested in the Baird television system, Baird now found himself under fire from a powerful competitor, Electric and Music Industries, Ltd., or EMI. For some years engineers at EMI had been working with great success to develop a British electronic television system. As with Zworykin and Alexanderson four years earlier, matters were quickly reaching a point at which a decisive competition would be necessary. In preparation, the BBC invited EMI to bring its equipment to London's Broadcast House for further experimentation.

The EMI apparatus had proved itself consistently superior to Baird's, but the BBC, which had been reluctant to embrace Baird's system years earlier, would now be equally reluctant to cast it aside. Baird, hoping to fortify his position, protested that EMI was nothing more than a puppet of the Radio Corporation of America. The American company, he insisted, "surely controls quite enough of the world's communications without the home of British broadcasting taking it under its wing." While it was true that EMI did make use of some RCA patents, the company had long since evolved technologies and patent structures of its own. Still, Baird's argument resonated with the British public.

Even as he rose to meet EMI's challenge, however, Baird faced dissension in his own ranks. Though he himself was clinging to the Nipkow disk as tenaciously as ever, the board of his company, Baird Television Ltd., wanted to go electric. While Baird repaired to his laboratory to wring further improvements from his spinning disks, his company brought on Captain A.G.D. West, a cathode-ray expert. West had served as a research engineer at the BBC and had even spent time in the United States as a liaison to the Zworykin team. At a stroke, he brought the latest electronic technology to Baird Television Ltd., with the result that the company was now eager to put aside all traces of the mechanical system—including Baird himself. "Daniel in the lion's den was a poor show compared to Baird in the Baird boardroom," the inventor reported indignantly. "Everything I did and had done was faulty."

In the meantime, EMI arranged a merger with the British Marconi company, creating an even more formidable adversary. Baird Television renewed the complaint that their rival was little more than a subsidiary of RCA, drawing a heated response from the new Marconi–EMI, Ltd., that "everything down to the last screw was home manufactured."

The BBC and the British Post Office had now set up a committee to make recommendations as to the future of British television. After weighing the merits of the various systems available, it was decided to arrange a two-year competition between Baird Television and EMI–Marconi. At the end of this time, one of the two systems would be adopted as the standard of British television, and the other would be cast aside.

Clearly, the stakes were enormous. Though Captain West had allowed Baird Television to make great strides, his advances were contingent on patents controlled by EMI and RCA. If it intended to compete, Baird Television would have to find another way forward. Ironically, given the company's loud protests against American interference, this left only one viable means of facing down the competition—Philo T. Farnsworth and his image dissector.

For Farnsworth, the benefits of striking a deal with Baird were obvious. First and foremost, he would get a quick infusion of working capital, which he sorely needed. With Everson's help he had been selling off further chunks of Farnsworth stock to raise operating funds, chipping away at his control over his own patents. In the circumstances, the promise of a foreign licensing deal must have seemed providential. Better yet, having his system taken up by Baird Television—and possibly by the BBC—would confer a new degree of credibility on Farnsworth Television Inc. and greatly strengthen his challenge to RCA.

In October 1934, Farnsworth set off for London aboard the SS *Bremen,* a German liner. While Cliff Gardner stayed behind to keep the Philadelphia operation running, Farnsworth brought along three trusted associates—Tobe Rutherford and Arch Brolly, both of whom had been with him since the Green Street days, and Seymour "Skee" Turner, a valued member of the lab team whose family had invested heavily in Farnsworth stock.

Farnsworth and his men were forced to carry a great deal of their television equipment as personal luggage. As the crossing had been made in a German-owned ship and British shipping regulations of the time did not permit the vessel to dock in England, the passengers and luggage had to be transferred to a British boat offshore. Baird Television sent a private launch to collect the Farnsworth party, but as a loading crane eased the television equipment onto the deck, a huge wave pitched the launch skyward, colliding with the suspended cargo. To make matters worse, the equipment was promptly impounded as it reached shore, leaving Farnsworth to fret over whether his tubes had survived the impact while a representative of the Baird company sorted out the import restrictions.

After several hours, Farnsworth's crates were transferred to Baird Television's laboratory facilities. Baird had come a long way since the Frith Street walk-up in Soho; his new lab and a staff of some two hundred engineers occupied an impressive space in London's famed Crystal Palace. Originally built in Hyde Park to house Britain's Great Exhibition of 1851, the immense glass-and-iron structure was dismantled and reerected in South London following the exhibition. There, in the building's south tower, Farnsworth and his colleagues were finally able to examine their equipment. As Farnsworth pried the lids off his crates, Baird engineers crowded around for a look at the miracle tubes that they hoped would save their jobs. Instead, as Farnsworth pushed aside the packing straw, they found a jumble of shattered equipment. Baird's men shrugged and went back to work, obviously expecting no further help from the American contingent.

As Farnsworth began cataloging the damage, however, he discovered that somehow his tubes had been spared. Most of the breakages had been restricted to the less critical elements of the apparatus, which had not been packed as carefully. Farnsworth undertook repairs and had a complete system up and running in short order. Soon the work area was crowded with Baird engineers straining to get their first look at the new electronic picture.

Leaving his men in charge, Farnsworth went off to find Baird himself. He could not be certain how long his battered equipment would function, and he was eager to have the great man see the picture for himself before anything else went wrong. For Farnsworth, the prospect of working alongside Baird was enormously exciting. Although he had rejected the mechanical principles upon which Baird had built his career, he felt a great deal of admiration for the man himself, whose struggles so closely paralleled his own.

Baird felt differently. He remained convinced that his problems could be resolved without American intervention, and he took the opportunity of his meeting with Farnsworth to belabor the merits of his mechanical system. Baird was still lecturing his young visitor as the two men made their way back to the lab. As they entered the room, Baird's eye fell upon the picture displayed on Farnsworth's oscillite. The older man fell silent, walking cautiously toward the monitor as though it were an exotic and perhaps hostile animal of some kind. He stood in front of the screen for several moments with his back straight and his arms folded. Then, without a word to Farnsworth, he turned and left the room.

Like Jenkins and Alexanderson before him, Baird had finally been forced to confront the end of the mechanical era. Skee Turner summed up the reaction of most of the men present: "I could have cried for the poor guy."

While Baird withdrew to ponder his fate, Farnsworth and Turner began a series of meetings with company officers to hammer out a licensing agreement. At the head of the Baird team was Sir Harry Greer, a member of a parliamentary committee on television standards who also served as Baird's chairman of the board. Greer was an imposing figure, and it soon became apparent that he was unwilling to enter into a conventional license agreement with the American upstarts. Greer felt that once Baird's team of two hundred engineers had a chance to work with the Farnsworth system, they would make important refinements, just as the EMI team had done with Zworykin's system. That being the case, he proposed a conventional cross-licensing agreement, in which neither side would pay patent royalties but each would be free to make use of the other's technology.

To Farnsworth's way of thinking, this amounted to trading away the image dissector for a Nipkow disk. He was inclined to drop the negotiations and head back to Philadelphia, but Turner reminded him of their desperate need for working capital. With Farnsworth's assent, Turner rejected Greer's offer and laid down his conditions. If Baird Television wished to make use of Farnsworth's image dissector in its competition with Marconi–EMI, the company would not only have to pay royalties but also offer an immediate cash payment equivalent to $50,000.

By all accounts, Greer regarded these demands as ridiculous. He made it clear that once Baird's financial officers got wind of these conditions, they would likely break off the discussions and send the Americans home empty-handed. Farnsworth and Turner were asked if they might wish to reconsider their position. Realizing that they were about to take an enormous gamble, Turner asked if he might have a moment alone with his boss.

Turner pulled Farnsworth into an adjoining office as the two men tried to gather their resolve. Greer did not appear inclined to bluff; if Farnsworth insisted on his conditions, they might very well come away with nothing. Farnsworth needed the money more than he was willing to let on, but at the same time, he needed some sort of licensing deal—even if it was simply a cross-licensing agreement—to help establish the worth of his system. As Farnsworth wavered, Turner spotted a bottle of whiskey on top of a cabinet. Reaching for the bottle, he poured a healthy measure into a glass and handed it to Farnsworth, who knocked it back. With a nod, Turner took the glass and poured a second drink for himself. Thus fortified, the two men returned to the conference table. "Gentlemen," Turner announced, "we want fifty thousand dollars or no deal."

Seeing that Farnsworth would not be dissuaded, Greer and the other Baird representatives withdrew for the night amid grave doubts as to whether any form of the deal could be salvaged. Back at the Grosvenor House Hotel that evening, Farnsworth despaired that he had aimed too high. As the discussions resumed the following morning, however, it became apparent that the Baird representatives had come to a full appreciation of the gravity of their own situation. Farnsworth was notified that $50,000 would be paid immediately, along with future royalties.

The Farnsworth team sailed home in triumph. At last, they believed, they had the money in hand that would allow Farnsworth to bring television to the public. "Now," Pem noted dryly, "all they had to do was convince Jess."

Indeed, it would soon develop that Jesse McCargar had other plans for the money. Farnsworth intended to use the cash infusion to build a broadcasting studio, just as he had done at Philco, in order to keep pace with the competition. In McCargar's view, an expensive studio was out of the question at a time when he and Everson had been regularly selling stock to raise basic operating expenses. The British money, he insisted, was needed for day-to-day operations.

It was only the latest in the long series of clashes between Farnsworth and McCargar. McCargar felt that Farnsworth was oblivious to the realities of running a business, while Farnsworth believed that McCargar's chokehold on the lab's budget was preventing him from making any real progress. Both positions had merit. Farnsworth was painfully aware that his patents would be in force for only seventeen years. He would not derive any benefit from them unless television went into commercial production during that time. He firmly believed, therefore, that he should spend whatever was necessary to bring television into the American home, in the certain belief that millions of dollars in royalty payments would follow.

From McCargar's perspective, however, the value of Farnsworth's system was eroding with every passing moment. Each time he was forced to sell off stock to keep the lab going, future profits slipped away. By the time they actually managed to get television out of the laboratory, McCargar believed, Farnsworth was likely to have frittered away all of their holdings.

The two men would never see eye to eye on this point, and George Everson was regularly caught in the middle. "Now for God's sake, George," McCargar fumed as the financial worries deepened, "don't toss this off with the expression that I am having a pathological outburst. This situation is terribly serious!" Farnsworth, too, often vented his frustrations to Everson. "I think we have to make allowances for Jess," Everson said at one stage. "He tells me his wife is divorcing him." But the continuing strain had left Farnsworth in an uncharitable frame of mind. "I'm not surprised," he answered. "I don't see how anyone could live with him."

Through the early months of 1935, as Farnsworth continued to press for an experimental broadcasting facility, it became clear that the rift with McCargar was having a serious effect on his health. "Feeling the hot breath of his well-funded competitors closing in on him, Phil continued to push himself unmercifully," Pem would write. "He had built his lab force up to the highest efficiency he had yet been able to achieve, but it had been a fight with Jess all the way." Worse, the fortifying whiskey he had downed outside the Baird Television boardroom would not be his last. "The strain of his long hours and the constant clashes over funding began to take a toll," Pem admitted, "and he began to seek relief in a cocktail before dinner, frequently followed by one or two more during the evening before he could calm down enough to go to bed. This change in his routine began to cause me some real concern."

The concern would be echoed by Farnsworth's sister Agnes. "It was around 1935 that I saw the beginning of the change in my brother," she would tell an interviewer years later. "At meals, instead of chattering away about what was going on like he used to, he was withdrawn. He would get these ideas and he couldn't turn his mind off. You go to bed and you usually want to sleep to restore your mental capacities and your body. He would be working on a problem, and he couldn't turn it off. He would work on it while he was sleeping. He paid a heavy toll for this brilliance."

Soon, however, it would become apparent that McCargar had not exaggerated the need to conserve resources. Soon the cost of running the lab would be dwarfed by a more urgent if less productive expense—legal fees to defend Farnsworth's patents against repeated challenges from RCA.

"Filing a patent on an invention is like planting a crop and waiting for it to germinate, and then nursing it through a hazardous season of growth to the harvest," Everson wrote. By the summer of 1935, the efforts of David Sarnoff's lawyers had placed the harvest very much at risk. Although Sarnoff had claimed that Farnsworth's lab contained nothing he would need, the same could not be said of Farnsworth's patent portfolio. Since Farnsworth had rejected RCA's offer of a buy-out, Sarnoff's legal team moved to disallow key Farnsworth patents in a court challenge. "It had cost the Farnsworth company about $30,000," Everson wrote, "at a time when the country was struggling through a major depression. To find money for such litigation fell on Mr. McCargar and me. It was a difficult and exhausting ordeal."

The experience was no less difficult for Farnsworth. "That lawsuit!" exclaimed Farnsworth's brother Lincoln. "That's why we all got so damned angry at RCA. They tried to steal the whole damn thing. Phil had to spend money on patent lawyers to prove that it was his idea, and it was money he didn't really have."

Though Farnsworth's patents had been bumping up against Zworykin's for many years, the primary case of interference—in which one patent holder challenges the rights of another—had begun three years earlier. In May 1932, RCA filed a suit claiming that Farnsworth's patent entitled "Television System," filed in 1927 and issued three years later, was infringing on the patent filed by Zworykin in December 1923, while he was an employee of Westinghouse. At issue was a claim that was absolutely essential to both sides, that Farnsworth's patent covered the means of "forming of an electrical image." For years the RCA lawyers had complained—and they would continue to complain—that the language of the patent was far too broad, extending protection to all electrical images, even those formed by an iconoscope, rather than an image dissector. In RCA's view, it was as if Thomas Edison had been granted control not just of the incandescent lightbulb but of light itself. "In the end," said Bill Eddy, one of Farnsworth's engineers at the time, "whoever would win was going to be the kingpin of television."

Obviously there was no question that Zworykin's 1923 patent application predated Farnsworth's of 1927. At issue was the matter of "priority of invention," encompassing not only the conception of the idea, but also the creation of a working model. In order to prove their case, Farnsworth and his lawyers would have to verify three essential steps in the creation of the image dissector—the conception of the idea, the disclosure of the idea to an outside party, and its eventual reduction to practice.

The latter steps were not at issue—Farnsworth had produced a written description of his system for the Los Angeles patent lawyers in 1926 and produced a working model in 1927. The critical issue, then, became when Farnsworth had conceived of the idea. His claim to have originated the concept as a high school student, sometime between the dates of January 1, 1922, and April 30, 1922, would be difficult to establish.

In hearings before patent examiners, both Farnsworth and Zworykin were subjected to grueling cross-examination by opposing counsel. Zworykin made a surprisingly poor showing, and his testimony did more to cloud the central issues than to strengthen his own case. "Zworykin has shown throughout that he is perfectly ready to make any statement on the stand which he believes, at the moment, will be to his advantage," declared Farnsworth's attorneys. "His memory is alternately superactive and distressingly vague, and throughout his cross-examination he was so evasive as to make the elicitation of any fact whatsoever extremely difficult." While this is undoubtedly an exaggeration, it must be said that years of working under the strict control of RCA patent lawyers had left Zworykin accustomed to guarding his words. It is entirely possible, however, that Zworykin did not wish to invite close scrutiny of the degree to which the camera tubes he eventually created conformed to the outlines of his 1923 application.

Farnsworth's lawyers threw a particular emphasis on Zworykin's visit to the lab on Green Street and seized on Zworykin's praise of the image dissector: "This is a beautiful instrument. I wish that I might have invented it." Zworykin's justification for this remark was far from satisfying. "Zworykin's explanation of why he made such a statement at the time is a marvel of ingenuity," declared the Farnsworth team. "It was considered for a period of many minutes, laboriously reduced to writing, and then read by him into the record." The gist of that statement, it emerged, was that Zworykin had simply wished to be polite.

Zworykin's legal team was no less severe in its treatment of Farnsworth. The seventy-page brief filed by Zworykin's lawyers made it clear that they intended to show that "Zworykin was first to conceive the invention" and also "first to reduce the invention to practice." In addition, the RCA legal team promised to show that "Farnsworth never conceived and/or disclosed to anyone, prior to Zworykin's filing date, a complete invention." In other words, according to the RCA lawyers Farnsworth had no way of proving that he had hit upon a workable idea prior to Zworykin's 1923 patent application.

Farnsworth himself was not particularly helpful on this point. Questioned about the drawings he had made of his television system while still in high school, he offered no compelling facts: "They were simply rough sketches of a vacuum tube containing a cathode and an anode with an external lens and a static machine. Further details I do not remember." His lawyers, led by Donald Lippincott, struggled to flesh out Farnsworth's testimony: "Counsel for Zworykin have attempted to impeach the testimony of Farnsworth on the grounds that the invention was too complex for a boy of fifteen and a half years of age to have made. Granting that inventions of the importance of the one now in issue are not usually made by high school boys, the other testimony adduced in this case effectively disposes of this contention. All who have testified in regard to the boy Farnsworth have spoken of his unusual ability. He was an omnivorous reader, he had but recently had, for the first time, the opportunity to dip into the storehouse of technical literature, and he was indulging that opportunity without stint. And while counsel for Zworykin has spoken of the invention as 'complex,' it is in fact extraordinarily simple considering the results accomplished."

As the testimony dragged on, however, it became apparent that Zworykin's team had the upper hand. Unless Farnsworth could prove decisively that he had conceived of electronic television in early 1922, as he was claiming, he would likely lose the case. If RCA gained control of the patents governing the formation of an electronic image, Farnsworth would be out of the television business forever. Reviewing the situation in Lippincott's office, Farnsworth agreed that the situation looked grim. Part of the problem, Farnsworth admitted, lay in

the fact that he had been so protective of his ideas, even at the very beginning. As his father had told him, ideas were "valuable and fragile,
and could be pirated easily." Farnsworth shook his head. His father had
been perhaps the only person in whom he had confided fully. He had
been dead for more than ten years, and in any case, the court would
have been unlikely to give much credence to his testimony. Lippincott
looked up at this. Had there been others to whom Farnsworth confided his ideas?

Farnsworth thought a moment. "Yes," he replied. "There was my
high school chemistry teacher. A man named Justin Tolman."

Twelve

Now We Add Sight to Sound

There are liars, damn liars, goddamn
liars, and patents experts.

—Ernst Alexanderson

Justin Tolman no longer lived in Rigby, Idaho, and it would be some time before Lippincott could establish that Farnsworth's former teacher was indeed still alive. At length, Lippincott tracked him down in Salt Lake City, where Tolman had moved some years earlier. Farnsworth's legal team had now come to believe that their case might well stand or fall on Tolman's testimony. Lippincott, along with an RCA attorney named Samuel Smith, made arrangements to fly to Utah to take Tolman's deposition.

On arrival, Lippincott was impatient to find out if Tolman would be able to help. In his initial contact by phone, the lawyer had been careful to give no details whatever, so as to avoid accusations of priming the witness. While Smith settled into a hotel room, Lippincott rented a car and, after losing his way once or twice, found the neighborhood where Tolman now lived. When he located the house, Lippincott spotted a portly, white-haired man working in a small rose garden.

The lawyer parked his car and approached the older man. "Are you Justin Tolman?" he asked.

The gardener looked up from his plants. "Yes," he said. "I am."

Declaring, "Now we add radio sight to sound," David Sarnoff opens RCA's Exhibition Hall at the 1939 New York World's Fair. BETTMANN/CORBIS

"Do you remember a student in Rigby, Idaho, by the name of Philo Farnsworth?"

A smile came to the older man's face. "I surely do," he said. "Brightest student I ever had."

Lippincott paused. Though he was anxious to question Tolman, he did not want to hand RCA the means of disqualifying the testimony. Treading carefully, he gave a brief explanation of the situation and asked Tolman if he would be willing to give a deposition the following morning. Tolman agreed, declaring that he would do whatever he could to help.

According to a newspaper account published some years later, Lippincott not only managed to impress Tolman with the gravity of the situation but also told him that simple oral evidence would likely not be enough to turn the tide in Farnsworth's favor. "We've got to have something real," Tolman was told. Pondering the matter later that evening, Tolman thought back over his after-school sessions with Farnsworth at Rigby High School more than ten years earlier. He vividly remembered the afternoon when Farnsworth sketched a diagram of the image dissector on the classroom chalkboard, but he could not be certain of the exact date. He seemed to recall that Farnsworth had wanted to check some calculations at one stage, and he remembered the boy's excitement as he elaborated a particular point, reaching for a page from Tolman's notebook to jot down some sketch or equation.

Tolman considered the matter for a moment longer. Then he stood up as a sudden thought struck him. Making his way down to his basement, Tolman found a pile of boxes coated with dust and cobwebs. It took perhaps twenty minutes of sorting before he came upon a small pocket notebook from the winter term of 1922. Flipping through the faded notations of reading assignments and attendance violations, Tolman soon found what he was looking for—a crude, spidery drawing that showed a tube, a lens, and a pair of surfaces marked "optical image" and "electron image." Though there had undoubtedly been changes made over the years, this was clearly a preliminary sketch of the famous image dissector. Looking down at the faded drawing, Tolman recalled what he had told Farnsworth that day: "Study like the devil and keep mum." Apparently Farnsworth had done both. Now, however, there was no longer any reason to keep mum.

Both Lippincott and Smith, the RCA attorney, were greatly impressed with Tolman's deposition the following day. "This was made for me by Philo in early 1922," Tolman said of the sketch, and the assertion appeared to be supported by subsequent notations in the notebook. When Tolman finished giving his testimony, Lippincott continued on to Philadelphia in high spirits.

Not surprisingly, Tolman's deposition came under fire from the RCA attorneys, who attacked it as "vague and incomplete," amounting to little more than the unsubstantiated testimony of a biased witness. As the Farnsworth side defended its position, the debate over Tolman's evidence would stretch out over a period of several months. Zworykin's attorneys, however, had now created an equally serious problem for themselves. The Farnsworth team had repeatedly pressed for Zworykin to produce an example of his early camera tube as evidence, so that its construction and operation might be checked against the claims of his 1923 patent application. The Zworykin side failed to do so and offered no explanation for the lapse. Although any number of witnesses had testified to the existence of the tubes and many had claimed to see them in operation, there would be no confirmation that the Zworykin system—as described in the 1923 application—could produce an electrical image of the type required to uphold the challenge to Farnsworth's patent.

In the end, this would be the point upon which the case turned. However compelling the evidence of Justin Tolman might have seemed initially, it would eventually be dismissed by the Patent Office examiner as "insufficient to corroborate the testimony of Farnsworth that he disclosed a complete and operative embodiment of the invention." As damaging as this seemed to Farnsworth's case, the Zworykin team appeared to have done themselves a greater injury. For all their attacks on Farnsworth's credibility, they had failed to corroborate the testimony of their own star witness.

Final briefs were given on April 16, 1934, and a final hearing took place the following week. More than a year later, on July 22, 1935, a forty-seven-page decision was handed down. It ruled, in effect, that the Zworykin application as filed did not disclose a device that would produce a scanned electrical image as defined by the Farnsworth patent. Because Zworykin's device had been found to produce a different kind of image, it was therefore not relevant to the patent at issue. That being the case, the decision ruled that "Philo Taylor Farnsworth, junior party, be awarded the priority of invention on his system of television."

Farnsworth and his team of supporters should have been ecstatic. The implications of the victory were momentous, and signaled to the electronics industry and to the world at large that Farnsworth was firmly in control of the future of television. As they reviewed their situation, however, a deadening sense of the reality of their position washed over the Farnsworth camp. The battle had leached away their assets, diverting time and money that they would otherwise have used to develop a commercial product. Worse, though the Patent Office had ruled in their favor, the struggle was far from over. RCA filed an immediate appeal, and the company's vast financial and legal resources promised to keep the matter tied up for years to come. Though the courts had upheld his vital claims, Farnsworth would be unable to capitalize on the victory and would instead be forced to stand by and watch as more and more time ticked off the life of the vital patent protection.

Sarnoff now had even less reason to hurry the introduction of television to the American public. Despite his frequent assurances that television would never supplant radio, Sarnoff had been surprised at the explosion of interest in mechanical television in 1928, and he knew that electronic television might well occasion a similar boom, undercutting RCA's radio income. With Zworykin's research program burning through millions of dollars, Sarnoff could ill afford a dip in profits. At the same time, any RCA effort to rush a product onto the market would be hamstrung by Farnsworth's patents. As a result, while Farnsworth seized every chance he could to declare that television was "just around the corner," Sarnoff continued to insist that it would be some years in coming.

It was during this period that Sarnoff signaled his confidence in the radio industry by turning the Empire State Building's broadcasting facility over to Howard Armstrong for his experiments in FM radio transmission. This effectively applied the brakes to television development throughout the industry and bought time for the Camden team to perfect an RCA system.

Soon enough, however, events would conspire to push Sarnoff into a more active posture. In England, the two-year competition between Baird Television and Marconi–EMI had resulted in a rapid push toward commercial television. Britain now appeared to be pulling ahead of America in both technology and programming, raising the possibility that RCA might find itself overtaken by a foreign rival. Sarnoff began to realize that he could no longer afford to "move television at my own pace," as he had remarked of his earlier stance. If the British were pushing toward production, RCA would have to push back. Armstrong was given notice to remove his equipment from the Empire State Building, and at the annual meeting of RCA stockholders in 1935, Sarnoff announced that he had renewed the company's commitment to television. "First Field Tests in Television, Costing $1,000,000, to Begin Here" ran a front-page headline in the *New York Times*. Under the ambitious new plan, Sarnoff promised to establish the best transmitting station in the United States, create receiving sets for testing purposes, and design an experimental broadcast service to "determine the most acceptable form of television programs." He estimated that the process would take between twelve and fifteen months. "While the magnitude and nature of the problems of television call for prudence," he told the RCA stockholders, "they also call for courage and initiative, without which a new art cannot be created or a new industry established. The Radio Corporation of America, with its coordinated units engaged in related phases of radio-communication services, is outstandingly equipped to supply the experience, research, and technique for the pioneering work which is necessary for the ultimate creation of a complete television system."

Sarnoff's new initiative would come to be known as the "Million Dollar Plan," though in truth he had already funneled more than $5 million into the Camden laboratories. The announcement, coming at a time when RCA had not made any public disclosures of its television work in several years, captured headlines around the world. For Farnsworth, the message was perfectly clear. He had won the battle, but Sarnoff had every expectation of winning the war.

In Philadelphia, Farnsworth returned to his lab and attempted to forge ahead. He could not be certain what effect Sarnoff's Million Dollar Plan would have on the continuing legal struggle, but it now seemed more urgent than ever to produce a practical alternative to the RCA system. When reporters asked him when a Farnsworth television receiver might be available, he gave an optimistic response of one year, but also took a moment to reflect on all the similar forecasts he had made in the past. "Some of my predictions haven't turned out too well," he admitted.

Sarnoff's prediction, by contrast, would prove to be right on the money. He had said that it would take between twelve and fifteen months to put his plan into operation. Thirteen months later, in June 1936, RCA and NBC began a series of all-electronic experimental television broadcasts from the Empire State Building. The effort started small, with the broadcasts going out from a modest 10-kilowatt transmitter to some one hundred RCA receiving units throughout the New York area. Sarnoff himself gave a speech to inaugurate the programming, and was followed by various entertainments of a less businesslike sort, including a kick line of twenty dancing girls. The program finished with a brief on-camera appearance by Zworykin and his engineering team. Sadly missing from the group was Gregory Ogloblinsky, who had joined the team after meeting Zworykin in Paris. The engineer, who had been an essential part of the development of the iconoscope, had died in an automobile accident a short time earlier.

The following month, on July 7, 1936, Sarnoff presided over a festive inaugural celebration at Radio City, designed to demonstrate RCA's television advances to a vast audience of licensees and other potential customers. Jesse McCargar, who was in New York at the time, sent an anxious report to Everson. "They showed film and direct pickup in Radio City, which was transmitted both by coaxial cable and beam transmission—so it is said—to the Empire State Building, and there broadcast and picked up in the auditorium," McCargar wrote. "One of the stunts they did was to take a picture of a horse race that day at Baltimore, flying the film to New York in a plane specially equipped for developing the film in transit. . . . The television pictures were shown to the spectators about three-quarters of an hour after the race was run."

While these bravura machinations were carried out behind the scenes, RCA salesmen swarmed through the crowd to ensure that the guests were properly impressed and, not incidentally, to make certain that no one looked inside any of the television receiver cabinets arrayed throughout the room. "There were, however, five of the guests who did look inside the receivers," McCargar reported. Inside each cabinet was a chassis holding no fewer than thirty-three glass tubes.

After the demonstration, the guests were ferried by taxi to a banquet at the Waldorf-Astoria. "Each guest," noted McCargar, "had his own waiter, whose duty it was to see that the guest at least got enough to drink—and in most cases, more than enough. All during the demonstration and the talks at the dinner they kept emphasizing that July 7th was a great day in history that they would be able to tell their grandchildren about."

Presiding over this bounty in a courtly and magnanimous spirit was David Sarnoff himself. Television, he insisted throughout the evening, was too wondrous an advance in human technology to be the exclusive preserve of one company. There would be enough room for all in this vast new industry, and RCA was eager to use the results of its television research for the benefit of all, including foreign licensees. Evidently Sarnoff was eager to signal that RCA would not participate in the kind of industry poaching and border skirmishes that had characterized the early days of radio; he conveniently forgot that most of those clashes had originated with him. In part, Sarnoff's seemingly charitable impulses can be understood in light of the fact that many of the people in the room were radio licensees whose agreements were due for renewal. Even so, Sarnoff had never appeared so willing to share RCA's wealth.

"After the dinner Sarnoff read a prepared statement in which he went over the history of the radio business and told what was ahead," McCargar reported, adding that before the speech Sarnoff could be seen "in most earnest conversation" with a representative of Philco. This conference brought an unexpected addendum to Sarnoff's remarks. "The surprising thing in his talk," McCargar explained, "was that he stated that there were other experimenters in television besides themselves—that they mustn't think that RCA was everything in television—that other people had been working on it, and that Farnsworth was a name that had to be reckoned with. Sarnoff then congratulated Mr. Skinner, of Philco, on his foresight in having made an arrangement with Farnsworth when he did—after which Mr. Skinner rose and took a bow. This statement, we understand, was a deviation from the prepared speech."

If so, the deviation was certainly an extraordinary one, and Sarnoff's nod to his competitor cannot have been entirely altruistic. RCA had lost an appeal of the patent infringement case four months earlier, but its legal department had not yet given up on breaking or evading Farnsworth's patents. At the same time, however, television researchers not yet affiliated with either RCA or Farnsworth were hard at work on television apparatus that wedded the best features of both systems. With foreign competitors knocking at the door and his legal options dwindling, it is probable that Sarnoff realized it might soon be expedient to seek an accommodation with Farnsworth. If so, it would have suited Sarnoff to appear as the benevolent godfather of television, with a tolerant attitude toward headstrong youngsters such as Farnsworth, so as to quiet any reservations that might be felt by the company's licensees. As McCargar observed, the last thing Sarnoff needed was "any accusation of an effort at monopoly."

The July 7 gala would bring many new licensees into the fold, but Sarnoff had good reason to tread warily. Philco still had a licensing deal with Farnsworth, and the company was making an all-out effort to begin full-scale television production, an effort widely seen within the industry as a bid to undercut Sarnoff and RCA. The rivalry between the two companies, which had its roots in the early days of radio, came to a very public climax in 1936 when Philco filed suit against RCA in the New York Supreme Court, claiming unfair trade practices. The complaint charged that representatives of RCA had set upon a group of female employees of Philco, plying them with "intoxicating liquors at hotels, restaurants, and nightclubs" in an effort to extract sensitive company secrets. In addition, the RCA representatives were said to have maneuvered the women into "compromising situations" in order to "induce, incite, and bribe said employees." The story created a brief tabloid sensation in New York, but would ultimately be dropped for lack of evidence.

Sarnoff had a more serious battle on his hands with the newly created Federal Communications Commission, which had been established to succeed the Federal Radio Commission two years earlier, in 1934. As each of the various contenders in the television race worked to bring its own apparatus into production, a potential nightmare was taking shape. In order for a television receiver to work, it had to be perfectly synchronized with the transmitter signal in terms of the number of scanning lines and the number of frames per second. Farnsworth and RCA had long been working with a standard of 441 lines and thirty frames per second. However, each of the other television concerns—Philco, Zenith, CBS, and the fledgling DuMont, among others—was working with its own individual standard. This meant that a Philco set could only receive a Philco signal, a Zenith set could only receive a Zenith signal, and so on. Unless a consistent standard could be established, the industry would fall into chaos even before mass production could begin.

At Sarnoff's urging, the Radio Manufacturers Association formed a committee to seek an agreement within the industry and recommend a set of standards to the FCC. It took more than a year of infighting and horse-trading among the various committee members to reach a fragile consensus, which closely accorded with the standards already in use by RCA and Farnsworth. No sooner had the report been presented to the FCC, however, than Philco withdrew its support, claiming that RCA had unfairly influenced the committee to fall in line with its wishes. When CBS and Zenith joined in the disapproval, the FCC found itself at an impasse. Hoping to encourage further testing, the FCC postponed its final decision.

The delay touched off a fresh round of clashes between RCA and its competitors. Zenith, in particular, concentrated its bile on Sarnoff personally, charging that his television crusade was premature for both economic and technical reasons. In a series of notices placed in trade journals, Sarnoff was pictured as a giant ape hunkered over the fallen form of the radio industry.

Once again, Sarnoff thrived under conditions of challenge. One of his engineers would recall that he was "never more alive" than when fighting to bring his television system out of the laboratory. Unlike during his earlier struggles in the "Radio Music Box" days, Sarnoff was no longer constrained by the agendas and sensitivities of superiors or the company's royalty partners. As a result, he came out swinging. All who opposed him, he told an attentive press, were "bloated parasites who feasted on the products of RCA research." These "scavengers" had done nothing to nurture television in its infancy, but now wished to reap the rewards of its maturation.

Ironically, one of the chief accusations against Sarnoff held that he was trying to rush television into production so that his standards would be accepted. In fact, he had been dragging his feet for years, and only now, under pressure from foreign competition, was he inclined to press ahead with actual production. Now that television had come to the point of commercial viability under his stewardship—at a cost of $20 million by 1938—he saw no reason to indulge his competitors.

In time, he would take much the same attitude toward the FCC. Seeking to sidestep the government's interference, Sarnoff made yet another bold prediction at the annual meeting of the Radio Manufacturers Association in October 1938. "Television in the home is now technically feasible," he declared. "The problems confronting this difficult and complicated art can only be solved from operating experience, actually serving the public in their homes." With that in mind, Sarnoff continued, he had no choice but to initiate complete television service. The commencement of RCA's television sales and programming would coincide with the opening of the New York World's Fair on April 20, 1939.

In other words, Sarnoff was telling the industry, RCA was no longer content to wait for the FCC to take action. RCA would move ahead with television production based on its preferred standards, and the rest of the industry could fall in line—or compete—as they wished. In the absence of government guidelines, Sarnoff himself would set the standard.

It was a typically bold and aggressive strategy, and fraught with ruinous potential. Sarnoff was gambling that RCA's resources and technological advantages would force the FCC to bend to his will. If, however, his display of hubris touched off a sufficient backlash, the FCC might well adopt a different set of standards, rendering any RCA apparatus obsolete.

Not unexpectedly, Philco and Zenith were quick to charge Sarnoff with an effort to "stampede" the communications industry, a charge he would readily acknowledge, but the FCC continued to sit on the fence, neither condoning nor condemning RCA's defiant plan. "Only Sarnoff could possibly have dared such a thing," said a Philco executive. "No one else had anything approaching that level of power, nor the willingness to risk it all so readily. But that's what made him Sarnoff." If his own board of directors felt any trepidation over Sarnoff's all-or-nothing campaign, they kept it quiet. Sarnoff's salary during this period rose to a staggering $100,000.

In Philadelphia, meanwhile, Farnsworth's men could barely keep themselves fed. "To eat, we'd go to the Italian market in South Philadelphia and buy a gunny sack of week-old bread for one dollar," recalled Bill Eddy. "Bread, and rabbits that I raised on our farm, constituted my family's menu. Still, there was no lack of enthusiasm. We were either naive or crazy. If morale dropped, Phil would get up on his platform and start spouting his ideas, and we were back in battery again."

Even so, finances were sufficiently precarious that Farnsworth could not ignore a second plea from Baird Television Ltd. in the fall of 1936. As the two-year competition with Marconi–EMI moved forward, Baird's engineers were having difficulty achieving an acceptable picture with their version of the image dissector. Baird's board of directors wanted Farnsworth himself to come and fine-tune the system.

The request came at an awkward time. Farnsworth did not want to leave his own operations unattended during a crucial stage of development, and he was in the midst of promising negotiations with both AT&T and CBS. At the same time, he admitted, he wasn't certain he felt up to making a long trip. He confessed to Pem that the long hours in the lab were grinding him down. To her dismay, his drinking grew worse.

In spite of poor health and concerns at the lab, Farnsworth could not afford to let Baird's request go unanswered—he stood to lose millions of dollars if Marconi–EMI triumphed over Baird. He and Pem decided to turn the trip into a working vacation, in celebration of their tenth wedding anniversary. Another son, Russell, had arrived the previous year, and though Pem felt a natural reluctance to leave him, the concern over her husband's health persuaded her to make the voyage. Farnsworth's mother was flown in to care for the children.

Typically, Farnsworth gave his wife only four days to prepare, leaving her flustered over the state of her clothing. Setting aside his money worries for the moment, Farnsworth sent her out to buy an entirely new wardrobe at Bonwit Teller, whose manager kept the store open late for her convenience. The Farnsworths were in high spirits as they sailed for England in October 1936; by the first night of the voyage, their anniversary celebrations had advanced to such a stage that they were mistaken for newlyweds. "We did not deny it," said Pem.

In London, Farnsworth was shocked to discover that Baird's engineers had undone nearly everything that he had accomplished two years earlier. Instead of embracing the all-electronic system, the Baird team had somehow orchestrated a cross-pollination of the Nipkow disk and the image dissector. Farnsworth spent long days at the Crystal Palace labs attempting to make the system competitive with Marconi–EMI.

At night Farnsworth was often too exhausted to stir from his hotel room, and Pem began to fear that London society would be denied a viewing of her new wardrobe. Happily, as the Baird lab shut down for the weekend, Farnsworth rallied for an evening of dancing at the Savoy, allowing Pem to model a "rather saucy and fetching" Spanish lace gown. "Phil was enchanted with it," Pem reported. Farnsworth had fitted himself out with a top hat and tails on his previous trip, and the results, according to Pem, were "very Fred Astaire-ish." Farnsworth seems to have found the dancing at the Savoy rather sedate compared to the lively steps to which he was accustomed in Philadelphia. "Suddenly," Pem recalled, "he broke into a fast doubletime step of his own creation." Pem kept pace as they danced in and out among the other, slower moving couples, pointedly ignoring the "down-the-nose" glances being cast their way. "We did have the grace to leave after that," Pem acknowledged.

In a matter of weeks Farnsworth had brought the Baird system to a competitive level, but the effort left him exhausted. Meanwhile, he received discouraging news from Philadelphia—Jesse McCargar had seized upon Farnsworth's absence to install Russell Pond, a former stockbroker, as a lab supervisor, prompting a revolt in the ranks. It was clear to Farnsworth that his relationship with McCargar had reached a crisis, but he did not feel well enough for a major confrontation.

Appointing Cliff Gardner as his proxy in the dispute with McCargar, Farnsworth left England for the French Riviera, hoping to recover his health. When a French doctor told him that he was near the point of physical collapse, Farnsworth agreed to a period of total rest. After two weeks, just as Pem felt that her husband was "looking better and eating well," he received grim news from London. A massive fire had destroyed the Crystal Palace, incinerating the Baird laboratories and all of the work Farnsworth had done on Baird's behalf. Over the objections of his doctor, Farnsworth returned to England to see what could be done. Sifting through the ruins of Baird's lab, he came upon the charred and melted remains of an image dissector. Baird, he realized, was officially out of the race. Two months later, the BBC adopted the Marconi–EMI system as the basis of the British television industry. Though Farnsworth's agreements with Baird were still in force, there would be no royalties forthcoming. The loss to his future finances would be incalculable.

As for Baird, he found himself in a situation that only Farnsworth would have truly understood. "In an amazingly short time," Baird wrote, "the Marconi publicity department had established in the public mind that Marconi invented television! Poor Marconi was dead and buried and when alive he never knew one end of a television apparatus from the other." It is regrettable that Baird was denied proper credit for his remarkable achievements. It is worth noting, however, that his own autobiography makes no mention of the name Philo T. Farnsworth.

With Baird sidelined, Farnsworth hoped that he might still derive royalties and recognition from other European television operations. Weighing up the social and political situation from Britain at the end of 1936, Farnsworth decided to focus his attentions on what he judged to be a promising new market: Germany. Through an alliance between Baird Television and Germany's Fernseh AG, Farnsworth had already established a strong foothold in the country. Earlier that year, Fernseh AG had helped to broadcast the Olympic Games from Berlin using Farnsworth equipment, in competition with the rival Telefunken, which was using a camera based on Zworykin's iconoscope.

Captain West, Baird's technical director, raised a strenuous objection, but Farnsworth had reason to believe he would be warmly welcomed in Germany. Dr. Paul Goerz, the director of Fernseh AG, had extended a warm invitation on an earlier visit to the Farnsworth lab in Philadelphia. More important, the German company's use of the image dissector entitled Farnsworth to collect royalties, which had been tied up in government channels. Farnsworth hoped that he might be able to free up some of the money owed to him if he applied in person.

The visit got off to an inauspicious start as Farnsworth's cash and traveler's checks were confiscated, and further difficulties arose as a pair of uniformed men who identified themselves as "courtesy drivers" insisted on serving as chaperons. In time, Dr. Goerz arranged to take charge of the Farnsworths, but there was no escaping the ominous political climate. The Farnsworths felt a growing sense of foreboding as they witnessed military parades featuring heavy artillery, columns of goose-stepping soldiers, and—on one occasion—Adolf Hitler himself.

Even at the Fernseh AG manufacturing plant the Farnsworths could not escape a sense of foreboding. One door, bearing a *Verboten* sign, had been left open, but as Dr. Goerz started to lead them inside, a guard stepped forward and blocked their path with a rifle. Nodding at Farnsworth, Goerz addressed the officer in German. After a moment, the party was allowed to pass. Farnsworth found himself inside a "secret lab" where his own image dissector was being produced.

Soon enough it became apparent that Farnsworth would not be permitted to take royalty payments out of Germany so long as the National Socialist Party was in power. Farnsworth resigned himself to going home empty-handed, and he made arrangements for a return passage. To his distress, he and Pem found that their exit visas had been canceled. Farnsworth applied for new visas, and when these, too, were canceled, Farnsworth threatened to take the matter to the American consulate.

Dr. Goerz managed to intervene. Through private contacts, their host made arrangements to get the Farnsworths aboard a train that would connect with a liner in Hamburg. Pem recalled being "smuggled" onto the train by a group of concerned friends, who then crowded into their compartment to give a champagne toast to the couple's safe departure.

Over the years there has been speculation to the effect that Hitler himself had taken an interest in the visit of the famous American scientist, perhaps with a view toward putting Farnsworth to work for the Nazi cause. Today there is no way of knowing why Farnsworth's exit visa might have been canceled, though he would not have been the only traveler inconvenienced by the German government in the 1930s. What is clear, however, is that the Farnsworths sincerely believed themselves to have had a narrow escape. "Not long after our return," Pem wrote, "Hitler began forcibly detaining visiting scientists." Dr. Goerz had presented Pem with a box of chocolates for the ocean crossing, and she had it signed by all present as a memento. Today, the wrapper is preserved among Farnsworth's papers at the University of Utah, with a notation from Pem reading: "We were celebrating the success of our escape from Hitler's men who had twice canceled our sailing arrangements."

Between the failure of Baird Television and the loss of the German royalties, Farnsworth's European trip had been a financial disaster. Worse, he arrived home to find the Philadelphia lab in a state of mutiny. McCargar's plan to have Russell Pond oversee the lab had created bitter feelings among the old hands. Matters deteriorated still further when McCargar dispatched his own son-in-law, George Sleeper, to shore up Pond's authority. Writing to Everson in New York, McCargar complained of insubordination from Arch Brolly and Frank Somers, two of Farnsworth's most trusted coworkers. "If Archie and Frank had our real interests at heart I think they would welcome any help they could get, even if it were from my son-in-law," McCargar insisted. "Either it is a petty, short-sighted professional jealousy, or it is a frantic cooperation with our competitors. This situation calls for a strong hand and very prompt action."

A few days later, McCargar renewed his complaints against the lab team in terms that appeared to border on paranoia. "They are pursuing a course that will wreck us unless we stop them. . . . Is it possible that some of the people in whom we have placed every confidence are working against us? Now do not dismiss that idea with 'oh, that isn't possible,' because *it is possible*."

As Farnsworth returned to the lab, McCargar insisted to Everson that he not be allowed to upset the work that Pond and Sleeper had been doing: "I hope you will keep this in mind constantly and keep Phil on the right track."

Farnsworth would not be kept on the right track. Upon arriving home in Philadelphia he immediately fired Pond and Sleeper and called McCargar in San Francisco to complain about his meddling. It proved to be the beginning of the showdown Farnsworth had been dreading. Four days later, McCargar arrived in Philadelphia and demanded that Farnsworth fire his entire lab team. When Farnsworth refused, McCargar exploded. "You're all fired!" he shouted, storming into the lab. "Pick up your stuff and leave!"

In the end, not even George Everson could smooth over the difficulty. Although Farnsworth assured his men that they would still have jobs as long as he had any say in the matter, many of his closest colleagues, including Tobe Rutherford and Arch Brolly, would not return to the lab, refusing to work under McCargar any longer. The episode was devastating to Farnsworth. He determined that one way or another he would find a way to free himself of McCargar.

In the meantime, Farnsworth had been pressing still harder for an experimental broadcasting studio—over McCargar's bitter objections—and Skee Turner, who was living with the Farnsworths in lieu of an actual salary, brokered a solution. As Farnsworth despaired over his lack of facilities one night during dinner, Turner blithely announced that he and his father had decided to shell out the money to build a station. "Don't worry about the expense," Turner insisted. "It will pay for itself."

Farnsworth did not have to be told twice. He began designing the building the following morning, and the foundation was laid two weeks later. By the end of 1936, experimental broadcasting station W3XPF took to the air from Mermaid Lane in the Philadelphia suburb of Wyndmoor.

As with the demonstration at the Franklin Institute in 1934, Farnsworth soon found himself struggling to fill airtime. The job of booking talent fell to Bill Eddy, who had some experience of staging shows from his navy days. "Puppet shows and ventriloquists were very popular," Pem recalled. "Our star was 'Little Smiles Blum,' a singing ten-year-old protégée, who earned the title of 'Little Miss Television.' "

While Farnsworth took advantage of the broadcasts to refine his equipment, his sister Laura plumbed the mysteries of television makeup and costume. At a time when television performers often appeared with black lipstick and blue face paint to achieve "normal" black-and-white values, it quickly became apparent that the image dissector had an aversion to the color red. This proved especially noticeable one afternoon when Eddy invited a pair of boxers to spar for the camera. One of the fighters was wearing vivid red trunks that appeared to melt away on the monitor, creating the impression of a nude boxing match. Farnsworth sent the fighter back to the dressing area to find something more telegenic.

As a result of the work at the station, Farnsworth continued to file a remarkable number of patent applications, with the total reaching twenty-two in 1936 alone. One of these applications, for the electron multiplier tube, drew a great deal of attention in the press. *Time* reported: "Mr. Farnsworth, who despite his flair for electronics has learned to talk like a tycoon, calls his new tube the multipactor."

"He is now just thirty years old," reported *Collier's* magazine, "and his fair hair, blue eyes and slender build make him seem even younger, although when one talks with him the maturity of his outlook often gives the impression that he is older."

By this time, Farnsworth had learned to use his media profile to get his message across to the competition. When a film crew arrived to interview him for a Paramount "Eyes and Ears of the World" short subject, Farnsworth made certain to follow his technical demonstration with something more accessible to the general public. In the reception area of the Wyndmoor studio, Pem and seven-year-old Philo were seen sitting before a Farnsworth television receiver. "Mother," asked young Philo, "may we see a television show?"

"Yes, Philo," Pem answered, "will you please turn it on?" The boy walked over and turned a knob; within seconds, a bright and clear picture appeared on the screen. Farnsworth had made his point—his television was so simple that a child could operate it.

At least one of Farnsworth's competitors was paying attention. In the early months of 1937, a contingent from AT&T's Bell Laboratories arrived in Philadelphia led by Dr. Herbert Ives, the man who had pioneered the historic Herbert Hoover broadcast ten years earlier. Hoping for a licensing deal, Farnsworth put his equipment through its paces. "I was proud of Phil," George Everson would write. "As always, he was modest in his presentation, but I could see that they were greatly impressed with the brilliance and originality of his conceptions."

When AT&T asked to inspect his patent portfolio, Farnsworth felt a natural hesitation. He had been entirely open with Zworykin and RCA, and now he found himself paying a heavy price in legal fees. The AT&T representatives, according to Everson, were "very fair in pointing out that such an inspection carried certain hazards," but after an initial hesitation Farnsworth decided that the potential reward was worth the risk. "You know," Everson declared as he handed over Farnsworth's portfolio of some 150 patents and applications, "approval of his work by the Bell Labs has been one of the dreams of his life."

Farnsworth waited anxiously for four months before AT&T

agreed to strike a deal. On July 22, 1937, Farnsworth traveled to New York and signed a contract allowing each party the full use of the other's patents, while maintaining the right to license to outside parties as well. Farnsworth freely admitted that it almost seemed too good to be true. The deal would bring him money, prestige, and recognition as an equal of one of the world's foremost research facilities. As he prepared to sign the document, the gravity of the moment caught up with him. "Phil finally broke down and confessed that he didn't know whether he would have a steady enough hand to sign his name," said Everson. In the end, Farnsworth fortified himself and was able to affix a "legible, though squiggly" signature to the agreement.

Across town at the RCA building, David Sarnoff was forced to sit up and take notice. As *Business Week* noted, the deal signaled that "the grip which the Radio Corporation of America was generally assumed to have on the future of television was relaxed." In some of the press coverage of the agreement, RCA was mentioned only as having an "alternative" to the Farnsworth system.

The Farnsworth team moved aggressively to capitalize on their new prominence. Throughout 1937, negotiations had been underway to reorganize the Farnsworth company, creating a new entity that would encompass not only research and broadcasting but also a potentially lucrative branch of equipment manufacturing. Under the guidance of Hugh Knowlton of Kuhn, Loeb and Company, a prominent New York banking concern, Farnsworth and Everson drew up a plan to launch the Farnsworth Television and Radio Corporation. Knowlton's firm not only structured the plan but arranged for financial backing in exchange for Farnsworth stock. To Everson, it seemed "a little better than having one's dreams come true." As he left one of his early meetings with Knowlton, he recalled, "I found it necessary to steady myself in the hallway by leaning against the wall."

Farnsworth, upon being assured that he would retain control of his patents, was enthusiastic. At last, he believed, he would have the power and resources to go head to head with RCA. "We will manufacture both receivers and transmitters," he wrote in a letter to his mother. "We will erect and operate television broadcasting stations. We will modify our licensing policy to provide the greatest use for all the radio industry. We will negotiate all the cross-licensing necessary to permit us to enter the entire radio and television field."

Best of all, as Farnsworth told his mother, Jesse McCargar would not be a part of it. "Phil was certain of one thing," Pem recalled, that "life was too short to put up with Jess McCargar any longer." As the dealings with Knowlton progressed, Farnsworth made it clear that he wanted McCargar fired outright, but Everson insisted that they make a token offer of a board position in the new company. McCargar would ultimately refuse, preferring to seek "fresh pastures."

With McCargar out of the picture, Farnsworth brought on Edwin A. Nicholas to head his new manufacturing division. Nicholas not only had extensive sales and engineering experience, he was also a vice president of RCA and would bring a useful experience of the company's methods. By hiring Nicholas away from its rival, the new Farnsworth company reinforced the message that it was ready to play rough.

Nicholas soon located a manufacturing facility that Farnsworth would be able to purchase outright—the Capehart Company, a phonograph producer with facilities in Fort Wayne, Indiana. To provide the necessary capital, Farnsworth Television and Radio planned to float $3 million worth of stock. Nicholas set to work to arrange the contracts and secure the permissions from the Securities and Exchange Commission.

The SEC, under fire as a result of recent abuses, withheld approval for several agonizing months, while Farnsworth's representatives dutifully sent a stream of lawyers and accountants to Washington. "The attitude seemed to be one of daring us to prove that we were not all a pack of dishonest rogues," said a dispirited Everson.

Adding to the pressures, a firm deadline had been established by the deal's underwriters. As the date approached, Pem recalled, "Phil and the rest of us were sweating it out in Philadelphia." At last, on the day before the deadline, a battery of lawyers, bankers, executives, and government officials gathered to ratify the deal. It seemed as though the long months of struggle would finally bear fruit when—at the last possible instant—it was discovered that a crucial promissory note had gone missing. This was the responsibility of a man named Allen G.

Messick, who was subsequently discovered to have gone to lunch. Don Lippincott, who watched in horror as the deal came to the brink of collapse, would later commemorate the afternoon in verse:

> *So here are ranks of men from banks*
> *And many secretaries*
> *And legal lights and parasites*
> *And fiscal functionaries*
> *But what's this pall that grips them all*
> *And stifles all this bunch:*
> *They're waiting for an IOU*
> *And by the Gods they need it, too*
> *And Messick has the IOU*
> *And Messick's gone to lunch.*

In the end, Messick was located and the deal concluded. Everson and Lippincott accepted a check for $3 million and proceeded to Fort Wayne to complete the purchase of the Capehart facility. Initially, the new corporation planned to generate revenue by producing radios, and by the summer of 1939, a complete range of Farnsworth home radio units was rolling off the assembly lines. At last, it appeared, Farnsworth would achieve what had been denied him at Philco—a stable source of revenue, an effective laboratory, and the esteem of the entire industry. In every respect, this appeared to be the culmination of the long journey that had begun in the hayfields of Idaho.

From the first, the new company moved to capitalize on the history and personal integrity of its founder. A "Farnsworth Radio Book of Facts," distributed to radio dealers in 1939, featured a large photograph of Farnsworth over the words "The Genius of Television." Farnsworth's "heroic struggle" to realize his dream was briefly detailed, along with an assurance that his name would soon take its place alongside those of Alexander Graham Bell and Guglielmo Marconi. "No great invention is ever wholly the story of one man," the account concluded, "but out of the story of television emerges the giant figure of Philo T. Farnsworth, guiding genius, lonely experimenter, scoffed-at dreamer—history already has a page reserved for this man who, convinced that mechanical principles were wrong, held fast to his theories and made television a practical reality—today's front-page scientific discovery."

Although it was not stated directly, Farnsworth's unblemished character was clearly meant to stand in contrast to certain other industry figures: "Farnsworth—television's greatest name—enters the radio industry with no past to live down. Its name is unsullied. . . . Farnsworth believes that in the values it offers, in its respected name, in its emphasis upon straightforward dealing lies the formula for your success as well as its own."

The strategy appeared to pay immediate dividends when a prominent biographer selected Farnsworth as one of "America's Top Ten Young Men" for 1939, along with Lou Gehrig, William Paley, and Spencer Tracy. Even Dale Carnegie weighed in with an enthusiastic rendering of the Farnsworth story: "Your life will be touched, and you will be a bit different, because of that farm boy," he concluded. "What an inspiration this farm boy is to every person young and old! His age today? Thirty-three!"

Even as his new company attempted to transform him into an icon of "story-book dreams," Farnsworth himself was absent from the scene. The previous year his health had taken another downturn, and the family had retreated to Maine in search of rest and isolation. George Everson had recommended a particular property—a two-hundred-year-old farmhouse on sixty acres of wooded land—and Farnsworth felt an instant affinity for the place. Hoping to fashion a private refuge for himself, he arranged to buy the house and the surrounding lands, and would spend several months on renovations. Not since the early days on Green Street had he thrown himself so wholeheartedly into physical labor, and soon he would be clearing land, repairing fences, and drawing up plans for a private laboratory in the Maine wilderness. "I can hardly tell you what acquiring this place in Maine means to us," Pem wrote to Everson. In Philadelphia, she insisted, her husband was often too nervous and upset to eat or sleep. In Maine, he allowed himself to forget about the patent interferences and the licensing deals that had plagued him for most of the decade. "He is no good to the lab the way he is," she concluded. "So we are making tracks for Maine."

While Farnsworth recovered his health, Zworykin and his research team were working flat out to prepare for RCA's promised unveiling of commercial television at the 1939 World's Fair. Farnsworth had every intention of competing directly with RCA at the fair and had even told reporters that "two trucks equipped with television cameras would be in use" as the ceremonies got underway. Had he found a way to make good on the promise, the remainder of Farnsworth's life might have played out quite differently. For all his vision, however, Farnsworth could not possibly have foreseen the enormous impact that the fair would have on the American public's awareness of television. It was to be, as the *Washington Post* observed, the "long-awaited debut of the television art." As the fair opened in April 1939, however, the Farnsworth Television and Radio Corporation was nowhere to be seen. The long delays with the SEC had not left Farnsworth enough time to prepare.

David Sarnoff, however, was very much in evidence. Though the Federal Communications Commission had not yet adopted a set of television standards or allocated broadcast frequencies, Sarnoff pressed ahead with his ambitious plan to launch commercial television service. His reasoning remained clear—if RCA set the pace, the rest of the industry, as well as the government, would have no choice but to fall in step.

"The World's Fair in New York is to differ from most World Fairs in being a forward-looking display," wrote the sixty-nine-year-old writer and futurist H. G. Wells in the pages of the *New York Times*. "Its keynotes are not history and glory but practical anticipation and hope. It is to present the World of Tomorrow. It is arranged not indeed as the visible rendering of a utopian dream—there is to be nothing dreamlike about it—but to assemble before us what can be done with human life today and what we shall almost certainly be able to do with it, if we think fit, in the near future. It is, to go back to the original meaning of the word, a prospectus, the prospectus of tomorrow. It is a promotion show."

This was certainly the case on April 20, 1939—ten days before the fair was to be officially opened by President Franklin D. Roosevelt—at the dedication ceremonies for RCA's Exhibition Hall. Inside, an array of television receiving units in ornate wooden cabinets stood ready to greet an eager public. The largest, with a price tag of $1,000, featured a seven-by-ten-inch picture screen, visible by means of a special angled mirror in the cabinet's lid.

As roughly one hundred invited guests gathered in front of kinescopes at the RCA Building, an iconoscope camera transmitted a strikingly clear sweep of images from the site of the fair in Flushing, Queens. "As the camera moved down the 'Avenue of Patriots,' " wrote Orrin Dunlap in the *New York Times,* "spectators in New York eight miles away saw the perisphere and trylon and other landmarks of the fair. They saw hundreds of workmen lined up along the curb at lunch hour watching the radio camera men at work. A bugle blew and the Stars and Stripes was seen to climb the mast opening the dedicatory ceremonies. Every detail was distinct, even the fleecy texture of the clouds."

After a word of introduction from Lenox Lohr, the president of NBC, David Sarnoff stepped to a podium draped with an RCA banner, with two NBC microphones positioned on either side to capture his remarks. "Now," Sarnoff declared, "we add radio sight to sound. It is with a feeling of humbleness that I come to this moment of announcing the birth in this country of a new art so important in its implications that it is bound to affect all society. It is an art which shines like a torch of hope in a troubled world. It is a creative force which we must learn to utilize for the benefit of all mankind.

"This miracle of engineering skill, which one day will bring the world to the home, also brings a new American industry to serve man's material welfare. In less than two decades, sound broadcasting provided new work for hundreds of thousands of men and women, added work in mines and forests and factories for thousands more, and aided the country and its citizens economically by causing the flow of hundreds of millions of dollars annually. Television bids fair to follow in its youthful parent's footsteps and to inherit its vigor and initiative. When it does it will become an important factor in American economic life."

As he intended, Sarnoff's remarks would come to be regarded as television's commencement address. "Today we are on the eve of launching a new industry based on imagination, on scientific research and accomplishment," he had declared. "Ten days from now, this will be an accomplished fact."

It was a sentiment strongly echoed in Orrin Dunlap's account of the fair's official opening the following week. "Today the curtain goes up," wrote Dunlap. "And so by sunset tonight television will have come from around the corner in quest of its destiny; to find its role in the art of amusing Americans, and to fit in with the social life of the land."

It was to be Sarnoff's finest moment, courtesy of Vladimir Zworykin and his iconoscope.

/ / /

Meanwhile, Philo T. Farnsworth was sliding toward a nervous breakdown.

Thirteen

The Lawyer Wept

My candle burns at both ends;
It will not last the night;
But, ah, my foes, and, oh, my friends—
It gives a lovely light.

          —Edna St. Vincent Millay

          (Farnsworth's favorite poem)

"Pem, I just can't go on like this," Farnsworth told his wife as television threatened to slip from his grasp. "It's come to the point of choosing whether I want to be a drunk or go crazy."

In the end, he chose the former. Throughout 1939, while Sarnoff consolidated RCA's dominance of the industry, Farnsworth did his best to mold the new Farnsworth Television and Radio Corporation into a viable competitor. He moved his family to Fort Wayne and applied himself to his laboratory work with his usual diligence. It seemed to him, however, that the fates were allied with Sarnoff. The Federal Communications Commission showed no inclination to hurry a decision on television standards. In the absence of a government sanction, only Sarnoff had the resources and the nerve to move ahead with actual television production—and for the moment, Sarnoff had yet to reach an agreement with Farnsworth. At one stage, Farnsworth was shown an RCA document listing each of his patents and its date of expiration. "All they have to do is hold commercial television off until

Identified only as "Dr. X," Farnsworth answers questions on the quiz show I've Got a Secret *in 1957.* BETTMANN/CORBIS

my patents expire," Farnsworth said, "and we will not collect a single royalty check."

Worse, Farnsworth had realized for some time that the growing crisis in Europe would likely knock several years off the useful life of his patents. If America entered the conflict, the television industry would be put on hold for the duration, effectively gutting the value of his portfolio.

In Fort Wayne, the sale of Farnsworth radios had placed the company on firm financial footing, but the working climate left Farnsworth feeling isolated. He no longer headed a small, intimate group of devoted engineers; instead he sat and listened as younger men sought to impress him with their own ideas for the future. The changing role left Farnsworth feeling that he had gone from boy genius to doddering has-been. For the sake of his colleagues, he attempted to put a brave face on his feelings. "This is a young man's game," he declared, "and we find that the enthusiasm of these young men more than overbalances their lack of years of experience. I do not mean to give the impression that youth is a substitute for ability, but I do believe that it constitutes a very important factor when coupled with aptitude."

At thirty-three, however, Farnsworth did not feel quite ready for the scrap heap. Even as television appeared to be leaving him behind, he found he could not let go of his inventive drive. "I guess I've trained my brain too well," he told Pem. "Now I have a hard time turning it off. I think I'm going crazy."

Pem insisted that he get medical advice, but this seems to have made matters worse. One doctor told him that a "finger-habit" might soothe his nerves, with the result that Farnsworth took up heavy smoking. At the same time, his drinking grew heavier—"not only in the evening," said Pem, "but all day long."

By now, the effects of Farnsworth's relentless work schedule and poor sleeping habits could be read plainly on his face. His once-boyish features were lined and mottled, and stomach troubles had left him pale and gaunt. As his drinking grew worse, Pem issued an ultimatum: she would leave him, she said, unless he gave the doctors another chance.

Farnsworth agreed, only to spiral into addiction when his new doctor prescribed chloral hydrate as a sedative. Enervated by the drug, Farnsworth took to his bed and refused to eat. Pem kept an agonized vigil as her husband began to waste away.

There was worse to come. Writing about her husband's mental collapse years later, Pem would find it difficult to address the matter directly. Instead, she described finding her youngest son sitting fearful and rigid in his bed one morning, unable to move for fear of crushing a pet mouse hiding beneath his pillow. "Like the mouse," she wrote, "Phil had found a haven from his tortured mind in his medication." In truth, Farnsworth's condition more closely resembled that of his terror-stricken son—anxious, discomposed, and unable to move. Farnsworth's sister Laura would be more blunt: "Phil had a nervous breakdown."

Arrangements were made to place Farnsworth under observation at a hospital in Boston. His weight had dropped to a skeletal 105 pounds, leaving him so frail that he had to be carried from his sickbed.

The recovery would be slow and painful. After several weeks in Boston, Farnsworth shook his addiction to chloral hydrate and retreated to the house in Maine under the care of a male nurse. To Pem, it seemed that her husband would never be the same. "Phil's dream," she said, "the quest that had occupied him for almost twenty years, had burst like a bubble."

Sadly, it was only now, with Farnsworth ill and broken, that Sarnoff began to give ground. Farnsworth's name was now cropping up in Sarnoff's public pronouncements, as it had at the Waldorf gala in 1936. Speaking before the Senate on the matter of television standards, Sarnoff made an unprecedented acknowledgment of his rival's contributions. "It is only fair that I should mention," Sarnoff declared, "an American inventor who I think has contributed, outside RCA itself, more to television than anybody else in the United States, and that is Mr. Farnsworth, of the Farnsworth television system."

Sarnoff had good reason to extend an olive branch. Although his broadcasts from the World's Fair had made use of a Zworykin iconoscope, it was clear that the next generation of camera tubes would combine elements of the Zworykin apparatus with the image dissector. With Sarnoff readying for mass production, he would finally have to come to terms with Farnsworth. "There's nothing here we'll need," Sarnoff had said of the work at Green Street. Now, after nearly ten years of legal contention, Sarnoff would have to admit that he had been wrong.

It would prove to be a bitter pill. Sarnoff's entire career had been built on the acquisition of patents, and never before in its twenty-year history had RCA ever paid a royalty—not even to Howard Armstrong, one of Sarnoff's closest friends. It was as Sarnoff had repeatedly said: "The Radio Corporation does not pay royalties, we collect them." Sarnoff had tried everything he could to outmaneuver his smaller and supposedly weaker rival—buyout offers, legal challenges, patent avoidance, and smear campaigns. In each case, Farnsworth had demonstrated an astonishing resilience, clinging to his image dissector as though, as he often suggested, it were his own child. Now, with the future of RCA dependent on his plan for commercial manufacturing, Sarnoff had run out of options. He ordered Otto Schairer, his vice president in charge of patents, to hammer out an agreement with the Farnsworth team.

If Jesse McCargar had remained at the head of Farnsworth's company, it is likely that the negotiations would have been resolved quickly, as McCargar had long dreamed of selling out to RCA. Farnsworth's new team, headed by Edwin Nicholas, was in no hurry. Nicholas, who had previously been an RCA executive, did not share McCargar's sense of awe. More important, he had a fairly realistic sense of what he could demand from his former employer. "At first, the two sides seemed so far apart that it looked utterly hopeless," wrote George Everson. "Only the clear underlying fact that neither company could get along without the other kept the discussions alive."

Negotiations began in May 1939, just days after the launch of the World's Fair, and continued through September. Amid much hard-nosed bargaining, the outlines of an agreement began to emerge: RCA would pay $1 million to the Farnsworth Radio and Television Corporation over a ten-year period, on top of licensing payments for the right to use Farnsworth's patents. At long last, RCA would pay a royalty.

After a last-minute flurry of revisions, a final contract was ready. On October 2, Otto Schairer led the Farnsworth team into the conference room of the RCA Building to close the deal. As he watched Nicholas sign the document, he felt keenly aware of the importance of the moment. For Schairer, there was more at stake than royalties. Schairer had been instrumental in bringing Zworykin to Westinghouse in 1923 and had been present two years later when Zworykin demonstrated his first crude scanning device. Next to Sarnoff himself, there was no one at RCA with a more personal investment in RCA's television program. As Nicholas pushed the contract across the conference table, Schairer was overwhelmed by a devastating sense of loss. Bending down to sign, the lawyer's eyes filled with tears.

As the historic agreement was made public, none of the original Farnsworth partners was at hand. Leslie Gorrell had long ago sold off his shares and withdrawn from the television scene. George Everson was tending to business in San Francisco. Farnsworth himself was sequestered in Maine, struggling to recover his health. "Though we were not all together to celebrate the success," Everson recalled, "each knew that the others rejoiced in the victory that had firmly established the Farnsworth inventions as vital patents in the field of television." Regrettably, Farnsworth was in no frame of mind to take pleasure in his moment of triumph.

Sarnoff, too, appeared to be somewhat distanced from the agreement. The accord with Farnsworth had come just as the rest of the industry was calling for his head. RCA, continuing its show of flagrant disregard for the FCC, had now launched a regular NBC broadcasting schedule. Although it was not a commercial service, Sarnoff believed it would be sufficient to establish NBC as the industry leader. At the same time, RCA television sets were available in New York stores at prices ranging from $395 to more than $1,000.

Still, though the broadcasting era had officially begun in America, the *New York Times* noted that there seemed to be "no rush on the part of New Yorkers" to join in. Sarnoff had anticipated that RCA might sell as many as forty thousand sets in the first year of production, but after three months, fewer than a thousand had actually been purchased. Sarnoff cut prices, but the public remained wary. In part, the imminent threat of war had made consumers more cautious than usual. However, the industry war had also taken its toll. Both Philco and Zenith were stressing that television was still in the experimental phase, and that RCA's receiving units might well become obsolete if the FCC adopted a different set of broadcasting standards. In the trade press, there were rumblings that RCA had jumped the gun, and television itself, according to a headline in *Radio Daily*, had become "Sarnoff's Folly."

As the battle over standards escalated, Sarnoff found himself subject to accusations that his drive for personal power was threatening the future of American business itself. "I've had plenty of cats and dogs thrown at me," he would say in later years, "but never like that. Philco and Zenith were more interested in getting me than in creating a television industry."

The FCC began public hearings on the matter of television standards in January 1940. Early on, it was announced that limited commercial service would be authorized later that year, although the standards remained to be finalized. Sarnoff, desperate to spark sales, seized on this slender advance to announce an enhanced broadcast schedule, along with a fresh wave of 25,000 television sets at reduced prices.

The FCC responded angrily, with its chairman, James Fly, accusing big business of "bullying the little fellows." The commercial authorization was formally suspended, and the familiar accusations of monopolistic practices were leveled against RCA. Publicly, Sarnoff dismissed this as little better than a "mildewed red herring," but the threat was clearly real. The production line in Camden was temporarily halted.

President Roosevelt himself attempted to mediate, suggesting that Fly and Sarnoff sit down together over lunch and iron out their differences. Sarnoff declined. "Our dispute is in the head," he told the president, "not the stomach." The mood in the press suddenly shifted, and the government was now seen to be standing in the way of progress. The FCC action was denounced as high-handed and punitive, with one editorialist railing against the "bureaucratic blackout of television." Seizing upon the change of tone, Sarnoff cannily pointed out that television—once approved by the FCC—promised to create half a million new jobs.

The dispute got a public airing during Senate hearings in Washington in April 1940, with Fly accusing Sarnoff of orchestrating a "blitzkrieg" to push the RCA standards through. Sarnoff countered that "substantial progress in the art can only come after its introduction on a commercial basis." When the hearings brought no resolution, the conflict was shunted back to the FCC. Under growing pressure to reach a solution, the FCC appointed a National Television System Committee, composed of engineers selected by the Radio Manufacturers Association. This group was charged with reaching a final consensus of standards, subject to approval by the FCC.

In the end, the NTSC recommended a system that closely accorded to the RCA and Farnsworth standards, and the plan would eventually be adopted by the FCC as the new foundation of American television. Sarnoff trumpeted this perceived victory in the press, and within weeks NBC aired its first paid commercial, which featured a Bulova watch face ticking off several seconds of television airtime. For this, the Bulova Watch Company paid NBC $4.

Though Sarnoff had scored another triumph, by this time it was clear that a more serious campaign was set to begin. "By the summer of '41," he would recall, "I was convinced we could not avoid war, and I knew RCA would be in the thick of it." When news of the attack on Pearl Harbor reached him on December 7, Sarnoff dispatched a telegram to the White House: "All our facilities are ready and at your instant service. We await your commands."

In Maine, Farnsworth was no longer in the thick of it. He knew full well that the coming of war would likely mark the end of his career in television. The manufacturing facility in Fort Wayne would now divert its resources to the war effort. By the time the conflict ended, Farnsworth realized, his crucial early patents were likely to be nearing expiration.

Strangely, the realization briefly reinvigorated him. As his health stabilized, Farnsworth began looking to the future. If television had left him behind, he reasoned, he would have to find a new scientific frontier to conquer. First, with Cliff Gardner's help, he would design his own private lab.

With revived enthusiasm, Farnsworth planned a series of improvements to the property in Maine, selling off thousands of shares of stock to finance the work. To avoid drawing attention to the transactions, he instructed his sixty-one-year-old mother to make the sales for him, excitedly telling her of his plan to create an estate worth "a hundred thousand dollars," without a penny's worth of debt. Energized by this fresh round of activity, Farnsworth decided to ride out the war in Maine.

Sarnoff, by contrast, was determined to see action. He rapidly converted RCA's facilities to defense production and spent time in Washington as a special assistant to the chief signal officer, overseeing the transfer of communications equipment to the front lines. As his sons entered the service and his wife, Lizette, volunteered with the Red Cross, Sarnoff found time to appear at bond rallies, once sharing a microphone with Bob Hope as he urged fellow Americans to do their bit.

For Sarnoff, it would not be enough. Since 1924, he had been an officer in the Signal Corps reserve, and occasionally he devoted weekends to technical seminars. With America at war, he longed for the opportunity to get into the action overseas, as he had failed to do during the Great War. The chance came in the spring of 1944. Sarnoff was ordered to active service—as a full colonel, owing to his reserve activities—and instructed to proceed to Europe on the first available military air transport. With no advance knowledge of his assignment, Sarnoff arrived in London in March 1944 to find that his services had been requested by General Dwight D. Eisenhower himself.

At a private meeting with Eisenhower, Sarnoff was given the task of coordinating the complex communications systems that would be involved in the Allied invasion of Europe. His title would be special assistant for communications to the supreme commander, and his first assignment would be the preparation of a broadcasting station powerful enough to reach all of the Allied forces under Eisenhower's command. At the same time, he was to devise a plan to coordinate all communications between headquarters and the invasion forces, as well as the distribution of information to the international press corps. All of this had to be ready by D-Day—June 6, 1944.

It was a job uniquely suited to Sarnoff's talents. He had the technical knowledge to see what needed to be done and the executive skills to make it happen. Sarnoff's lifelong habit of cultivating the men in power served him well; at one stage, when he encountered resistance from Britain's minister of information, he made a direct appeal to Winston Churchill.

Decades earlier, during the *Titanic* crisis, Sarnoff had claimed that he stayed at his post for seventy-two hours to be certain that every message had been properly relayed. Now, as the Allied invasion began, Sarnoff spent three days overseeing operations at London's Ministry of Information, in battle dress and with a pistol on his hip, ensuring that all went according to plan. The first news flash reached him at 7:31 a.m., and within one minute he had sent the official bulletin around the world. Now, as the RCA publicity department had said of his younger self, the world "hung on his every word."

Sarnoff's duties continued well beyond the initial phases of the campaign. Within weeks, he had been dispatched to North Africa and Rome to advise on communications matters. Soon after the liberation of France, he followed the American forces into Paris—arriving, he later boasted, a full day ahead of Charles de Gaulle—to oversee the restoration of the war-ravaged French communications network. By the time Sarnoff returned to New York at the end of 1944, his services had drawn a letter of commendation to the Allied high command from Eisenhower himself.

As Sarnoff resumed his duties at the helm of RCA, he received word from Washington of his promotion to brigadier general. Thereafter he would be known throughout the company and across the industry simply as "the General." Along with his new rank, Sarnoff would proudly wear miniatures of two of the medals he had been awarded for his service overseas—one to note the U.S. Army's Legion of Merit and the other signifying his election as a Commander of the French Legion of Honor.

As he settled back into Rockefeller Center, the General returned quickly to business. "Gentlemen," he told his top executives, "the RCA has one priority: television. Whatever resources are needed will be provided. This time we're going to get the job done. There's a vast market out there, and we're going to capture it before anyone else."

Sarnoff had never lost sight of his television goals through the conflict, and even found time to discuss the new medium with both Eisenhower and Churchill. Now, as RCA prepared for the postwar era, Sarnoff unveiled a point-by-point plan to convert improved wartime electronics into a stepped-up television production plan. Less than two years later, while most of his competitors were still retooling their wartime machinery, RCA's 630-TS television sets rolled off the production line in Camden. The set, soon to be known as the Model T of television, featured a ten-inch screen and retailed at $385. This time, "Sarnoff's Folly" found its audience. In its first year, the set sold ten thousand units. The following year, the number rose to 200,000. Sarnoff's commitment to the electronic television program, stretching back to the day in 1929 when Vladimir Zworykin first appeared in his office, to date had cost the company nearly $50 million. Now, as he told his board members, it was time to reap the rewards.

In Fort Wayne, the Farnsworth Television and Radio Corporation was determined to get its share. Though Farnsworth himself had taken a leave of absence, the company had pressed ahead without him. "It has given me a great deal of pleasure," Farnsworth wrote to Edwin Nicholas in 1944, "and I have watched with pride not unmixed with envy, what you have all been accomplishing in the war effort, and in laying the foundation for postwar activity in television. Please accept my sincere congratulations."

The company had distinguished itself during the conflict by helping to produce critical elements for sniper scopes and guided missile systems, earning the Army-Navy Production Award. The patriotic stance was reflected in an aggressive advertising campaign in national magazines. In one notable image, a cartoon likeness of Hitler was flattened by a large hammer, which bore the words "It's Organizations Like Farnsworth that is giving the Ax to the Axis."

Like RCA, however, the company managed to look ahead to postwar prosperity. As early as 1942, the Farnsworth Television and Radio Corporation offered the homefront a glimpse of coming wonders. "Ever look through a blank wall?" ran an advertising headline that appeared in *Life, Time, The New Yorker, Newsweek,* and several other national magazines. "It's really not as fantastic as it sounds. For *television* is ready to lead you into a realm of magic and surprise . . . to let you see through walls and over mountains, around corners and across plains.

"We cannot describe these instruments to you," the ad continued. "But it would do your heart good to see them, and the almost incredible things many of them accomplish. And you can rest assured that no enemy country has equipment so fine or so far-reaching as that supplied to our fighting men by the American electronics industry. We are glad to be able to tell you that progress in television is still going on, hand-in-hand with vital war production. You cannot have this marvelous new television until peace once more is ours. But your purchase of War Bonds *now* will speed that day of Victory! And when tomorrow comes, Farnsworth Television will be ready to bring the pageant of history, the splendor of art, the flourish and romance of life, *in bright parade daily through your home!*"

Unfortunately, the bright parade appeared to have left Farnsworth himself watching from the sidelines. As he continued to struggle with his health in Maine, Farnsworth offered repeated assurances that he expected to be "back on my feet" in a matter of months. In fact, it would be several years before he rejoined the company in Fort Wayne. Colleagues sent him plaintive notes asking for assistance, but Farnsworth's replies were sporadic. "No," he told one Farnsworth executive, "I haven't died. Quite the contrary, I've been as busy as a bird dog. Whenever I get so busy my correspondence goes to pot."

Even George Everson had difficulty getting through to him. "Don't you think it is about time that you answered at least one of the many letters I have written you?" Everson asked at one stage. "You know," he chided after another long silence, "writing is a matter of habit and becomes easier with practice." In 1943, when Farnsworth Television and Radio shares were admitted to trading on the floor of the New York Stock Exchange, Everson sent a beseeching note: "Our baby is really of age now and can fend for itself. How are you getting on? Take time out and write to me."

At least part of Farnsworth's reticence had to do with feelings of mortification over his continuing health problems. "My illness has been very embarrassing to me," he admitted to Edwin Nicholas in 1944. "My health has been slowly but steadily improving during the last year and a half. At times, though, I have almost felt that my patience would give out first." When he felt well enough, Farnsworth began work in the lab he had built for himself on his property, though much of his time during the war years went to organizing Farnsworth Wood Products, with the goal of aiding the war effort with "boxes for bullets." Together with his brothers Carl and Lincoln, Farnsworth purchased three thousand acres of forest near his property and constructed a sawmill and shop to fulfill government contracts for ammunition cases.

By 1945 it became clear that the Farnsworth Television and Radio Corporation would have difficulty making the adjustment to peacetime manufacturing. The company had overextended its resources in military production, and the transition to television manufacturing was now creating an enormous debt. As the company drifted into serious financial trouble, the board grew impatient with Farnsworth's withdrawal from Fort Wayne. In an effort to force him either to return or resign his position, the company challenged his involvement in Farnsworth Wood Products as a conflict of interest. Furious, Farnsworth sent a heated response. "I feel very strongly that if you really believed that this work constituted a breach of my contract with you, you should and would have advised me of the fact when you first became aware of it. That you should raise the question at this late date implies strongly that you are merely seeking an excuse to void a contract which is unsatisfactory to you for other reasons."

In the resulting uproar, Farnsworth resigned as vice president of the company, but remained as a consultant at a greatly reduced salary. Farnsworth now had to sell off more stock to fund his operations in Maine, and Cliff Gardner, who had been working in the Maine lab, would be forced to seek employment elsewhere. The departure of Gardner, who had been at Farnsworth's side since their street-sweeping days in Salt Lake City, was devastating to Farnsworth. He sank into a painful depression, and began drinking heavily again.

Soon Farnsworth was back in the hospital, with Pem cooking steaks at his bedside over an electric broiler in a desperate effort to get him to eat. When a subsequent hernia operation left him dependent on painkillers, Farnsworth made a drastic bid to regain control of his health. Checking himself into the Baldpate Sanatorium in Massachusetts, Farnsworth submitted to an aggressive course of treatment that included shock therapy. The man who had spent his life learning to control electrons now lay strapped to a table with electrodes wired to his head while doctors sent charges of 150 volts through his brain. The experience left Farnsworth weakened and the family shaken.

As his health slowly returned, Farnsworth suffered another blow. His brother Carl, who had taken an active role in the Farnsworth lumber business, was killed while piloting a private plane. Farnsworth's grief was compounded by feelings of guilt; he blamed himself for bringing his brother to Maine and encouraging his interest in flying.

Still reeling, Farnsworth suffered a second tragedy when a massive forest fire destroyed his property in Maine, two days before a scheduled meeting to raise his insurance coverage. At a stroke, the retreat into which he had poured his energy and resources was gone, along with his laboratory, his treasured science books, and most of the family's possessions.

In his mind, much of the misfortune he had suffered could be traced directly to television, and for a time Farnsworth resolved to put everything associated with television behind him. "For a while," Pem would tell an interviewer, "he wouldn't even allow the word 'television' to be used in our home. When the *Encyclopedia Americana* asked him to do the article on television, he just threw the letter in the wastebasket." A letter from Hugo Gernsback, the editor of the magazines that had fired his scientific curiosity as a boy, seemed to underscore Farnsworth's disenchantment. Gernsback was soliciting a statement of tribute to celebrate the anniversary of what he called "perhaps the greatest invention of modern history"—Lee de Forest's audion radio tube.

Soon, however, an offer from Farnsworth Television and Radio in Fort Wayne appeared to offer a way forward. In December 1947, Farnsworth attended his first board meeting in six years, and was greeted as a returning hero. Feeling a rekindled sense of obligation to the company's employees and stockholders, Farnsworth agreed to return as vice president and director of research, in an attempt to bring the company back to a competitive level. Along with his duties in the lab, Farnsworth was also given a role as the public face of the company. He made appearances at dealers' meetings across the country, and company promotional materials once again emphasized "the inspiring leadership of Philo T. Farnsworth." Farnsworth would confide to Pem that such displays made him feel uncomfortably like "a show fish in an aquarium."

Apparently Farnsworth's return to Fort Wayne brought at least a temporary boost to his vitality. In September 1948, just weeks after the wedding of his eldest son, Farnsworth accompanied Pem to a Fort Wayne hospital for the birth of another son, Kent Morgan Farnsworth. At age forty-two, Farnsworth delighted in having a new baby in the house.

By 1949, it had become clear that he could do little to shore up the losses at Farnsworth Television and Radio. As the company fell deeper into debt, the International Telephone and Telegraph company launched a takeover bid. In April 1949, Farnsworth sent a melancholy letter to his company's shareholders: "Most of you know that my entire working life has been devoted to the development of electronic television, the last 11 years with this company which bears my name. None of you can be more deeply concerned than I have been by the bitter facts which our company has had to face. I write to you now as a Farnsworth stockholder holding over 10,000 shares, which I am voting in favor of the IT&T plan."

Asked to comment, Jesse McCargar could not resist twisting the knife: "It missed the boat. It booted the best chances in the industry." *Newsweek* attempted a more positive spin: "Nonetheless, the name Farnsworth will still appear on the company's sets, and the genius of Farnsworth will continue to light up every cathode-ray tube."

Farnsworth remained as vice president in charge of research, and he was the only management officer retained by IT&T. The new company was relaunched as the Capehart-Farnsworth Corporation, capitalizing on Farnsworth's name recognition as well as that of Homer Capehart, whose phonograph manufacturing facilities had been bought out by Farnsworth ten years earlier. The new company got off to a promising start with television orders in excess of $3 million, but it proved unable to sustain long-term competition with RCA and the other manufacturing powerhouses. As the company's television program sputtered, Farnsworth's role was diminished. Though he would be associated with IT&T for many years, Farnsworth would eventually become little more than a contract engineer, with the company offering only scant acknowledgment of his contributions as a television pioneer. At one stage, IT&T would even refuse to pay his disability benefits.

In March 1954, Farnsworth began to complain of severe stomach pain, and early one morning he was taken by ambulance to a hospital. When Pem arrived, after arranging care for her children, she learned that her husband had been diagnosed with a perforated ulcer. The doctor blandly notified her that two-thirds of Farnsworth's stomach had been removed. Once again, Farnsworth entered a slow and difficult period of recovery, and he emerged in more fragile health than ever before.

Though Farnsworth no longer had a leading role in the television industry, it was not unusual for reporters to seek his opinion on the progress of the new medium. In 1957, a Fort Wayne newspaper reported that Farnsworth's feelings were much like those of any other father of an eight-year-old son—he thought there were "too darned many cowboy movies on at the dinner hour." Later that year, after refusing two prior invitations, Farnsworth traveled to New York to appear on the quiz show *I've Got a Secret*. Identified as "Dr. X," Farns-

worth looked composed and comfortable in his only national television appearance, and responded in good humor as celebrity panelists
Jayne Meadows and Bill Cullen failed to guess the secret that had been
displayed to the studio audience: "I invented electronic television."
When Cullen asked if the secret might involve some machine that
could be painful when used, Farnsworth's response drew a huge laugh:
"Yes," he said with a grin, "sometimes it's most painful." As time ran
out, Farnsworth walked away with his prize for stumping the panel—
$80 and a carton of Winston cigarettes. "We'd all be out of work if it
weren't for you," declared host Garry Moore.

Instead, it was Farnsworth himself who appeared to be out of
work. As his patent portfolio dwindled with each passing year, his
name began its slow fade from the television scene. Vladimir
Zworykin, meanwhile, found himself thrust into the national spotlight
by an enthusiastic RCA publicity department, which lost no opportunity to promote Zworykin as the "father of television" and Sarnoff as
the "clear-sighted and steadfast godfather." Upon Zworykin's retirement in 1954 a seminar was held in his honor at Princeton University,
where Sarnoff repeated the story of their fateful meeting and the initial
budget estimate of $100,000. "Look at Zworykin, how he deceived
me," Sarnoff cried. "Before we got a dollar back from television, we
spent fifty million dollars!"

Through all the honors and fame of his later years, Zworykin appears to have had an understated and occasionally ambivalent view of
his achievements. "I hate what they've done to my child," he told one
interviewer. "I would never let my own children watch it."

It was not a sentiment likely to be echoed by Sarnoff. Though
Zworykin had withdrawn from television, Sarnoff would continue
to dominate the new medium and its industry for years to come. As
he reached retirement age in 1956, Sarnoff declined to relinquish
power. There were still battles to fight, he told his board of directors,
not least of which was the ongoing contest for control of television's
latest advancement—color technology. At age sixty-five Sarnoff signed
a ten-year contract as RCA's CEO, at a salary of $200,000. The occa-
sion was celebrated with a banquet at the Waldorf-Astoria, where

Sarnoff looked back fifty years to his beginnings in radio. "Teddy Roosevelt was president then," he recalled. "Horsecars plied the streets of New York. You could get a schooner of beer for a nickel, and a free lunch at the bar. Gaslight was used in most homes. The horseless carriage was a novelty. Radio broadcasting was unheard and television was unseen. I was only fifteen years old and life for me was a blank page—challenging and a bit frightening in its clean white emptiness. Well, I have done a good deal of scrawling over it in half a century. I'd gladly make some erasures and edit out errors if I could. Yet on the whole I am content. For they have been endlessly fascinating years for me and for the world of science, business, and industry where fate has placed me."

While Sarnoff looked back over a prosperous career, Farnsworth resolved to look ahead. More and more, as he worked to regain his health, Farnsworth found his thoughts returning to the electron. The creation of atomic weapons had appalled him, and he determined to spend his declining years finding a peaceful application for nuclear energy. The idea had been on his mind since his days in Philadelphia, when he observed a "minute, bright, starlike glow" in one of his multipactor tubes. Although he did not pursue it at the time, the "very puzzling" phenomenon never left his mind, and he would eventually conclude that the reaction he had observed held the secret to a "low cost nuclear fusion process." As he turned his full attention to the matter, Farnsworth came to believe that he could bring safe, economical nuclear power to the American home.

Throughout the 1960s, Farnsworth often spoke to the press about "grapefruit-sized power packs" capable of producing more electrical energy than the Grand Coulee Dam. The potential of this new energy, he insisted, would be limitless. It would allow for weather control devices capable of "untwisting" tornadoes, and electronic force fields that would protect American cities from enemy attack. New York City, he insisted, could be heated for thirty cents a month. "This may sound a little like science fiction," he wrote in 1962, "but we will be using this process in this decade." Farnsworth seized on every possible opportunity to expound on his ideas. Even an address to a local Art

League was broadened to include a discussion of the "new fourth dimension" and the prospects for travel to Alpha Centauri.

If the members of the Art League found themselves baffled, there were others willing to listen seriously to Farnsworth's proposals. With limited funding from IT&T, Farnsworth began work on a preliminary apparatus, with the Atomic Energy Commission keeping tabs on his progress. "ITT Hopeful on Experiments to Harness the H-Bomb's Power," declared the *New York Times,* and even Albert Einstein found time for a lengthy telephone conversation with Farnsworth to address various aspects of the fusion process.

To this day, there are some within the scientific community who believe that Farnsworth's theories were sound, and a few who contend that he actually achieved a controlled fusion reaction in his early experiments. To others, his fusion work is taken as evidence of a fine mind gone to ruin, the last misguided obsession of a forgotten genius. Little is certain except that Farnsworth believed this to be the most important work of his lifetime. When IT&T cut off funding, he took a second mortgage on his home and cashed in his life insurance policy to raise funds to continue his work.

In the end, when he found himself stonewalled in his efforts to obtain a patent, Farnsworth lost the will to continue. "I've given you all the material you need," he told a patent attorney, "now I'm going to go home and get drunk."

Leaving the attorney's office, Farnsworth stopped to pick up two cases of beer and went home intent on drinking it as fast as humanly possible. He was tired of fighting, he told Pem; now he simply wanted to die.

Farnsworth appeared serious in this resolve. When the two cases of beer were gone, he ordered four more from a neighborhood liquor store. Pem did her best for him—even trying to coax a scholarly treatise on nuclear fusion out of him one page at a time—but Farnsworth continued to decline. "It was torture to see him gradually waste away," said Pem. "His doctors had said unless I could instill in him some will to live, there was nothing they could do."

The will to live arrived in the form of a granddaughter, the child of his son Philo, who arrived for a visit just as Farnsworth reached his lowest point. At the sight of the three-month-old baby, Pem insisted, Farnsworth visibly pulled back from the brink. "At that moment," she declared, "Phil decided life was worth living after all."

By now, Farnsworth had come to accept that he himself would not be making the trip to Alpha Centauri, but on July 20, 1969, he and Pem set aside their distaste for television viewing long enough to watch astronauts Neil Armstrong and Buzz Aldrin prepare for their walk on the moon. As Armstrong emerged from the lunar module and made his way down the access ladder, Farnsworth leaned forward for a better view of the television screen. A friend, watching with them, mused aloud over the incredible scene playing out on television screens across the world: "I just can't understand how we can get a television picture to earth all the way from the moon."

"I can tell you the reason the picture is as good as it is," Farnsworth offered. "They're using a miniature version of my image dissector tube."

Pem, her eyes glued to the screen, offered a word intended as clarification. "Phil's image dissectors still give the best detail to the picture because of their direct scan operation," she said matter-of-factly.

Farnsworth did not appear to have heard. He kept his eyes trained on the screen as Neil Armstrong's foot touched the lunar surface. Leaning back in his chair, Farnsworth gave a heavy sigh. "Pem," he said, "this has made it all worthwhile."

In January 1971, Farnsworth fell ill with pneumonia. He refused hospitalization, insisting that he would never come out alive. He died on March 11, 1971, at the age of sixty-four, having left an epitaph which reads: "He loved his fellow man."

His obituaries were respectful, if understated, with more than one newspaper describing him as an important figure in the "pioneering days of radio." By contrast, the death of David Sarnoff later that year at the age of seventy-nine made headlines around the world.

Farnsworth was often asked, "What will television be like in the future?" His answer was characteristic of the life he had lived: "What do you want television in the future to be like? If you can imagine something, sooner or later we may be able to achieve it; and conversely, unless we can at least imagine it there can be no hope of it becoming a reality.

"Well then," he asked, "what do we want?"

Bibliography

Abramson, Albert. *Electronic Motion Pictures: A History of the Television Camera.* Berkeley: University of California Press,1955.

———. *The History of Television, 1880 to 1941.* Jefferson, N.C.: McFarland, 1987.

———. *Zworykin: Pioneer of Television.* Chicago: University of Illinois Press, 1995.

Barnouw, Erik. *The Golden Web: A History of Broadcasting in the United States, 1933–1953.* New York: Oxford University Press, 1968.

———. *A Tower in Babel: A History of Broadcasting in the United States to 1933.* New York: Oxford University Press, 1966.

———. *Tube of Plenty: The Evolution of American Television.* New York: Oxford University Press, 1975.

Bilby, Kenneth. *The General: David Sarnoff and the Rise of the Communications Industry.* New York: Harper & Row, 1986.

Binns, Joseph J. *Those Inventive Americans.* Washington, D.C.: National Geographic Society, 1971.

Dreher, Carl. *Sarnoff: An American Success.* New York: Quadrangle/New York Times Book Co., 1977.

Dunlap, Jr., Orrin E. *The Future of Television.* New York: Harper & Brothers, 1942.

———. *The Outlook for Television.* New York: Harper & Brothers, 1932.

Eckhardt, George. *Electronic Television.* New York: Arno Press (reprint), 1974.

Eddy, William C. *Television: The Eyes of Tomorrow.* New York: Prentice-Hall, 1945.

Everson, George. *The Story of Television: The Life of Philo T. Farnsworth.* New York: W. W. Norton, 1949.

Farnsworth, Elma G. *Distant Vision: Romance and Discovery on the Invisible Frontier.* Salt Lake City: Pemberly Kent Publishers, 1989.

Fisher, David E., and Marshall Jon Fisher. *Tube: The Invention of Television.* Washington, D.C.: Counterpoint, 1996.

Head, Sydney W., and Christopher H. Sterling. *Broadcasting in America: A Survey of Electronic Media.* Boston: Houghton Mifflin, 1990.

Hubbell, Richard W. *Four Thousand Years of Television.* New York: G. P. Putnam's Sons, 1942.

Inglis, Andrew F. *Behind the Tube: A History of Broadcasting Technology and Business.* Boston: Focal Press, 1990.

Kempner, Stanley. *Television Encyclopedia.* New York: Fairchild, 1948.

Kisseloff, Jeff. *The Box: An Oral History of Television.* New York: Penguin, 1995.

Lessing, Lawrence. *Man of High Fidelity: Edwin Howard Armstrong.* Philadelphia: Lippincott, 1956.

Lewis, Tom. *Empire of the Air.* New York: HarperCollins, 1991.

Lyons, Eugene. *David Sarnoff: A Biography.* New York: Harper & Row, 1966.

McArthur, Tom, and Peter Waddell. *The Secret Life of John Logie Baird.* London: Century Hutchinson, 1986.

Morgan, Jane. *Electronics in the West: The First Fifty Years.* Palo Alto, Calif.: National Press Books, 1967.

Ritchie, Michael. *Please Stand By: A Prehistory of Television.* New York: Overlook Press, 1994.

Ross, Gordon. *Television Jubilee: The Story of Twenty-five Years of BBC Television.* London: W. H. Allen, 1961.

Sarnoff, David. *Looking Ahead: The Papers of David Sarnoff.* New York: McGraw-Hill, 1968.

Shiers, George, with May Shiers. *Bibliography of the History of Electronics.* Metuchen, N.J.: Scarecrow, 1972.

Sterling, Christopher H., and John M. Kittross. *Stay Tuned: A Concise History of American Broadcasting.* Belmont, Calif.: Wadsworth, 1990.

Tiltman, Ronald F. *Baird of Television.* New York: Arno Press (reprint), 1974.

Udelson, Joseph H. *The Great Television Race: A History of the American Television Industry, 1925–1941.* University: University of Alabama Press, 1982.

Waldrop, Frank, and Joseph Borkin. *Television: A Struggle for Power.* New York: William Morrow, 1938.

JOURNALS, MAGAZINES, AND NEWSPAPERS CONSULTED

All About Television, Amazing Stories, Arizona Republic, Broadcasting, Business Week, Collier's, Coronet, The Electrical Experimenter, Fort Wayne Journal-Gazette, Fort Wayne News-Sentinel, Hollywood Reporter, The Journal of Broadcasting, Journalism History, Literary Digest, Manchester Guardian, Modern Electrics, Modern Mechanix, Newsweek, New York Times, New York World, The New Yorker, Philadelphia Inquirer, Philadelphia Record, Popular Mechanics, Popular Radio, Popular Science, Radio-Craft, Radio News, Salt Lake City Tribune, San Francisco Chronicle, San Francisco Examiner, Science and Invention, Scientific American, Screenland, Technical World, Television, Television News, Television Quarterly, Time, Times (London), Video Eighties, Washington Post, Wireless World and Radio Review.

Acknowledgments

The author wishes to acknowledge the generous assistance of the following people and institutions: Toby Linden, Sonny Wareham, Professor Donald Godfrey of Arizona State University, Marilyn Wurzburger and the staff of the Special Collections Department of the Arizona State University Libraries, Elizabeth Rogers and the staff of the Special Collections Department of the University of Utah, the Broadcast Pioneers Library of American Broadcasting at the University of Maryland, the Sarnoff Corporation and the David Sarnoff Library, the Library of Congress, the British Library, the National Archives, the Electrical Collections of the National Museum of American History, the Jefferson County Historical Society, Farnsworth TV and Pioneer Museum, the Museum of Television and Radio of New York City, Jack Berman, Charles Conrad of Broadway Books, and Donald Maass of the Donald Maass Literary Agency.

Index

A

advertising, 37, 46, 89, 119, 178, 246
  in magazines, 12, 18, 44, 76, 250–51
Alexanderson, Ernst, 41, 68–71, 82,
    122–25, 128–29, 135, 165–68,
    182, 214
  commercial savvy of, 123–25
  Farnsworth system as viewed by,
    165–66
  Jenkins compared with, 125
Alexanderson alternator, 41, 68–69
All About Television, xviii, 125
Alpine, N.J., transmitting station in, 8
Amazing Stories, xiv, 125
American Institute of Electrical
    Engineers, 70
American Marconi Company, 3, 31,
    34–42, 159
  John Wanamaker station of, 35–37,
    172
  World War I and, 38, 39–40
American Telephone and Telegraph
    Company (AT&T), 40, 42, 70,
    125, 156, 169, 182, 225
  Farnsworth's deal with, 231–32

Hoover broadcast and, 116–19,
    121
  RCA's competition with, 119–22,
    131
antitrust actions, 81, 169–71, 172,
    182
Appleton, Victor, 92
Armstrong, Edwin Howard, 2–9, 14,
    17–18, 182, 243
  FM radio and, 5–9, 125–26
Armstrong, Neil, 258
Atomic Energy Commission, 257
audion tube, 18, 20, 28, 109, 134,
    251
automobiles, 22, 51, 53, 59, 85

B

"Back to Methuselah" (Shaw), xvii
Baird, John Logie, xvi–xvii, 55, 62–68,
    69, 95, 127–28, 143
  Alexanderson compared with, 70–71
  demonstrations of, 65, 68, 127
  Farnsworth's dealings with, 201–203,
    204–205
Baird's Speedy Cleanser, 64

Baird Television Ltd., 202–208, 218, 224–27, 228
Baird Undersock, 63
Baldpate Sanatorium, 251, 252
Barkin, Joseph, 186
Barthélemy, René, xvi
Baruch, Bernard, 172
Batchelor, John, 161
Belin, Édouard, 19, 23, 129–30, 154, 155, 161
Belin tube, 129–30
Bell, Alexander Graham, xvii, 15, 16, 234
Bell Telephone Laboratories, 117
Belmar, N.J., transmitting station at, 3, 4, 9
Bishop, Roy, 104, 105, 138–40, 151
"black box" transmitter, 5, 29
Blue Network, 121
Branly, Édouard, 29
Braun, Karl Ferdinand, 28, 83
Brigham Young University, 44, 47, 48, 49, 51, 108
British Broadcasting Corporation (BBC), xvii, 202, 203
Brolly, Arch, 203, 229
Brown, Maxine, 126
Buker, Lola, see Gardner, Lola Buker
Bulova Watch Company, 246

C

Camden, N.J., RCA manufacturing and research facility in, 131, 156, 158, 160, 165, 166–67, 170, 190–92, 201, 218
Campbell Swinton, A. A., 20, 23, 67, 87, 128
Capehart, Homer, 254
Capehart Company, 233, 234
Capehart-Farnsworth Corporation, 254
Carnegie, Dale, 235

Carpentier, Georges, 76, 78–79
Cartlidge, Harry, 93, 110
cartoons, 190
cathode rays, 14, 20, 23, 24, 107
cathode-ray tube, 83, 86, 87, 129–30, 155, 161, 165
Chevallier, Pierre, 130
Christensen, Carl, 111–12, 141
Churchill, Winston, 248
Collingswood, N.J., mechanical-electronic systems competition in, 167
Columbia Broadcasting System (CBS), 126, 192, 222, 225
Commercial Cable Company, 33
Compton, Betty, 127
Coolidge, Calvin, 119
Crocker, William H., 138–39, 142
Crocker, Willie, 142
Crocker First National Bank, 103, 148
Crocker group, 104–105, 135, 138–48, 174, 178–79, 187
    Philco agreement and, 187
    RCA overtures of, 161, 164
    Zworykin's visit and, 161, 162, 163
Crocker Research Laboratories, 106, 108
Cullen, Bill, 255
Cummings, Bill, 107, 111

D

Daniels, Josephus, 40–41
Davis, Harry, 88–89
Dean, Louis, 123
de Forest, Lee, xviii, xx, 2, 4, 14, 38, 134, 150, 175–76
    audion tube of, 18, 20, 28, 109, 134, 253
De Forest Radio Company, 126
Dempsey, Jack, 76, 78–79, 143

Depression, Great, 169, 173, 181, 193, 209
   stock-market collapse and, 159, 160, 161, 166, 168–69, 172
DuMont, 222
DuMont, Allen, 173
Dunlap, Orrin, 154, 237, 238
   Alexanderson demonstrations and, 122, 123, 124, 128–29
   AT&T demonstration and, 116–17, 118

E

Eddy, Bill, 209, 224, 230
Edison, Thomas, xx, 4, 15, 16, 66, 182, 209
Edison Kinetoscope, 59
Edison Vitascope, 59
Edward, Prince of England, 30
Einstein, Albert, 14, 68, 257
Eisenhower, Dwight D., 247–48, 249
Electrical Experimenter, xv, 17, 18, 19, 20, 29
electrical telescopy, 83–84
Electric and Music Industries, Ltd. (EMI), 202, 205–206
electricity, 14, 16, 19, 25, 26, 60
electromagnetic waves, 15, 35, 46
electron multiplier (multipactor), 148, 199, 230, 256
electrons, 20, 24, 25, 46, 71, 129, 192, 256
electrostatic focusing, 130, 155, 166
Empire State Building, RCA facility on, 5, 6, 192–93, 217–18, 219
Essing, Sanford, 191
Everson, George, 52–56, 71–73, 93, 95–98, 100–105, 143, 146, 162, 166, 175, 177–78, 179, 188, 199, 203, 208, 229, 231–35
   AT&T deal and, 231

Crocker group and, 105, 111, 135, 138, 142, 145, 148
Farnsworth-McCargar conflicts and, 198, 207–208, 229–30, 233
Farnsworth's correspondence with, 110, 116, 135, 180, 186–87, 193–94, 250–51
Farnsworth Television and Radio Corporation and, 232–33
image dissector trials and, 113, 135–39
RCA-Farnsworth agreement and, 243, 244
Sarnoff's visit and, 179–81
TV research fund-raising efforts of, 103

F

Fagan, James, 103, 105, 135, 138–39
Fairbanks, Douglas, 143, 150, 199
Faraday, Michael, 28
Farnsworth, Agnes, 45, 51, 208
Farnsworth, Carl, 251, 252
Farnsworth, Elma Gardner (Pem), 49, 50–52, 92, 97, 105–108, 110, 141, 144, 179–80, 194–99, 201, 231, 240, 241, 253, 257–58
   on Baird deal, 204–205, 207
   Bridal Veil date of, 44–45, 179
   cooking of, 94, 252
   European travels of, 225–29
   health concerns of, 145–46, 194, 235, 241, 242, 252, 254, 257
   as husband's co-worker, 93, 107, 109, 112, 127, 136, 149
   at image dissector trials, 117, 138, 139
   marital problems of, 195–97
   marriage of, 73–74
   pregnancies and childbirths of, 149, 225, 253
   Washington trip and, 176, 177

on Zworykin visit, 164

Farnsworth, Kenneth Gardner, 150, 179, 189, 194–96, 197, 199

Farnsworth, Kent Morgan, 253

Farnsworth, Laura, 149, 230, 242

Farnsworth, Lewis, 15, 17, 22, 44, 47, 112
death of, 49, 195, 212

Farnsworth, Lincoln, 164, 201, 209, 251

Farnsworth, Philo Taylor, II, xvi, 12, 14, 45, 70, 90–113, 134–56, 177–91, 193–201, 222, 224–36, 238–44, 249–59
appearance of, 104, 179, 189, 225, 231
AT&T deal of, 231–32
automobile anti-theft contest and, 22
boyhood ambition of, 15–16
Bridal Veil date of, 44–45
budget worries of, 108, 142, 144, 145, 187, 194, 207
child welfare concerns of, 199
clipping service used by, 127, 154–55
communication problems of, 110, 250–51
Crocker group and, 103–105, 111, 135, 138–41, 145, 149, 178–79
death of, 258–59
drinking of, 206, 208, 225, 240, 241–42, 252, 257
drug addiction of, 242, 252
engagement of, 52
European trips of, 204–207, 225–29
Everson-Gorrell partnership with, 72–73, 93, 95–97, 101, 110–11, 113, 148–49
experimental broadcasting studio ambition of, 175, 188, 190, 207, 229–31
health problems and exhaustion of, 225, 226, 235–36, 241–42, 244, 251, 252, 258
at image dissector trial, 111
journal entries of, 112–13, 135, 148, 162–63
lawsuits of, 179, 182, 187, 209–17
Mann's adversarial relationship with, 141, 146
marital problems of, 195–97
marriage of, 73–74
medical research of, 199
motion picture film experiments of, 142–43
name change of, 49
at Naval Academy, 49
nervous breakdown of, 238–42
odd jobs of, 46, 52
patent concerns of, 47, 49, 71–72, 95, 101–103, 108, 109, 135, 139, 143, 146, 155, 162, 164, 174, 180, 181, 188, 197, 203, 207–17, 230, 231, 232, 240–41, 244, 246, 256–57
personal tragedies of, 194–96, 197, 252
at Philco, 187–191, 193–98, 207, 221, 234
at Rigby High, 12–14, 22–26, 215
Sarnoff compared with, 121, 181, 258
Sarnoff's buyout offer and, 180–86, 198, 208–9
scientific and technical magazine reading of, xx, 17–21, 22, 51, 58, 60, 67
stock sold by, 194, 201, 203, 207, 247, 252
Television Laboratories and, 148, 161, 178, 181–83
TV research of, xx, 18–21, 23, 48, 54–56, 68, 70–74, 92–116, 134–55, 161–68

wave band requirements and, 147,
    175, 177–78
work schedule of, 110, 196,
    241–42
World War II and, 241, 246,
    249–50
W3XE and, 190–91
Zworykin compared with, 129–30,
    155, 156, 161, 162, 181
Farnsworth, Philo Taylor, III, 150,
    179, 190, 195–97, 231, 242, 253,
    258
Farnsworth, Russell, 225, 242
Farnsworth, Serena, 15, 44, 48, 49,
    73–74, 105–8, 149, 225, 247
"Farnsworth Radio Book of Facts,"
    234
Farnsworth Television and Radio
    Corporation, 232–36, 240–41,
    246, 247, 249–54
    IT&T's takeover of, 253–54
    stock of, 232, 247, 251, 252, 253
Farnsworth Television Incorporated,
    198–201
    AT&T deal of, 231–32
    Baird's deals with, 201–7, 224–25
    financial problems of, 207–8, 209,
        217, 224–25
    lab conflicts at, 226, 228–29
    patent litigation of, 208–17
Farnsworth television system, 148
    breakdown of, 150–51
    demonstration of, 111–13, 116,
        136–40, 150–51, 200–1
    publicity about, 143–45, 148, 150,
        178, 186–87, 199, 201, 230–31,
        232
    see also image dissector; oscillite tubes
Farnsworth Wood Products, 251,
    252
Federal Communications Commission
    (FCC), xviii, 222–24, 236, 240,
    244–46

Federal Radio Commission, 147,
    175–77, 222
Federal Trade Commission, 120
Fernseh AG, 227–28
Fessenden, Reginald Aubrey, 4–5, 18,
    38
Fleming, John Ambrose, 28
France, 129–30, 154, 161, 226, 248
Franklin Institute, 200–1, 230
frequency modulation (FM), 5–9, 218

G

Gamble, John, 128
Gardner, Cliff, 50, 51, 53, 54, 106–7,
    110, 146, 198, 203, 226, 252
    glassblowing of, 98–100, 107, 136,
        163, 189
    Grimditch's confrontation with, 189
    at image dissector trials, 112–13,
        137–39
    Zworykin's visit and, 163, 164–65
Gardner, Elma, see Farnsworth, Elma
    Gardner
Gardner, Lola Buker, 146
Gardner, Verona, 51
General Electric (GE), 41–42, 68, 69,
    70, 77, 78, 82, 121, 128, 159,
    167–71
    antitrust actions and, 169–71
    Bishop's negotiations with, 140–41
    Farnsworth's demonstration for,
        139–40
    first regular TV broadcasting of,
        123–24
Germany, 157–58, 227–29
Gernsback, Hugo, xiv–xvii, xx, 17, 18,
    20–21, 61, 125, 252–53
Gifford, Walter, 120, 180
glassblowing, scientific, 98–100, 107,
    136, 163, 189
GM Radio Corporation, 169
Goerz, Paul, 227–28

Goldsmith, Alfred, 77, 171
Gorrell, Leslie, 52–56, 93, 95–97, 100–3, 105, 110–11, 113, 148–49, 244
Great Britain, 30, 201–7, 225–27, 247–48
  TV research in, 62, 64–67, 201–5, 218
  U.S. competition with, 41–42, 218
Green Street lab, 105–13, 134–52
  Crocker group's visit to, 138–41
  description of, 106–7
  disassembling of, 188
  fire at, 146–47
  Holland's visit to, 187
  Philco agreement and, 187–88
  Pickford-Fairbanks visit to, 150–51
  radio control unit sideline of, 145
  reconstruction of, 146–47
  Sarnoff's visit to, 174, 179–85, 186, 243
  Zworykin's visit to, 151, 152, 161–66, 173–74, 180, 210
Greer, Sir Harry, 205–6
Griffen, R. S., 39
Grimditch, William, 189

H

Hamilton, Sir William, 102
Hanna, R. J., 138–39
Harbord, James B., xix
Harding, Warren G., 21, 60
Henry, Joseph, 28
Hertz, Heinrich, 28, 29
Hitler, Adolf, 157, 227, 228, 250
Holland, Walter, 187
Hollywood, Calif., 93–94, 105–6, 150–51
Holweck, Fernand, 130
Honn, Harlan, 104–5
Hoover, Herbert, 116–19, 121, 231

"How I Telegraph Pictures," 19
Humphries, Robert, 111, 112

I

Iams, Harley, 161
iconoscope, xx, 25, 166–67, 191–93, 209, 219, 237, 243
image dissector, 98–105, 119–113, 144, 161, 181, 199, 243, 258
  Baird Television and, 202–3, 224–25, 226–27
  Farnsworth's problems with, 95, 97–99, 109–10, 141–43
  in Germany, 227–28
  patent litigation and, 209, 210, 215–16
  RCA verification tests and, 165–66
  tests and demonstrations of, 100–1, 112–13, 135–40, 199
  Zworykin's duplicates of, 164–67
  Zworykin's experiments with, 166–67, 180, 190–91
image-scanning, xvii, xix, 23, 25–26, 87, 92, 94, 148
  Zworykin's views on, 163, 165, 210
Institute of Radio Engineers, 7, 122, 155
International Telephone and Telegraph Company (IT&T), 178, 180, 253–54, 257
"I've Got a Secret" (TV show), 254
Ives, Herbert, 117, 177, 231

J

Jazz Singer, The (movie), 130
Jenkins, Charles Francis, 58–62, 65, 68, 70, 94, 135, 143
  Alexanderson's dismissal of, 69

stock market crash and, 166
TV broadcasting of, 61–62, 126
Jenkins Laboratories, 60, 61, 125,
    161
Jenkins Television Corporation, 126,
    166
J. P. Morgan & Co., 158
Justice Department, U.S., 80, 168–69,
    171, 172, 174, 182

K

Karloff, Boris, 97
KDKA (radio station), 15, 77
Keener, Hazel, 97
Keith-Albee-Orpheum theaters, 131
Kennedy, Joseph P., 131
kinescope, 155–56, 161, 166, 167, 181,
    193
Kintner, Samuel, 86, 88, 89, 130
Knouse, Joe, 190
Knowlton, Hugh, 232, 233
Kreisler, Fritz, 45, 50

L

Langevin, Paul, 84
Lippincott, Donald, 146, 176, 177,
    211, 212–16, 234
Lodge, Oliver, 29
Lyon, Leonard, 101
Lyon, Richard, 101–02
Lyon and Lyon, 101, 109

M

McCargar, Jesse, 103, 105, 135, 148,
    161, 178, 187, 207, 208, 219–21,
    243, 253
  Farnsworth's conflicts with, 175,
    197, 198–99, 207–8, 209, 226,
    229–30, 233

Farnsworth's correspondence with,
    175, 176
  patent litigation and, 208
magnetic focussing coils, 111, 129–30,
    136, 166
Mann, Albert, 141, 146, 151, 163
Manners, J. Hartley, 124
Marconi, Guglielmo, 4, 5, 28–31, 34,
    38, 77, 78, 150, 159–60, 172, 182,
    226, 234
Marconi–EMI, Ltd., 203, 205–6, 218,
    224, 225
Marconi Wireless Telegraph Company,
    Ltd., 30–31, 41, 42, 65, 77, 84,
    203
May, Joseph, xvi
Meadows, Jayne, 255
Messick, Allen G., 233–34
Metcalf, Herbert, 107–111
mica, silver-covered, 191
Mihaly, Dionys von, xvi
Millay, Edna St. Vincent, 240
mirrored scanning drum, 122, 125,
    165
Mitchell, William, 169
Modern Electrics, xv
Morgan, J. P., 157–58
Mormons, 15, 49, 107, 110
motion picture film experiments,
    142–44
movie projectors, 59, 142
movies, movie industry, 167
  "persistence of vision" and, 94
  talking, 130, 145
  television's competition with, 150
multipactor (electron multiplier), 148,
    199, 230, 256

N

Nally, Edward, 38, 41, 42, 79
National Broadcasting Company

(NBC), 119, 121, 160, 169, 237,
244, 246
new headquarters for, 171
National Radio Institute, 46, 134
National Television System Committee
(NTSC), 246
Nature, 19
Navy, U.S., xvii, 38, 39–41, 49, 60, 78
Nazi party, 157, 227–28
New Brunswick, N.J., Marconi
installation at, 40, 41
Newsweek, 250, 254
New York *American*, 36
New York *Daily News*, 128
New Yorker, 126, 250
New York *Herald*, 33, 36
New York Herald Tribune, 126
New York Times, 36, 154, 156, 172,
181, 218, 236, 244, 257
TV demonstrations covered by, 62,
67, 116–17, 118, 122, 123, 124,
128–29, 155, 201, 237
New York World, 127
New York World's Fair (1939), 223,
236–38, 242, 243
Nicholas, Edwin A., 233, 243, 249,
251
Nipkow, Paul, xvii, xix, 58
Nipkow disks, xix, 23, 24, 58–59, 65,
67, 68, 117, 122, 131, 145, 167,
202, 225
Northwestern University, 126
nuclear energy, 256, 258

O

Ochs, Adolph, 158
Ogloblinsky, Gregory, 130, 161, 219
oscillite tubes, 135–39, 144, 147–48,
155, 161, 165, 180, 201

P

Paley, William, xviii, 173, 192, 234
Paramount, 231
Paris mission (1929), 157–58
Passaic *Herald*, xix
Patent Office, U.S., 86, 109, 162,
216–17
patents:
disputes over, 8, 60, 163, 209–17,
221
of Essing, 191
Farnsworth's concerns about, 47, 49,
71–73, 95, 101–3, 108–9, 135,
139, 143, 146–47, 155, 162, 164,
174, 181, 182, 188, 197, 203,
207–17, 231, 232, 238, 240–41,
243–44, 246, 256–57
interferences and, 162, 174
of Jenkins, 58, 59, 69, 166
RCA's control of, 8, 42, 69, 70, 78,
79–81, 119–20, 165–66, 168–70,
181–82, 197–98, 203, 208–11
of Rosing, 83
Westinghouse's filing of, 154,
155–56
of Zworykin, 86, 87, 162, 166, 192,
209–11, 216–17
Pennsylvania, University of, 191,
199
Perkins, Thomas, 157
"persistence of vision," 94
Phantoscope, 59, 60
Philadelphia Storage Battery Company
(Philco), 178, 187–91, 193–99,
207, 221, 222, 234, 245
RCA vs., 187, 188, 190, 197–98,
221–22, 224
phonograph, 66, 131, 173, 254
photoelectric chemicals, 87, 94–95, 98,
99, 107, 136
selenium, xvi, xix, 24, 95
storage principle and, 166, 191

photographs, 111
    radio transmission of, 60, 61, 69–70,
        129
    telegraphing of, 19, 23
"photophone," xvii
Pickford, Mary, 143, 150, 199
Pond, Russell, 226, 253
"Possibilities of Television with Wire
        and Wireless, The" (Campbell
        Swinton), 86–87
potassium, 99, 146
Preece, Sir William, 30
Princeton University, 255

Q

Queen's Messenger, The (Manners), 124,
    128

R

radio, radio waves, xix, 2–9, 14, 18,
        50–51
    background static and, 5
    dials for, 46, 47, 49
    frequency modulation (FM), 5–9,
        217
    government control of, 40–41
    Marconi's experimentation with,
        28–31
    RCA operations and, 2–6, 76–82,
        118–22, 123, 157, 160, 193, 217,
        220–21
    TV signals transmitted by, 19, 23, 24
    in World War I, 40
radio alternator, 41, 68
Radio City, 171–72, 219
Radio-Craft, 12, 30, 44, 76, 117, 122
Radio Keith Orpheum (RKO), 131,
    167
Radiola, 77, 82, 119, 132, 157
Radio Manufacturers Association, 222,
    223, 246

"Radio Music Box" memo, 37, 40, 77,
    80
Radio News, 18, 50, 51, 61, 67, 68,
    118, 121, 125
Radiovision, 60–61
"Radiovisor," 125
Radio World's Fair (1929), 126
RCA (Radio Corporation of America),
    xvi, xviii, xx, 2–9, 76–81, 109,
    141, 167, 216–24, 231, 232
    advertisements of, 18
    Alexanderson's work at, 68–71, 82,
        122–23, 165–69, 182
    Annual Report of (1930), 168, 175
    antitrust actions and, 81, 168–70,
        172, 175, 182
    AT&T's competition with, 119–22,
        130
    board of directors of, 79, 130, 159,
        160, 170, 224, 255
    Crocker group overtures to, 161,
        163
    EMI and, 202, 203
    Farnsworth's agreement with,
        242–44
    formation of, 41–42, 68
    gala of July 7, 1936, 219–21
    Jenkins Television absorbed by,
        167
    new headquarters of, 171–72
    Paris mission of, 157–58
    patents controlled by, 8, 42, 69, 70,
        78, 79–80, 119, 166, 168–69,
        181–82, 197–98, 203, 208–11
    Philco vs., 187, 188, 190, 197–98,
        221–22, 224
    press campaign against Farnsworth
        by, 186–7
    publicity department of, 35–36, 186,
        255
    radio operations of, 2–6, 77–82,
        118–21, 123, 156, 160, 193, 217,
        220

size problem of, 80–81
stock of, 4, 6, 42, 119, 159, 160
TV commitment made by, 5–6,
    81–82, 118, 121–25, 130–32,
    156–57, 160–69, 172–74, 180–86,
    190–93, 217–24, 236–40, 243–45,
    248–49, 255
Victor purchase of, 131, 158, 160,
    169
World's Fair and, 223, 236–38,
    242
Zworykin's report and, 165
RCA Building, 171–72, 237, 244
Red Network, 121
Rickard, Tex, 76
Rigby High School, 12–14, 22–26,
    215
Robertson, Andrew, 159
Robertson, Guy (Mephy), 62
Rockefeller, Nelson, 31
Rockefeller Center, 171
Rockefeller family, 171
Roosevelt, Franklin D., 41, 170, 237,
    245
Rosing, Boris, xvi, 83–86, 87, 94
royalties, royalty partners, 42, 72, 80,
    82, 87, 89, 158, 159, 164, 182,
    188, 241
  Baird Television and, 205, 206
  German, 227–28
  RCA-Farnsworth agreement and,
    242, 243–44
Russian Wireless Telegraph and
    Telephone Company, 84
Rutherford, Robert (Tobe), 141, 145,
    198, 203, 229

S

Sanabria, Ulysis, 126
San Francisco Chronicle, 144, 199
Sarnoff, Abraham, 32–34
Sarnoff, David, xvi, xx, 3–9, 26,
    31–40, 76–82, 118–23, 154,
    156–60, 242–49
  Alexanderson's correspondence with,
    167–68
  Alexanderson system as viewed by,
    82, 122, 123, 129, 167–68
  at American Marconi, 3, 30–31,
    34–42, 159–60, 172
  antitrust actions and, 80, 168–70,
    172, 174, 182
  Armstrong's alliance with, 3–5
  background of, 4, 31–34, 130–32,
    172
  career turning point of, 77–78
  death of, 258
  early jobs of, 32–34
  Farnsworth's agreement with,
    242–44
  Farnsworth system and, 165–66,
    173–75, 179–83, 198, 208, 232
  finances of, 121, 158, 172, 224
  FM radio and, 4–9
  Green Street lab visited by, 174,
    179–86, 243
  Jewish background of, 31–34, 39,
    77, 120
  late years of, 255–56
  Million Dollar Plan of, 218
  named president of RCA, 159
  New York Times interviews of, 156,
    172
  Paley's competition with, 173, 192
  Paris mission of, 157–58
  patent control and, 8, 41–42, 69, 80,
    119, 166, 170, 182
  "Radio Music Box" memo of, 37,
    40, 77, 80
  resignation threat of, 159
  Titanic disaster and, 35–36, 248
  TV commitment made by, 6–7, 70,
    81–82, 156–57, 160, 163, 165–69,
    173–75, 180–86, 193, 217–24,
    236–40, 242–45, 249, 255

Victor deal and, 131, 158, 169
wedding of, 39
World's Fair and, 223, 236–37, 242
World War II and, 246–49
Zworykin and, 131–32, 151, 160, 167, 181–82
Sarnoff, Leah, 31–32, 39
Sarnoff, Lizette Hermant, 39, 121, 158, 172
Saturday Evening Post, 36, 81, 158
Schacht, Hjalmar, 157
Schairer, Otto, 86, 88, 243, 244
Science and Invention, 20–22, 47, 51, 60, 70
Scientific American, 17, 19, 58, 61
Securities and Exchange Commission (SEC), 233, 236
selenium, xvi, xix, 24, 95
Selfridge, Gordon, 65
Selfridges Department Store, 65–66
Shaw, George Bernard, xviii
Shields, Frank, 201
shoes, inflatable, 62
Sleeper, George, 229
Smith, Alfred E., 124
Smith, J. E., 134
Smith, Mott, 101–3
Smith, Samuel, 214, 216
Smith, Ted, 193
Somers, Frank, 229
stock market, 170
  crash of, 159, 160, 161, 166, 169, 171
Stoefen, Lester, 201
storage principle, 166, 191, 199
Supreme Court, N.Y., 221
Swope, Gerard, 159

T

Taft, William Howard, 35
Takayanagi, Kenjiro, xvi
Tall, William, 16

Taming of the Shrew, The (film), 143
Taynton, William, 66
Telefunken, 227
telegraph, 19, 23, 29–31, 34–42
telephone, xiv, xx, 16
telephot, use of term, xiv, xv
television:
  etymology of word, xv
  first license granted for, 125
  future of, 258
  "Model T," xx, 249
  problems in development of, xix–xx, 19
  standards issue and, 222–24, 236, 240, 243, 245–46
  wave band requirements of, 147–48, 175–76, 177–78
"Television and the Telephot" (Gernsback), xvii–xviii
Television Laboratories, Inc., 148, 161
  Philco's agreement with, 187
  Sarnoff's buyout offer for, 180–83
  stock of, 178, 194
"Television Song, The," 126
"Television with Cathode-Ray Tube for Receiver" (Zworykin), 155–56
teloramaphone, 59
Tesla, Nikola, 17–18
Time, 36, 158, 230, 250
Titanic, sinking of, 35–36, 248
Tolman, Justin, 12–14, 22–26, 47, 55, 58, 212–16
Tom Swift and His Television Detector (Appleton), 92
"Top Notchers," 193
transmitters:
  radio, 29
  television, xix, 24, 67, 86, 87, 112–13, 181, 186, 222; *see also specific transmitters*
"Transmitting Photographs and Drawings by Radio" (article), 19

Tunney, Gene, 143
Turner, Seymour (Skee), 203, 204,
    205–6, 230

U

United Artists Film Corporation,
    150–51

V

vacuum pumps, 107, 130
vacuum tube, 28, 83–84
    De Forest audion, 18, 20, 28, 109,
        134, 253
    Farnsworth's envisioning of, 24, 25
        see also image dissector
        see also cathode-ray tube
Vance, Arthur, 161
Varian, Russell, 189
Vasilieff, Tatiana, see Zworykin,
    Tatiana Vasilieff
Victor Talking Machine Company,
    131, 158, 169

W

Waldrop, Frank, 186
Walker, Jimmy, 127
Washington Post, 134, 236
WCFL-TV, 126
Wells, H. G., 236
West, A. G. D., 202, 203, 227
Westinghouse, 40, 42, 70, 77, 78, 121,
    159
    antitrust actions and, 168–70
    tube laboratory of, 165
    Zworykin's work for, 85–90, 129,
        131–32, 154–56, 164, 209, 244
White, Andrew, 79
Whitehead, Alfred North, 16
Wilkins, Leslie, 122–23

willemite, 136, 155
Wilson, Woodrow, 19, 39, 40, 41
"Windmill Broadcast," 61, 125
Winters, S. R., 60
Wireless World and Radio Review,
    86
World War I, 38, 39–41, 76, 84–85
    Versailles Treaty and, 157
World War II, 246–50
W3XE-TV, 190–91
W3XK-TV, 125
W3XPF-TV, 230

Y

Young, Owen, 41, 42
    financial losses of, 159, 170
    Paris mission of, 157–58
    presidential ambitions of, 158, 159
    resignation of, 171, 172
    Sarnoff's relationship with, 77, 78,
        119–20, 157, 159, 170

Z

Zenith Radio Corporation, 80, 222,
    223, 224, 245
Zworykin, Nina, 85
Zworykin, Tatiana Vasilieff, 84, 85
Zworykin, Vladimir Kosma, xvi, xx,
    82–89, 128–31, 151–56, 238,
    190–94, 217, 231, 238, 244,
    249
    background of, 82–83, 131
    Belin's lab visited by, 129–30, 154,
        161
    career turning point of, 129–30
    engineering team of, 161, 192–93,
        219, 235
    Farnsworth compared with, 129–30,
        155, 156, 161, 162, 181
    Farnsworth's clippings on, 155

Farnsworth's competition with, 190,
    193–94, 197, 199, 201, 209–11,
    216–17
financial estimates of, 174, 255
Green Street lab visited by, 151, 154,
    161–66, 173–74, 179, 210
Green Street report by, 165
immigration of, 82, 85–86

late years of, 255
new camera tube of (iconoscope),
    xx, 166–67, 191–93, 199, 200
patent applications of, 86, 87, 162,
    166, 192, 209–11, 216–17
Sarnoff as protector of, 160, 167
Sarnoff's meeting with, 130–32, 181
test broadcasts of, 190

About the Author

DANIEL STASHOWER is the author of *Teller of Tales,* a biography of Arthur Conan Doyle (Holt, 1999). He is also the author of five mystery novels, the most recent of which is *The Houdini Specter* (Avon, 2001). As the recipient of the Raymond Chandler Fulbright Fellowship in Detective and Crime Fiction Writing, he spent a year as Visiting Fellow at Wadham College, Oxford. Stashower has been a freelance journalist since 1986, and his articles have appeared in the *New York Times,* the *Wall Street Journal, Smithsonian Magazine, National Geographic Traveler,* and *Connoisseur.*